French Reaction to
British Slave Emancipation

LAWRENCE C. JENNINGS

FRENCH REACTION
TO BRITISH
SLAVE EMANCIPATION

Louisiana State University Press
Baton Rouge and London

Copyright © 1988 by Louisiana State University Press
All rights reserved
Manufactured in the United States of America
DESIGNER: *Sylvia M. Loftin*
TYPEFACE: *Trump Mediaeval*
TYPESETTER: *The Composing Room of Michigan, Inc.*
PRINTER: *Thomson-Shore, Inc.*
BINDER: *John H. Dekker & Sons, Inc.*

97 96 95 94 93 92 91 90 89 88   5 4 3 2 1

Library of Congress Cataloging-in-Publication Data
Jennings, Lawrence C.
    French reaction to British slave emancipation / Lawrence C.
Jennings.
        p.   cm.
    Bibliography: p.
    Includes index.
    ISBN 0-8071-1429-4 (alk. paper)
    1. Slavery—Great Britain—Emancipation—Public opinion.
    2. Public opinion—France.   I. Title.
HT1163.J46   1988
306'.362'0942—dc19   88-15511
                                                      CIP

The paper in this book meets the guidelines for permanence and
durability of the Committee on Production Guidelines for Book
Longevity of the Council on Library Resources. ∞

CONTENTS

PREFACE

While researching the topics of French slavery and the movement for its abolition in the 1830s and 1840s, I constantly encountered references to the British precedent in French primary sources, and that drew me to investigate the interconnections between French and British emancipationism at the time. As my work progressed, I found that the British example of eliminating colonial slavery in 1834 seemed to impinge on, not only the colonial policies followed by the French government from the early 1830s to the Revolution of 1848, but the attitudes and actions of the French proslavery and antislavery factions. Because of the shadow that British slave liberation seemed to cast on every aspect of the slavery and emancipation issues in July Monarchy France, I began to fix my attention on the interaction of French and British abolitionism during the decade and a half prior to the Revolution of 1848 (when the monarchy was overthrown and slavery abolished), viewing the problem from the French perspective. The major question I asked myself, of course, concerned the extent to which the British example influenced France and the French. This led me to examine such subsidiary issues as how the British precedent was viewed by all the interested parties in France, what effect French views of the British achievement had on antislavery forces in France, and how much the French image of the British experience was influenced by Anglo-French rivalry. My attempts to answer these queries have led to the writing of this monograph.

This book focuses primarily on France; essentially, it examines French perceptions of and reaction to British emancipation rather than British views on French abolitionism as such. Although my research obliged me to peruse both primary and secondary sources on British antislavery activities, my main concern was not with the British phenomenon, for the policies of British abolitionism have already been well explored by historians, who have built up a voluminous historiography on the British slavery and emancipation problems. British efforts to encourage slave liberation elsewhere in the world have also been analyzed by scholars. Relatively little is known, however, about French attitudes toward and response to British abolitionism. The present study proposes to fill this historical lacuna.

The reader should be forewarned that this work is limited to the period of the July Monarchy, a time when nascent French emancipationism was influenced and marked by the monumental transformation that British slave liberation brought to Britain's colonial possessions. Moreover, this book does not purport to be a definitive examination of French policies toward slavery and its eradication in general or of the French abolitionist movement in particular, even though it does constitute the most detailed discussion of these issues available so far. I am planning to write a subsequent volume to deal with the more general question of French slavery and emancipationism, but these topics cannot be understood without an intensive preliminary analysis of the French reaction to the British experience.

As few secondary studies touch on my subject, this book is of necessity based almost entirely on primary material, much of it hitherto unexploited by historians. The most essential set of sources has been the extensive documentation contained in the numerous dossiers of France's Archives Nationales, Section Outre-Mer. The material preserved in this holding has proved indispensable, especially for evaluating the French government's position toward the British process. In an attempt to fathom the attitudes of important elements of French public opinion to Britain's moves, I have relied heavily on French newspapers, pamphlets, brochures, and parliamentary debates for the entire period 1830 to 1848. Particular importance has been placed on the French press, a source that previously was largely untapped by scholars interested in French slavery and its abolition. Consequently, I have covered on a day-to-day basis all of the important July Monarchy dailies from the crucial ports of Le Havre and Bordeaux—available in the municipal libraries of these cities—and many of the dailies of Paris. Moreover, I have sounded for key periods during the fifteen years prior to 1848 newspapers of the other important colonial ports: Marseille, Nantes, Rouen, and La Rochelle. It is hoped that this intensive and systematic use of primary materials will provide the basis for evaluating the attitudes of the French government, proslavery and antislavery elements, and those sectors of the Parisian, provincial, and colonial elites that were interested in the problems of slavery and British emancipation during the reign of King Louis Philippe.

In the course of researching and writing this monograph I have become deeply indebted to a number of institutions and individuals. My research has been facilitated by the friendly efforts of the following libraries and archives and their staffs: the Bibliothèque Nationale and the Bibliothèque de l'Arsenal in Paris, the municipal libraries of Le Havre, Bordeaux, Nantes, Rouen, and La Rochelle, the University of Ottawa Library, the Robarts Library of the University of Toronto, the Rhodes House Library in Oxford, the Archives départementales de la Gironde, the Archives départementales de la Loire-Atlantique, the Archives Nationales in Paris, and, in particular, the Section Outre-Mer of the Archives Nationales, now in Aix-en-Provence, though previously in Paris. Mademoiselle Menier and Madame Pouliquen, administrators of the latter institution, have been especially kind and helpful. Madame Gruner Schlumberger graciously granted me permission to consult the Guizot papers. I am most grateful to Professors David Brion Davis (Yale University), David Eltis (Algonquin College), and Stanely Engerman (University of Rochester) for reading my work in the manuscript stage and improving it with their suggestions, although the ultimate responsibility for it, of course, remains mine. Finally, I wish to extend my thanks particularly to the Social Sciences and Humanities Research Council of Canada, which has facilitated my research with several grants.

French Reaction to
British Slave Emancipation

ONE

INITIAL FRENCH REACTION TO
BRITISH EMANCIPATION

French abolitionism always had close ties to its British counterpart. The French antislavery movement during the late eighteenth century was deeply indebted to the British abolitionist "Saints" for encouragement and assistance, although when French slaves were finally freed in 1794, it was due more to revolutionary principles, politics, and developments in Saint Domingue than to emancipationist ideals. Concurrently, French abolitionist ranks were decimated by the Terror and discredited during the regimes that followed; Napoleon even reestablished slavery and the slave trade in 1802. By 1807 the British had again emerged as the leading humanitarian power with the banning of the transatlantic slave trade and the adoption of a universal anti–slave trade policy, which they attempted to impose on the reluctant French Restoration government in 1814 and 1815. French abolitionism languished under the early Restoration, partially because of its association with Jacobinism, but the movement had begun to revive by 1819, and it once again looked to British philanthropy for succor and support.[1]

1. For a discussion of French abolitionism during the French Revolutionary period see Robert Louis Stein, *Léger Félicité Sonthonax: The Lost Sentinel of the Republic* (Cranbury, N.J., 1985); Robert Louis Stein, "The Revolution of 1789 and the Abolition of Slavery," *Canadian Journal of History*, XVII (1982), 447–67; David Brion Davis, *The Problem of Slavery in the Age of Revolution, 1770–1823* (Ithaca, 1975); Daniel P. Resnick, "The Société des amis des noirs and the Abolition of Slavery," *French Historical Studies*, VII (1972), 558–69; and Valerie Quinney, "Decisions on Slavery, the Slave Trade, and Civil Rights for Negroes in the Early French Revolution," *Journal of Negro History*, LV (1970), 117–30. The most complete treatment of French antislavery and anti–slave trade actions under the Restoration is afforded by Serge Daget, "La France et l'abolition de la traite des Noirs de 1814 à 1831: Introduction à l'étude de la répression de la traite des Noirs au XIXᵉ siècle"

With Franco-British emancipationist ties being renewed, it was apparent that the series of events between 1823 and 1833 that marked the acceleration in Britain of the campaign against slavery might have great importance for France.

Following the abolition of the British slave trade, British emancipationists made few concerted attacks upon the structure of colonial slavery until the early 1820s. Then, in 1823, ten years before the enactment of the British slave liberation law, the British abolitionist movement began to gain momentum. Thomas F. Buxton of the newly formed Anti-Slavery Society introduced a proposition in Parliament calling for the improvement of the condition of British colonial slaves. This action prompted the London government to institute a policy of encouraging individual colonies to initiate reform and amelioration aimed at facilitating the eventual elimination of slavery. Many emancipationists in the late 1820s acquiesced to this gradualist approach, though they continued to publish tracts and preach against servitude and to build up a provincial antislavery network. Only in the period just before actual emancipation did British abolitionists repudiate the gradualist model and become ardent proponents of immediate slave liberation.

British abolitionists' disappointment with the achievements of the British government's ameliorative program was becoming apparent by 1830. As a result, in 1831 the more radical emancipationists formed a new organization, the Agency Committee, which abandoned gradualism and espoused immediatism as its platform. The committee launched itself into spreading its doctrine by founding numerous branch societies and by rousing public opinion through mass meetings and petitioning. A slave revolt in Jamaica in 1831 further shook the confidence in gradualism of both abolitionists and elements in the British Colonial Office in London. Moreover, by the early 1830s many influential members of the British governing class, convinced by the laissez-faire precept that slave labor was uneconomical, had become opposed to slavery

---

(Doctorat de 3ᵉ cycle, Paris, 1969); and Yvan Debbasch, "Poésie et traite: L'opinion française sur le commerce négrier au début du XIXᵉ siècle," *Revue française d'histoire d'outre-mer*, XLVIII (1961), 311–52.

in principle and determined to free British slaves. When the British Reform Act of 1832 brought into Parliament a number of younger members prone to accept additional reform and cleared the Commons of many of the more implacable defenders of West Indian interests, the stage was set for striking the fatal blow against bondage. Indeed, in the spring of 1833 a Select Committee was appointed by the House of Commons to consider measures to implement slave liberation.

In 1832 and 1833 the abolitionists stepped up their activities and undertook a massive petitioning campaign. Faced with these new circumstances, the British government, already leaning toward abolition, feared that Parliament might introduce its own emancipation bill and undercut administrative initiative in the matter. Accordingly, the Colonial Office abandoned its gradualist approach in early 1833. After considerable debate within Parliament and the Colonial Office in the spring of 1833, a bill to eliminate slavery was introduced by the government and passed by the two houses that summer. The British Slave Emancipation Act, which received royal assent on August 28, 1833, called for the termination of British colonial slavery eleven months hence, on August 1, 1834. It provided for ample compensation for slave owners, a £20 million indemnity, in order to assuage the plantocracy and preserve the sanctity of private property. Moreover, in an attempt to avoid an abrupt transformation that might cause colonial upheaval, or at least major disruptions of work, the act did not immediately free Britain's approximately 776,000 slaves of all restrictions. Instead, it established an interim period during which former slaves would continue to serve their masters before obtaining complete liberty. Only slaves below age six were to be freed outright, while all others were to be transformed into "apprentices" for a period of four years for nonpraedial (domestic or artisanal) and six years for praedial (agricultural) laborers. Under this status they were to toil without compensation for a minimum of forty-five hours per week for their former owners, who would continue to provide for their physical needs; special magistrates would be appointed to oversee the welfare of the apprentices and settle any disputes that might arise between them and the colonists. The bill of 1833, then, while stipulating immediate emancipation, actually established a transitional regime, which British abolitionists accepted begrudgingly even at first and would soon vociferously attack as perpetuating servitude.[2]

Despite their disappointment over the apprenticeship system, the success of their campaign in pressuring the Whig government into freeing the slaves led many British abolitionists to believe that they had achieved an initial victory in the long battle for universal slave liberation. Even before the Act of 1833 went into effect, British emancipationists tended to be optimistic about the potential international repercussions of the measure. In the autumn of 1833 the noted abolitionist Joseph Sturge advocated "a general campaign" against servitude "throughout the civilized world." That December the Glasgow Emancipation Society professed its belief that Britain's actions presaged "the Abolition of slavery throughout the World," while in early 1834 the radical Agency Committee proclaimed its intention to encourage the universal freeing of slaves.[3] Once emancipation had become a reality, British abolitionist spokesmen continued to entertain internationalist objectives. In early 1838 the London *Courier* predicted confidently that England's example would soon be followed by all nations possess-

---

2. This and subsequent discussions of the mechanics of British slave liberation and of the postemancipation era in the British colonies are based on: David Eltis, *Economic Growth and the Ending of the Transatlantic Slave Trade* (New York, 1987); Seymour Drescher, *Capitalism and Antislavery: British Popular Mobilization in Comparative Perspective* (London, 1986); David Brion Davis, *Slavery and Human Progress* (Oxford, 1984); Michael Craton, "Slave Culture, Resistance and the Achievement of Emancipation in the British West Indies, 1783–1836," in James Walvin (ed.), *Slavery and British Society, 1776–1846* (London, 1982), 100–22; Seymour Drescher, "Public Opinion and the Destruction of British Slavery," *ibid.*, 22–48; Walvin, "The Propaganda of Anti-Slavery," *ibid*, 49–68; James Walvin, "The Public Campaign in England Against Slavery, 1787–1834," in David Eltis and James Walvin (eds.), *The Abolition of the Atlantic Slave Trade: Origins and Effects in Africa and the Americas* (Madison, Wisc., 1981), 63–79; James Walvin, "The Rise of British Popular Sentiment for Abolition, 1787–1832," in Christine Bolt and Seymour Drescher (eds.), *Anti-Slavery, Religion and Reform: Essays in Memory of Roger Anstey* (Folkstone, Kent, 1980), 149–62; Roger Anstey, "The Pattern of British Abolitionism in the Eighteenth and Nineteenth Centuries," *ibid.*, 19–42; William A. Green, *British Slave Emancipation: The Sugar Colonies and the Great Experiment, 1830–1870* (Oxford, 1976); Howard Temperley, *British Antislavery, 1830–1870* (Columbia, S.C., 1972); D. J. Murray, *The West Indies and the Development of Colonial Government* (Oxford, 1965); David Brion Davis, "The Emergence of Immediatism in British and American Anti-Slavery Thought," *Mississippi Valley Historical Review*, XLIX (1962–63), 209–30; William L. Burn, *Emancipation and Apprenticeship in the British West Indies* (London, 1937); and Frank J. Klingberg, *The Anti-Slavery Movement in England* (1933; rpr. London, 1964).

3. Quoted in Temperley, *British Antislavery*, 23–25.

ing slaves.[4] Two years later the official organ of the British and Foreign Anti-Slavery Society (founded in 1839) suggested: "The French, the Dutch, the Dane, the Spaniard, the Brazilian and the American . . . have felt the influence of the extinction of slavery in the British colonies on their respective systems as the shock of an earthquake is felt in distant regions. . . . They look to us as conquerors; they have read their destiny."[5] The enthusiasm of the London *Times* had not flagged even in 1843. Referring to the "moral effect produced by the example of Great Britain" on France and the influence that it exerted in favor of liberating French slaves, the daily was "intimately convinced" that "at no very distant period the cause of good policy will universely prevail." In the same year, the aging Thomas Clarkson, dean of the British abolitionists, expressed his belief that British actions had dealt bondage "its Death Blow in every part of the World."[6] Indeed, it appears that an entire generation of British antislavery advocates was convinced that the success of English slave liberation would undermine servitude everywhere it still existed.[7] After their victory at home British abolitionists turned their gaze on the rest of the world. They developed a deep-seated optimism that other nations—with the encouragement of British humanitarians and the British government—would take note of England's initiative in the noble cause of emancipationism and imitate her example. In truth, however, the English achievement was to be viewed differently on the other side of the Channel than British abolitionists had hoped and expected.

Theoretically at least, France had good reason to be highly concerned about British slave liberation. By 1830 the French colonial empire had declined dramatically in size and importance from its flourishing state under the ancien régime, but the four French colonies of Guadeloupe, Martinique, Bourbon (Réunion after 1848), and Guiana still contained approximately 285,000 black slaves, who provided much of the manual labor for their plantation economies. The major French colonial staple produced by these slaves remained sugar, which accounted for 92.3 and 90.1 percent

4. Reported in the Parisian newspaper *Le Courrier français*, February 20, 1838.
5. Quoted in Temperley, *British Antislavery*, 184.
6. London *Times*, May 29, 1843; Davis, *Slavery and Human Progress*, 118.
7. Green, *British Slave Emancipation*, 191–92.

of French imports from the two leading slave colonies, Guadeloupe and Martinique, in the 1830s and 1840s. In these decades cane sugar production was regaining some of the momentum it had experienced prior to the French Revolution, for the French colonies exported to metropolitan France an annual average of 84,371 tons for the years 1837 through 1846, despite the growing competition of domestically grown beet sugar.[8] Although this amounted to a decrease of 22,000 tons from the amount sent to France in 1788, it still constituted a dramatic recovery from the 29,450 tons exported to the mother country in 1806.[9] In a sense, then, the French colonial establishment, though in decline from the position it had held in the eighteenth century, was still a significant economic entity in the 1830s. Between 1830 and 1848 the French colonies might have been experiencing major political, social, and economic difficulties, in particular a lack of confidence in the future that discouraged the inflow of investment capital and caused these entities to languish. Nevertheless, the colonial system was still perceived by both the *colons* and metropolitan authorities as a viable one that must be maintained by France. Both the government and the plantocracy also agreed that France could preserve its colonies only by prolonging the system of coerced labor, slavery, on which they depended.

Surprisingly, then, despite the relative economic importance of her colonial holdings and the potential threat of British emancipation to them, France reacted somewhat lethargically to the circumstances between 1830 and 1833 that led up to British slave liberation. This was undoubtedly due to the fact that during these years Frenchmen and their government were largely preoccupied with the problems and events surrounding the Revolution of 1830 and the establishment of the new, liberal July Monarchy under King Louis Philippe. This was certainly the case with most French newspapers, which, when not covering internal political questions, were interested primarily in spectacular foreign developments accompanying the 1830 upheaval. The proslavery *Journal*

8. France, Administration des douanes, *Tableau décennal du commerce de la France avec ses colonies et les puissances étrangères, 1837–1846* (Paris, 1848), 58–61, 150. Interesting statistics on the growth of sugar beet production are provided by Augustin Cochin, *L'abolition de l'esclavage* (1861; rpr. Fort-de-France, 1979), 401.
9. Seymour Drescher, *Econocide: British Slavery in the Era of Abolition* (Pittsburgh, 1977), 129.

du Havre (Le Havre), though, distracted itself long enough from other affairs to contemplate the possibility of future slave liberation and predict that it would result in the annihilation of both the British and French colonies.[10] In the early 1830s other French journals also made passing reference to questions related to British slavery. *Le Temps* (Paris), a left-center daily at the time, noted that British colonial authorities had decided to give refuge to fugitive slaves from France's nearby possesions and that some sixteen slaves had fled from French Guiana to Trinidad. Referring to similar developments, *Le Journal du Havre* suggested that England was attempting to ruin France's Caribbean islands by luring slaves away from them.[11] The liberal *Courrier français* made a direct reference to the British gradualist approach when it reported in 1831 that London's efforts to convince colonial legislatures to institute reforms were proving unsuccessful, while the following year *Le Constitutionnel* (Paris) opined that the Jamaican slave revolt had been caused by rumors of impending abolition.[12] *La Re-*

10. *Le Journal du Havre*, September 3, 1830. For an analysis of *Le Journal du Havre* as a model defender of slavery under the July Monarchy, see Lawrence C. Jennings, "La presse havraise et l'esclavage," *Revue historique*, CLXXII (1984), 45–71. All mid-nineteenth-century French newspapers displayed two dates on the upper part of their first page—the publication date on the masthead at the top and, just below this, the date on which the news or articles were compiled, the previous day. In this work all newspapers are identified by their publication date.

11. *Le Temps*, October 28, 1830; *Le Journal du Havre*, December 3, 1831, January 31, 1832. Between the early 1830s and the late 1840s the slave population of France's four plantation colonies declined from approximately 285,000 to near 245,000, but these declines probably resulted more from natural attrition—the last remnants of the overt French slave trade having been extirpated in 1831—and individual manumissions than from evasions to Britain's dependencies. The slave populations of the colonies for the period 1834–1847, for which full statistics are available, are as follows.

   Guadeloupe: 96,684 in 1834; 87,752 in 1847.
   Martinique: 78,233 in 1834; 72,859 in 1847.
   Bourbon: 68,785 in 1834; 60,260 in 1847.
   Guiana: 17,645 in 1834; 12,943 in 1847.

France, Ministère de la marine et des colonies, *Etats de population pour 1834* (Paris, 1836), 1, 9, 17, 32; *Tableau de population, de culture et de navigation* . . . (Paris, 1844, 1851). Still, Frenchmen were quite aware of the proximity of French and British possessions. Guadeloupe and Martinique were approximately 26 miles from Dominica, Martinique was only some 20 miles from Saint Lucia, Bourbon about 102 miles from Mauritius, and French Guiana in contact with, though somewhat distant from, British Guiana.

12. *Le Courrier français*, February 8, 1831; *Le Constitutionnel*, February 23, 1832. The French—and British, too—in the 1830s and 1840s tended to use the terms *abolition* and *emancipation* interchangeably. Although some Anglo-American scholars now differentiate between these two terms, this study will conform to the contemporary usage of the words.

vue de Paris, a literary bimonthly favorable to slavery, preferred for its part to cite French colonial sources that mocked English "humanitarianism" for replacing the whip, "which made much noise but little harm," with the cat-o'-nine-tails, "which made much harm but little noise." *Le Journal des débats* (Paris), close to the doctrinaire Orleanists usually in power during the July Monarchy, chose to approach the problem of British emancipation as it applied to the French scene. It expressed concern that rapid British abolition would foment unrest in neighboring French dependencies and suggested that Paris and London discuss together the issue of slave liberation.[13]

Although the view of *Le Journal des débats* was probably of abolitionist inspiration, similar remarks by other French metropolitan newspapers undoubtedly reflected French colonial apprehension that widespread reform—or the ending of servitude—in Britain's colonies would destabilize France's slave holdings. Such was evidently the case when *Le Journal du Havre* published a letter from an important Martinique *colon*, L. Cicéron, warning Frenchmen not to emulate British colonial reforms. It is revelatory, however, that even the rabidly proslavery Le Havre organ simply printed Cicéron's missive without commenting on it or openly endorsing it. An examination of French journalistic and archival source material for the period preceding 1833 gives the impression that at this time France felt no sense of urgency concerning developments touching on British slavery. While the pages of France's major newspapers were overflowing with articles relating to the establishment of the July Monarchy in France and with foreign reports about the independence of Belgium and the revolt in Poland, matters pertaining to British antislavery were rarely covered and, even when mentioned, were relegated to a position of strictly secondary importance.[14]

Following the Revolution of 1830 the July Monarchy introduced

13. *La Revue de Paris*, XLII (September, 1832), 267; *Le Journal des débats*, October 22, 1832.
14. *Le Journal du Havre*, December 21, 1831. During the early 1830s the French press was equally uninterested in British anti–slave trade activity and in developments concerning slavery in the United States. See Lawrence C. Jennings, "The French Press and Great Britain's Campaign Against the Slave Trade, 1830–1848," *Revue française d'histoire d'outre-mer*, LXVII (1980), 5–24, and "French Views on Slavery and Abolitionism in the United States, 1830–1848," *Slavery and Abolition*, IV (1983), 19–40.

its own plans for applying moderate reforms to the French colonial system, a program apparently inspired by the new government's liberal proclivities rather than by Britain's efforts along the same lines. Authorities in Paris began in 1831 and 1832 by issuing ordonnances to facilitate individual slave manumissions and followed this in the spring of 1833 with regulations ending the branding and mutilation of slaves and granting civil and political rights to free men of color. More important still, a law of April 24, 1833, afforded the colonies more autonomy, establishing local legislatures, or Colonial Councils (*Conseils coloniaux*), and granting these bodies the right to hire representatives, colonial delegates (*délégués coloniaux*), to plead their cause in Paris before the Chamber of Deputies and Chamber of Peers. Over the next fifteen years these highly paid plantocratic spokesmen would do their best to defend French slavery, oppose any tendency toward abolition, and besmirch the British emancipation record.

Within this context of gradual colonial reorganization, it is perplexing to note that an examination of the archives of the French Ministry of the Navy and Colonies affords little evidence indicating that the Paris government was closely attuned to British developments concerning slavery or abolitionism during the period July, 1830, to March, 1833.[15] This is all the more remarkable because France and Britain consulted each other regularly at this time over the closely related topic of the repression of the slave trade, negotiating and finally signing the conventions of 1831 and 1833, which provided for cooperation through the implementation of mutual right-of-search procedures to achieve this aim. Indeed, the apparent indifference in official French circles toward British slavery matters could be explained only by neglect and oversight on the part of French administrators or by their belief that the cautious policy of gradualism pursued by London through 1832 was not particularly noteworthy or different from the French program. The French minister of the navy and colonies, Henri Gauthier, comte

15. The Ministry of the Navy and Colonies was responsible for French colonial affairs and all matters concerning slavery during the July Monarchy. Its records are now held by the Section Outre-Mer of the Archives Nationales, in Paris until 1986 and then transferred to Aix-en-Provence. For a discussion of the colonial reforms passed under the July Monarchy see the old but still useful studies by Cochin, *L'abolition de l'esclavage*, 35–62, and Christian Schefer, *La politique coloniale de la Monarchie de Juillet: L'Algérie et l'évolution de la colonisation française* (Paris, 1928), 85–120, 189–217, 489–503.

de Rigny, seemingly became cognizant of impending British slave liberation only through reports in the March 11, 1833, issue of the official French newspaper, *Le Moniteur universel* (Paris), which reproduced news from the English press to the effect that the Whig government was considering a proposal for immediate emancipation.[16]

Suddenly the French government became aware of the possibility of British slave liberation and of its potential implications for France. Rigny notified Prince Charles Maurice de Talleyrand-Perigord, then ambassador in London, that the French government had "the greatest interest in finding out exactly what" was happening in England concerning abolitionism, for "France's colonies everywhere touch closely upon England's and no violent perturbation there could shake property interests without the repercussions being felt immediately in France's possessions."[17] Talleyrand's initial reply was somewhat reassuring, for he noted that, although considerable pressure was being put upon London officials by "inhabitants of the countryside" influenced by the religious congregations, the British Cabinet would not act immediately. In early April, however, the authorities in Paris learned from their agent in London that the British government was cautiously leaning toward abolition.[18] A month later, after it had become clear to French administrators that Britain would proceed with emancipation, the navy and colonial minister issued his first directive touching on the matter in the form of a circular to France's four slave colonies. In Rigny's opinion, the effects of an emancipation law, "which will be so grave for England's colonies, could not be without importance for those that France possesses." He feared that trouble would break out in England's sugar islands when the law was implemented and that "*provocateurs* or even emissaries will try at this time to disrupt the peace of our slave establishments." Accordingly, Rigny instructed his colonial governors to act with all necessary zeal to maintain order. He reminded them, too, that it was their "most urgent duty" to gather "with the great-

16. Minister to Talleyrand, March 13, 1833, in Généralités 206 (1513), Archives Nationales, Section Outre-Mer, Aix-en-Provence, hereinafter cited as ANSOM.
    17. *Ibid.*
    18. Talleyrand to Rigny, March 19, April 9, 1833, both in ANSOM.

est exactitude" all information possible on the situation in the neighboring English dependencies.[19]

Rigny's attitudes were echoed by a proslavery spokesman in the Chamber of Deputies during a report he made in May, 1833, on the French naval budget. Baron Charles Dupin, later a prominent colonial delegate, suggested that England's "adventurous experiments" would cause disruptions in her colonies, that "a period of innovation will follow the seventeen years of peace in the West Indies." The French, he continued, being "friends of humanity," hoped that the British experience would succeed better than emancipation efforts at the time of the French Revolution, because France could profit from such an example; but Dupin's doubts about the matter led him to reiterate the need to take precautions necessary to "preserve our colonies from the revolutionary blacklash which such great changes will produce in the British colonies." That Dupin believed the English measures to be ill advised was evident from his statement that British officials wished to "transform at enormous cost generations of slaves into citizens," with little time to alter attitudes imprinted by three centuries of bondage, and "substitute the love of work for the passion of laziness."[20] The remarks of both Rigny and Dupin show to what extent initial French official reaction to British events was intermingled with uneasiness about British slave liberation and fear that it could prove disruptive to France's colonial establishment. Contrary to the expectations of British abolitionists, France's first response to the impending termination of British slavery was one of surprise, concern, and guarded disapproval.

The British Parliament's debate on the emancipation bill in the spring of 1833 and the passage of the measure in August of that year removed any doubts that might have persisted in French minds about the reality of British abolition. The French press, which had been largely impervious to British slavery issues prior to

19. Minister to Governors, May 24, 1833, in Correspondance Générale, Colonies françaises, 1833, ANSOM.

20. *Le Moniteur universal*, May 31, 1833. This official newspaper provides the most complete accounts of the proceedings in the two French legislative bodies under the July Monarchy and will henceforth be cited for all debates in these bodies. Unless indicated otherwise, legislative discussions always occurred on the day prior to the date given, that of the newspaper's publication.

the spring of 1833, reacted diversely to the realization that emancipation definitely would be implemented. Indifference continued
to mark the attitude of some important dailies. The major newspapers of Bordeaux, the doctrinaire *Mémorial bordelais* and left-
center *Indicateur,* either overlooked or chose to ignore the question. During the summer of 1833 both journals displayed profound
interest in developments across the Pyrenees and in foreign issues
in general but not in colonial affairs. *Le Mémorial,* for example,
reported on British policy toward Portugal and discussed the British reform movement in general but disregarded the emancipation
problem. For its part, the legitimist *La Guienne* (Bordeaux) made
no editorial comment on British antislavery actions until 1835. *Le
Sémaphore de Marseille,* another major newspaper from a port city
engaged in extensive commercial contact with the colonies, was
preoccupied with English commercial affairs in 1833 while barely
mentioning British abolition plans. The Parisian *Courrier français*
reacted somewhat similarly, referring to British slave liberation
without comment and treating it simply as one of the British reforms of the early 1830s. *Le Moniteur du commerce* (Paris), a doctrinaire organ that steadily promoted French colonial interests,
was more specific when covering the issue. It cited British antiabolitionist newspapers like the *Globe,* which had reported that
Jamaica was much agitated by slave liberation, and the *Sun,* which
had said that blacks were highly disappointed over their failure to
obtain complete and immediate freedom. In a report that clearly
reflected French colonial anxieties, *Le Temps* made direct reference to Britain's actions and suggested that British governors in the
West Indies were obsessed with maintaining order and work after
the implementation of the Emancipation Act. That implacable
apostle of slavery, *Le Journal du Havre,* focused on the French
scene by praising France's navy and colonial minister for opposing
antislavery measures similar to Britain's, which would result in
the "pillaging" of France's colonies.[21]

Two other newspapers, *Le Journal du commerce* (Paris) and *Le
Constitutionnel,* displayed concerns akin to those of the navy and
colonial minister in their comments on British slave liberation.
The former daily, favorable to colonial interests but in the early

21. *Le Moniteur du commerce,* September 17, 28, 1833; *Le Temps,* September
18, 1833; *Le Journal du Havre,* July 30, 1833.

1830s still not opposed to abolition, remarked that the British initiative "sooner or later, cannot but reoccur"—an obvious reference to 1794—in France.[22] The latter organ displayed its attitude in a series of articles in the spring and summer of 1833. In April *Le Constitutionnel* noted that the antislavery question had "too little sympathy" in France. Three months later the paper hailed the introduction of the British emancipation bill as a "great measure," though adding that a similar development could cause unrest in France's territories. Expressing its own predilections, *Le Constitutionnel* intimated that Paris should react to London's action, not by reinforcing repressive measures in France's holdings, but by improving the condition of French slaves, inasmuch as England's example showed that such moves would not destroy the colonial structure. Finally, in August the newspaper predicted that England's "great act" would have "a profound repercussion" in France's possessions and suggested that only slave liberation could end the threat of disorder there.[23] Liberal spokesmen like *Le Constitutionnel* mixed uneasiness over the reverberations Britain's act could have in the French West Indies with the expectation that it could advance abolitionism in France.

The response of French colonial administrators and spokesmen to British emancipation showed that they shared the anxiety but lacked the enthusiasm of French liberal elements. Once French colonial governors received Rigny's circular of May 24, they could be expected to echo the concern expressed by the French minister of the navy and colonies. Their reaction, though, proved to be even more negative than that of their superior. Louis Henri, baron Desaulses de Freycinet, governor of French Guiana, reported to Rigny on August 3, 1833, that news of forthcoming British slave liberation had produced a great sensation within his jurisdiction. Although less exposed to English influence than other French colonies, Guiana was not sheltered from it, he explained, and agitation

---

22. *Le Journal du commerce*, August 29, 1833. This daily, like many July Monarchy newspapers, underwent frequent and radical changes in name, editorship, and policy as time went on. By the mid-1830s it had become a fierce defender of slavery, probably in the pay of the French plantocracy. In 1844, however, it was a very liberal organ, whose driving force was Alexis de Tocqueville. For the latter's association with the journal see Roger Boesche, "Tocqueville and *Le Commerce*: A Newspaper Expressing His Unusual Liberalism," *Journal of the History of Ideas*, XLIV (1983), 277–92.

23. *Le Constitutionnel*, April 22, July 9, August 17, 1833.

among the slaves might increase as they became aware of Britain's intentions. While claiming that malaise and discouragement were extreme in British Guiana, he concluded that disquietude had decreased in his colony as the planters had become aware of "the efforts Your Excellency has made for the defense of their cause."[24]

The report sent to Paris a day earlier by the governor of Martinique, Admiral Jean Henri Joseph Dupotet, was even more pessimistic. According to this official, misery, incertitude, and negligence reigned in the British West Indies, where blacks took advantage of the situation by showing "their laziness" and "their habitual apathy." He boldly predicted that freeing of the slaves "will bring, without any doubt, a general conflagration in the British possessions of this archipelago." After nearly three months of additional reflection, he still lamented the lack of wisdom of the English decision, which menaced British holdings in the Caribbean with "a horrible upheaval." When Depotet reported on the reaction in Martinique to the British initiative, his tone resembled that of Freycinet: word of the British measure had caused profound uneasiness, which had soon given way to confidence inspired by Dupin's reassuring words in the Chamber of Deputies about the need for maintaining order.[25]

The third French Caribbean governor, Admiral René Arnous Dessaulsay of Guadeloupe, declared that masters on the neighboring English isles no longer dared be demanding of their slaves; and subsequently he issued a warning that French imitation of Britain's actions would cause "the complete loss" of France's possessions, "their complete ruin."[26] The tenor of the remarks by all three governors shows that, at a time when their sources of information on the British colonies were incomplete and probably limited to items from the colonial press, local French administrators were often allowing their own fears and prejudices to dominate their reporting on British developments concerning slavery. At the same time, they were obviously counting on French contingency measures for strengthened security to ward off the spreading to

24. Freycinet to Minister, August 3, 1833, in Gén. 156 (1302), ANSOM.
25. Dupotet to Minister, August 2, 1833, October 23, 1833, both in Gen. 178 (1420), ANSOM.
26. Arnous to Minister, December 20, 1833, January 29, 1834, both in Gén. 156 (1302), ANSOM.

French territories of what they believed to be the disruptive effects of British abolition.

As 1833 gave way to 1834 colonial advocates continued to emit occasional negative or alarmist reactions to Britain's commitment to freeing the slaves. In late 1833 and early 1834 the short-lived *Revue mensuelle d'économie politique* (Paris) published two articles, one by the noted economist Jean Charles Léonard de Sismondi, the other by Baron A. de Cools, colonial delegate of Martinique. After denouncing slavery and praising the justice and generosity of England's actions, Sismondi charged that Great Britain had proceeded with undue precipitation, and suggested that blacks would be no better off under apprenticeship than slavery. Cools, as might be expected from a representative of the French *colons*, picked up and elaborated on the negative aspects of Sismondi's arguments, citing statements from British colonial defenders in the House of Lords to underscore the imprudence of British emancipation.[27] Commenting on Sismondi's article, *Le Temps*, which wavered on the slavery issue throughout the July Monarchy, insisted that France need not fear the British example, for slave liberation was not advocated in France with the "religious fanaticism" that prevailed in England. Consequently, the daily added, Frenchmen would have time "to profit from the lessons" of the British "before throwing themselves thoughtlessly into the path [down] which England appears to wish to lead us." In June, 1834, *Le Moniteur de commerce* printed a letter from the island of Mauritius which also predicted that eliminating slavery would consummate the ruin of that colony.[28] In the same month, Alphonse Barrot, the French consul in Colombia, on a visit to Jamaica, painted an equally dismal picture of the prospects for abolition; according to Barrot, the measure was not only misinformed and hasty but destined to destroy Britain's tropical establishments.[29] On occasion, then, French procolonial voices were prepared to vent their ire upon Britain's decision to emancipate even before the abolition act had been implemented. Already at this

27. *La Revue mensuelle d'économie politique*, December, 1833, and February, 1834.
28. *Le Temps*, January 6, 1834; *Le Moniteur du commerce*, June 20, 1834.
29. Barrot to Minister of Foreign Affairs, June 18, 1834, in Gén. 178 (1418), ANSOM.

time they also noted that popular support for abolitionism was greater in Britain than in France. Still, in early 1834 most French newspapers and officials seemed to feel it best to wait until the British bill had actually gone into effect before making extensive comments upon it. As *Le Journal du commerce* perspicaciously remarked in the late summer of 1834, the French press awaited "not without impatience" the first reports from England's dependencies following the implementation of emancipation on August 1.[30]

In British establishments the initial reaction of most slaves on becoming apprentices was to celebrate their newfound freedom, rejoice, and stop work temporarily. However, apprentices rapidly came to realize that they were not entirely free, that they were required to labor forty-five hours per week under the new regulations, and that it was necessary to earn a living. Consequently, within a period ranging from days to a few weeks, most black men—though not necessarily the women and children—returned to work of some kind, either on their former plantations, on their own plots, or in the towns. The results were uneasiness among whites, a mutation in work structures, and at least a temporary decrease in the output of tropical staple products, primarily sugar. Although the outcome varied greatly both temporally and spatially, in the long run plantation production was negatively affected. This effect was most pronounced in areas, such as Jamaica, in which the ratio of laborers to land acreage was low; in areas with a high ratio, such as Barbados, work remained much more steady.[31] These diverse developments were duly reported by British colonial authorities or the local press, then picked up by the various British dailies, and, in the end, often reproduced by French newspapers, which borrowed widely and freely in this matter from London journals. Because the numerous British colonial and metropolitan publications were widely divided in their opinion on slave liberation, many favoring but others opposing it, French newspapers had a plethora of sources from which to choose.

As news from British territories reached France throughout September and October, 1834, it received a mixed reception from the French press, though more coverage than previously. Some French

30. *Le Journal du commerce*, September 8, 1834.
31. For scholarly examinations of this situation, see the works by Green, *British Slave Emancipation*, and Burn, *Emancipation and Apprenticeship*, in particular.

organs, such as *Le Journal des débats*, *Le Courrier français*, and *L'Indicateur* of Bordeaux, made no editorial comment but simply reproduced reports that they drew apparently haphazardly from the English press, a procedure that perhaps best reflected the uncertainties of the moment. However, others took advantage of the fluid situation to choose information and make statements in line with their own stand on slavery. For example, a legitimist, proslavery daily, *La Quotidienne* (Paris), cited news from Saint Kitts, claiming that in early August martial law had been proclaimed and that everywhere in the British Caribbean, except Antigua, Negroes refused to work.[32] Similarly, *Le Moniteur du commerce*, while publishing some items indicating stability in British possessions, tended for the most part to quote from various London dailies about the uncooperative and insubordinate attitudes of the apprentices.[33] In the autumn of 1834 *Le Temps* also had a penchant for news from the British colonies about troubles, arrests, and demonstrations. Conversely, the liberal, proabolitionist *Le National* (Paris) waxed poetic about "this noble example" of English philanthropy, this act "of humanity and of national honor." Although *Le National* felt obliged to carry some English reports about "nonreassuring news" from Trinidad and Antigua, it was obviously more pleased to cite the *Courrier* about the "exemplary conduct" of apprentices in Barbados.[34] *Le Sémaphore de Marseille*, a port city journal favorable to emancipation in the 1830s, spoke, too, of "the happy attempts" being made in British holdings, where "indolent slaves" were being transformed into "happy and contented workers."[35] French newspapers' early reactions to the reality of

32. *La Quotidienne*, September 9, 1834. This study will employ the currently preferred term *blacks* rather than *Negroes*, except when the latter is actually cited in the source itself. My research, however, indicates that in the 1830s and 1840s Frenchmen often used the terms interchangeably, not as value judgments but as devices of literary alternation, with vociferous proslavery advocates like T. M. A. Jollivet using the term *black* almost exclusively and determined abolitionists like Victor Schoelcher often preferring to employ the term *Negro*. For an attempt to quantify the use of these words as they pertain to the French slave trade in the eighteenth and nineteenth centuries, see Serge Daget, "Les mots esclave, nègre, Noir, et les jugements de valeur sur la traite negrière dans la littérature abolitionniste française de 1770 à 1845," *Revue française d'histoire d'outre-mer*, LX (1973), 511–48.
33. See especially *Le Moniteur du commerce*, August 30 and December 6, 1834.
34. *Le Temps*, September 28, 30, October 11, December 13, 1834; *Le National*, August 12, September 21, 28, 1834.
35. *Le Sémaphore de Marseille*, September 25, 1834. In the 1830s and 1840s

British slave liberation were as varied as their responses to the prospect of emancipation had been in the summer and autumn of 1833 and as closely related to the stance on slavery adopted by the individual organs.

In an editorial of October 22 *Le Constitutionnel* reflected an impression that would emerge in both French press and government circles in late 1834 when it reassured its readers that, despite early news of an alarming nature from the British Caribbean, everything now indicated that order was restored, that "this great act of colonial regeneration" would be accomplished peacefully. Later that year the newspaper insisted again that "sinister predictions" about British abolition bringing disorders to the West Indian archipelago were being belied. *Le Constitutionnel* was not alone in noting this development. *Le Sémaphore de Marseille*, too, pointed out that rumors about troubles in British dependencies had been exaggerated.[36] The fact that the transition from slavery to apprenticeship had been effected rather smoothly was beginning to sink into the French mentality.

This reassuring tendency was reinforced by further reports in 1835. Even newspapers that preferred printing the worst about the British experience were now obliged to face up to the facts. *Le Moniteur du commerce* avowed that the situation in Britain's sugar isles was satisfactory, with no indication of insubordination by blacks. As late as December, 1834, *Le Temps* had dwelt upon past occurrences, insisting that disruptions had been widespread in British possessions; but in early 1835 it cited British sources about the good effect of liberation, with blacks submitting to apprenticeship and the adjustment being realized with calm.[37] This altered tone discernible in the discourse of the metropolitan press

---

Marseille was the second most important French port for commercial contact with the French West Indies, following only Le Havre in both number and tonnage of ships dealing with these sugar colonies. Marseille had far outdistanced both Bordeaux and Nantes, the third and fourth most important colonial ports at this time, ports that in the eighteenth century had dominated French colonial trade. For statistics on the colonial trade of the major French seaports, see Jennings, "La presse havraise et l'esclavage," 68–71.

36. *Le Constitutionnel*, October 22, December 16, 1834; *Le Sémaphore de Marseille*, September 20, October 5–6, 1834.

37. *Le Moniteur du commerce*, March 8, 1835; *Le Temps*, December 13, 1834, February 13, 1835.

was echoed by dispatches from the colonies, although French Caribbean officials still had little firsthand information about neighboring British holdings. Two successive governors of French Guiana, Louis Jean Guillaume Jubelin and André Aimé Pariset, reported in the same sense to their superiors in the navy and colonial ministry: after an initial refusal by blacks to work, there had been no significant trouble in British Guiana, where tranquillity reigned. Admiral Ange René Mackau, at the time visiting Antigua as commander of the French West Indian naval station, also informed Paris that freedmen had taken up work again amidst general calm.[38] A turning point was occurring in French perception of British emancipation by the mid-1830s as Frenchmen began to realize that British colonial establishments had not been swept away by upheavals after all.

To be sure, some French apostles of slavery could not, or would not, forget the minor problems that had accompanied the implementation of British slave liberation. When the Chamber of Deputies brought up the slavery question in its discussions in late April, 1835, the abolitionist Hippolyte Passy proudly proclaimed that order and peace had not been troubled by the freeing of British slaves. His statement was challenged, however, by the colonial spokesman François Mauguin, who insisted upon those disturbances that had taken place, magnifying their importance in the process.[39] Nevertheless, as time went on, an ever greater consensus developed on the issue, with even most organs favorable to the colonies conceding that British emancipation had been a generally tranquil experience. In 1837 *Le Temps* admitted that in the two years following the granting of freedom there had been hardly any agitation and that any difficulties which had arisen had been "partial and short-lived." Likewise, *La Paix* (Paris), an inveterate defender of slavery, granted that the English proceedings had been peaceful and without grave perturbations.[40] No colonial sympathizer contradicted the abolitionist François Mongin de Montrol when he asserted in a pamphlet in 1835 that not one drop of blood

38. Jubelin to Minister, November 13, 1834, Pariset to Minister, April 6, 1835, both in Gén. 165 (1337), Mackau to Minister, June 8, 1835, in Gén. 144 (1225), ANSOM.

39. *Le Moniteur universel*, April 23, 1835.

40. *Le Temps*, October 15, 1837; *La Paix*, October 14, 1836.

had been spilled in the English emancipation process.[41] When the doctrinaire Charles de Rémusat submitted to the Chamber of Deputies in 1838 his report on Passy's proposal to free slave children at birth, he noted that from the point of view of peace and security the English experiment had succeeded beyond all hope.[42] There was little doubt by the late 1830s about the generally pacific nature of the transformation from servitude to apprenticeship in the British Caribbean.

A corollary to early French concerns about difficulties in Britain's colonies was the fear that any disruptions, or even the example of the peaceful implementation of freedom, would have detrimental effects on France's possessions. The proximity of the French and British islands, the impossibility of preventing interchanges between them, and the fact that some French slaves had fled to British holdings even before 1834 combined at first to convince French *colons* and their government that the security of the French West Indies was endangered by British emancipation. When the British measure went into effect, *Le Journal du Havre* voiced colonial anxiety about France's Caribbean isles being "submitted to a rather difficult test." The Le Havre organ then went on to advocate strengthening garrisons and improving the slaves' condition to ward off danger. The question in most colonial minds, as clearly articulated by *Le Journal du commerce*, was whether France's "300,000 slaves [a slightly inflated figure] could breathe the air of liberty which blew from the English colonies" and still remain tranquil.[43] As General Henri Bertrand, who had been Napoleon's faithful companion on St. Helena and who was now a proprietor on Martinique, told Jules Lechevalier in 1838 when the latter visited the island: "It is not the abolitionist tribunal in the Chamber of Deputies that we dread the most. Dominica to the north and Saint Lucia to the south . . . there is the real abolitionist

41. François Mongin de Montrol, *Des colonies anglaises depuis l'émancipation des esclaves et de l'influence de cette émancipation sur les colonies françaises* (Paris, 1835), 14.

42. Société française pour l'abolition de l'esclavage, *No. 9. Rapport fait au nom de la commission chargée de l'examen de la proposition de M. Passy, sur le sort des esclaves dans les colonies françaises* (Paris, 1838), 44, hereinafter cited as Rémusat Commission, *Rapport*.

43. *Le Journal du Havre*, October 8, 1934; *Le Journal du commerce*, April 24, 1835.

tribunal which speaks to the Negroes, and from which emanate menaces and warnings for the masters."[44]

Throughout the 1830s both procolonial and antislavery elements tended to view the constant trickle of fugitive slaves from French to British territories as evidence of the destabilizing effect of British slave liberation. Still, there was little consensus on the extent of the problem, and the presumed significance of these evasions vacillated according to the personal proclivities of the reporter. For example, *Le Journal du Havre* in July, 1835, bemoaned the continued flight of blacks from Martinique; *Le Moniteur du commerce* asserted in January, 1836, that the number of fugitive slaves from Martinique had not increased since 1834; the colonial spokesman Baron Dupin claimed in the legislature in the spring of 1836 that the practice of escaping to Britain's holdings had practically ceased; and in the autumn of that same year *Le Bulletin colonial* (Paris), a determined plantocratic organ, denounced the "scourge of evasions."[45] In 1836 the Colonial Council of Martinique also complained of the flight of slaves to the British Caribbean isles and requested the implementation of preventive measures by the government.[46] Colonial spokesmen might continue to point to the threat that slave evasions posed to the French West Indies, but such complaints were probably intended primarily to draw additional funds from Paris for increased colonial defenses and internal security measures. The actual number of fugitive slaves appears to have been relatively small.[47] The insignificance

44. Jules Lechevalier, *Rapport sur les questions coloniales . . . à la suite d'un voyage fait aux Antilles et aux Guyanes pendant les années 1838 et 1839* (2 vols.; Paris, 1843–44), I, 26. For more information on Lechevalier, see Jack Hayward, "From Utopian Socialism, via Abolitionism to the Colonisation of French Guiana: Jules Lechevalier's West Indian Fiasco, 1838–44" (unpublished paper presented to Colloque International sur la traite des Noirs, Nantes, 1985).

45. *Le Journal du Havre*, July 18, 1835; *Le Moniteur du commerce*, January 9, 1836; *Le Moniteur universel*, May 26, 1836; *Le Bulletin colonial*, October 3, 1836.

46. As reported in *Le Courrier français*, August 10, 1836.

47. Although no exact figures are available in French depositories, even the most exaggerated estimates point to a total of only about 2,000 fugitive slaves from the 1830s to the mid-1840s. At the time, however, there was considerable disagreement as to the extent of the problem. In a discussion in the Chamber of Deputies in 1836, Baron Dupin agreed with the British claim that some 600 French slaves had fled to English possessions in the previous three years (*Le Moniteur universel*, May 26, 1836), while the commander of the West Indian naval station, Admiral Arnous, insisted in 1840 that only 500 to 600 French slaves had fled to British dependencies since 1816 (Arnous to Minister, October 15, 1840, in Gén. 144 [1225], ANSOM). In

of the problem is attested to by the fact that the navy and colonial ministry was never preoccupied with the issue, though French colonial garrisons were temporarily strengthened and the governor of Martinique took the precautionary measure of briefly stationing troops along his shores in August, 1834, to preclude the escape of slaves to Saint Lucia.[48]

In reality, most French slaves seem to have been little influenced in the short term by British emancipation, despite the close proximity of the British refuge. As early as 1834, reports arrived from the French Caribbean indicating that, apart from occasional evasions—which could act as an escape valve to drain off the most discontented or desperate elements—French slaves displayed few signs of being moved by British colonial developments. Governor Emmanuel Halgan of Martinique indicated that British abolition had caused no incidents on his island. Admiral Arnous, then the governor of Guadeloupe, also reported in 1834 that news of the British action "produced no noticeable effect here."[49] Not all French colonial fears were quieted, because escapes did continue; and in the mid-1830s French colonists realized that the real test might come only when British apprenticeship ended and French slaves felt the attraction of complete freedom in the British West Indies. One might surmise that British emancipation contributed in the long run to the general feeling of inquietude that gripped the French plantation colonies in the 1830s and 1840s, but a recent study has shown convincingly that the growing pressure within France for slave liberation was the overwhelming factor behind this malaise.[50] As for the possibility that British emancipation adversely affected the price of French slaves, it is noteworthy that a major official in the French navy and colonial ministry and the

1845 the abolitionist Count Beugnot asserted in the Chamber of Peers that there were some 700 or 800 escaped French slaves in Dominica and 600 each in Saint Lucia and Antigua (Le Moniteur universel, April 5, 1845). Schoelcher indicated that between 1845 and 1847 a minimum of 185 additional slaves fled to the British West Indies (Victor Schoelcher, Histoire de l'esclavage pendant les deux dernières années [2 vols.; Paris, 1847], I, 439–54).

48. Halgan to Minister, August 9, 1834, Gén. 156 (1299), ANSOM.

49. Arnous to Minister, January 29, August 10, 1834, both in Gén. 144 (1225), ANSOM.

50. Christian Schnakenbourg, La crise du système esclavagiste, 1835–1847 (Paris, 1980), vol. I of Histoire de l'industrie sucrière en Guadeloupe.

former governor of Guiana and Guadeloupe, Jubelin, informed the Broglie Commission on slavery in 1842 of his belief that British abolition had caused a decline in the pecuniary value of French colonial slaves since 1835.[51] However, this tendency, too, is more attributable to apprehension about eventual French moves against slavery than to uneasiness about British developments. There is as a whole, then, little evidence that British emancipation had a marked disruptive effect upon the everyday operation of the French colonial slave system.

As time went on, French *colons* became more comforted and reassured by the relative stability of slave structures, which continued to prevail in France's territories. When British apprenticeship was terminated in 1838, Jubelin, then the governor of Guadeloupe, reported that this, plus the possibility of French emancipation, had caused a relaxation of discipline toward, though no disorder among, slaves under his jurisdiction.[52] It appears that the situation in the British West Indies had induced at least some French slave owners to treat their slaves more humanely in order to forestall slave agitation. Still, this too might have been a limited phenomenon, for it was not mentioned in other reports, and it seems to contradict traditional colonial claims that French slaves were generally treated more leniently than those of other slave-holding nations. Admiral Mackau, a former governor of Martinique, testified in 1838 before a Chamber of Deputies commission investigating the possibility of French slave liberation that his colony had remained calm and virtually unaffected by Britain's actions.[53] (The commission was chaired by François Guizot, with Rémusat acting as reporter.) Testimony deposed a year later by the colonial delegates before a new Chamber of Deputies commission (presided over by Count Xavier de Sade and having Alexis de Tocqueville as reporter) confirmed the fact

51. France, Ministère de la Marine et des Colonies, *Commission instituée, par décision royale du 26 mai 1840, pour l'examen des questions relatives à l'esclavage et à la constitution publique des colonies. Procès-verbaux* (Paris, 1840–42), session of April 25, 1842, hereinafter cited as Broglie Commission, Minutes.

52. Jubelin to Minister, June 30, 1838, in Corr. Gén., Guadeloupe 85, ANSOM.

53. "Procès-verbaux de la commission nommée par la Chambre des Députés pour l'examen de la proposition de M. Hippolyte Passy sur le sort des esclaves dans les colonies françaises" (hereinafter cited as Rémusat Commission, Minutes), session of April 3, 1838, Gén. 161 (1322), ANSOM.

that tranquillity had reigned in France's establishments despite the British initiative. E. de Jabrun, a wealthy plantation owner representing Guadeloupe, affirmed that so far no fermentation had manifested itself in his colony, while Vidal de Lingendes of Guiana pointed out that slaves were aware of what was happening in England's territories but were as submissive as ever. Cools of Martinique assured the commission that French slaves remained calm and had not been excited by their knowledge of occurrences in the neighboring British islands; and Th. Ruyneau de Saint-Georges of Bourbon insisted that "English emancipation has in no way affected, until now, the discipline in slave workshops."[54] Mackau had perfectly reflected colonial sentiments when he assured the Rémusat Commission that, despite British moves, "there is no urgency for emancipation."[55] French planters were coming to realize that much of their initial apprehension had been unfounded, that the freeing of British slaves would not provoke significant unrest or perturbations within French colonial holdings.

Even before the British Emancipation Act had gone into effect in 1834, one of the primary assumptions of Frenchmen had been that England's decision would cause agitation and disorder within its colonies and that troubles would subsequently spread to France's possessions. Already in the mid-1830s these fears were being assuaged. Not only had the British precedent of a peaceful slave liberation process quieted many French concerns about unrest in France's dependencies, but it had done much to negate the legacy of fear left in the French mentality by the uprising in Saint Domingue some forty years earlier. Although a historian has suggested that from the time of the French Revolution until 1845 Saint Domingue was a constant theme in French literature on slavery and the slave trade,[56] a thorough analysis of sources of the time indicates that in reality its importance as a term of reference was declining markedly in the late 1830s and that it was seldom men-

54. Société française pour l'abolition de l'esclavage, No. 14. Rapport fait au nom de la commission chargée d'examiner la proposition de M. de Tracy, relative aux esclaves des colonies, par A. de Tocqueville (Paris, 1839), 63–64, hereinafter cited as Tocqueville Commission, Rapport. An English translation of this document is available in Seymour Drescher (ed.), Tocqueville and Beaumont on Social Reform (New York, 1968), 98–136.
55. Rémusat Commission, Minutes, April 3, 1838.
56. Daget, "Les mots esclave, nègre, Noir," 534.

tioned in either proslavery or antislavery discourse in the 1840s. There is no doubt that the peaceful transition between servitude and freedom that had transpired in the English colonies was reassuring Frenchmen and destroying the fear-inspiring image of Saint Domingue. The abolitionist Passy noted in 1838 that the English experiment was influencing the French to forget Saint Domingue by demonstrating that liberty for blacks did not mean "conflagration and ruin."[57] As the abolitionist Guillaume Adam de Félice pointed out in the 1840s, to try to draw a parallel between Saint Domingue and slave liberation after the orderly and peaceful example set by England would be to display "gross ignorance."[58]

After having weighed the early results of British abolition from the point of view of security and order, at least those Frenchmen favorable to similar action by France could conclude that the British experience had been a success. Accordingly, French advocates of slave liberation were quick to point out the implications of the British precedent for France. In the Chamber of Peers the moderate abolitionist Achille Charles Léonce Victor, duc de Broglie, said the British model showed that concerns about undertaking emancipation had been exaggerated and that destroying slavery was possible "without trouble, without disorder."[59] Le Journal du commerce, still in its early liberal phase, insisted in 1835 that all initial fears about abolition in England's colonies being "the signal for anarchy and pillage" had been dissipated and that "civilized nations" like France should follow in England's footsteps. Similarly, L'Indicateur of Bordeaux, somewhat favorable to emancipation in the mid-1830s, affirmed that England had abolished servitude without bloodshed and asked why France could not do the same.[60] During debate in the lower house on April 22 and 23, 1835, Passy also exclaimed that England had liberated her slaves while maintaining order and that the time had come for France to consider eradicating bondage.[61]

French abolitionists were citing the British example as one that France should emulate. It was now up to the French Ministry of the

---

57. Le Moniteur universel, February 16, 1838.
58. Guillaume de Félice, Emancipation immédiate et complète des esclaves: Appel aux abolitionistes [sic] (Paris, 1846), 28–29, 93.
59. Le Moniteur universel, February 25, 1835.
60. Le Journal du commerce, March 7, 1835; L'Indicateur, April 26, 1835.
61. Le Moniteur universel, April 23, 1835.

Navy and Colonies to weigh the issue of British slave liberation and its implications for France. Indeed, during the mid-1830s the French government was closely examining the British emancipation process and coming to its own conclusions about it.

TWO

THE BRITISH EXPERIENCE AND THE FORMULATION OF FRENCH POLICY

In March, 1841, the French Protestant biweekly *L'Espérance* declared to its readers that "the example of England was the major motive that determined France to take up" the question of slave liberation.[1] Speaking on emancipation in the Chamber of Deputies three years later, the noted abolitionist and opposition leader Alexandre Auguste Ledru-Rollin also exclaimed that "the impetus [for antislavery] was given by England."[2] Proponents of French abolitionism obviously tended to attribute great importance to the influence of the British precedent on France. In a sense they—and their British colleagues who harbored similar beliefs—were right. As has been shown, the realization that Britain was freeing her slaves had obliged Frenchmen and their government to weigh the ramifications of this development on France's colonial structure. French officials were compelled to take notice of emancipation, formulate a policy toward it, and in the process consider the possibility of imitating British actions.

The first step in the formulation of French government policy was the gathering of adequate information on the British experience. When the French navy and colonial minister first realized that abolition was about to be effected by Britain, his initial reaction was to request information on the situation in the British

1. *L'Espérance*, March 8, 1841. This statement was cited with pride by the British abolitionist journal the *British and Foreign Anti-Slavery Reporter* (hereinafter cited as the *BFAS Reporter*), on March 24, 1841.
2. *Le Moniteur universel*, May 5, 1844.

colonies.[3] At the same time his department launched a concerted effort to analyze thoroughly French and British newspaper reports on the issue. Throughout the period of the July Monarchy the French government would look to the press as a source of data on the process of British slave liberation, but never was it as dependent on journalistic accounts as during the years immediately following the British decision to emancipate.

It is significant that administrators in Paris first became aware of Great Britain's intention to free its slaves through French (and, indirectly, English) press accounts.[4] In the period 1833 through 1835 the French navy and colonial ministry continued to depend on this medium as a source of intelligence on British colonial events. In most of the numerous dossiers of the holdings of the Archives Nationale, Section Outre-Mer, relating to British emancipation there are clippings, extracts, and summaries from both French and British dailies, though the British sources are usually drawn from translations made by French journalists. The frequent citation of the British press by French organs indicates how dependent the French newspaper establishment was on its British equivalent for information. The fact that the vast majority of British articles cited provide news reports rather than editorial comment also shows to what extent French newspapers were content to give factual accounts rather than opinionative analyses of the emancipation issue. Besides the scattered newspaper clippings in the archival holdings, there is an entire dossier devoted to press entries relating to the British situation from 1833 through January, 1836, along with a neatly drawn up index to the diverse listings.[5] The register meticulously notes the different articles, indicating whether they deal with evaluations of British colonial developments in general or within a particular colony, and giving the date, the French journal in which the item appeared, and often the British organ from which it was drawn. This cataloging process demonstrates on the one hand how ineffective the navy and colonial minister's intelligence-gathering initiative was—for a thorough examination of the French press proves the indexed listing of 104

3. Minister to Governors, May 24, 1833, in Corr. Gén., Colonies françaises, 1833, ANSOM.
4. Minister to Talleyrand, March 13, 1833, in Gén. 206 (1513), ANSOM.
5. Gén. 82 (716), ANSOM.

articles to be far from complete—and on the other hand how reliant on journalistic reports the French government was during the early stage of the British abolition process.

Besides scrutinizing French press accounts of English news items, French ministers of the navy and colonies endeavored to tap British sources directly. In Rigny's first dispatch to France's ambassador in London on the British emancipation question, he not only displayed his concern about the matter but also solicited all possible information on it.[6] Undoubtedly as a result of this request, the French embassy in London began sending diverse documentation on the subject to Paris, although apparently in a rather haphazard fashion. In January, 1837, the navy and colonial minister, Admiral Claude Charles Marie du Campe de Rosamel, wrote to the French consulate in London to stress the importance of information that could enlighten his administration on the British approach, asking particularly for newspapers from Jamaica, Barbados, and Antigua, where, he argued, freedom of the press permitted the disclosure of a variety of data. Rosamel followed this up in March with an order for subscriptions to the Jamaica *Herald, West Indian Barbados,* and Antigua *Register.* The receipt of these publications, along with various other documents from London, enabled Rosamel to attest in August, 1838, that he was well informed on events in the British Caribbean.[7]

That the navy and colonial ministry was not always entirely satisfied with these intelligence sources, however, was evidenced by a series of notes emanating from this department in the middle to late 1830s. In 1835 Rosamel's predecessor as minister of the navy and colonies, Admiral Victor Guy, baron Duperré, had explained to the governor of Martinique that, because British dailies were "far from meriting full confidence," representing the opinions of their editors more than anything else, it was desirable to send an observer incognito to Jamaica to witness the emancipation process.[8] Four years later Duperré, who had by then returned as navy and colonial minister, asserted that it was essential for his department "to procure prompt and sure means of information" on

6. Minister to Talleyrand, March 13, 1833, in Gén. 206 (1513), ANSOM.
7. Minister to Consul in London, January 25, March 31, 1837, both in Corr. Gén. 189, Minister to Governor of Guadeloupe, August 28, 1838, in Gén. 144 (1225), ANSOM.
8. Minister to Governor of Martinique, July 4, 1835, in Corr. Gén. 187, ANSOM.

British occurrences, for journals and public documents from London could be prejudiced or inconclusive.[9] Duperré was still more explicit in a note written shortly thereafter to the commander of the West Indian naval station to request that he send an emissary to the British colonies. English newspapers, he explained, were no "means of learning the truth," for "in them facts are often dissimulated, altered, or contested in passionate polemics." Nevertheless, the ministry did not stop receiving British dailies and documents; and in 1840 it renewed its order for them.[10] The government also continued to glean data on British colonial affairs from the French press. Indeed, when the abolitionist Agénor de Gasparin requested documentation on British abolition, the minister of the navy and colonies at the time, Jean Marguerite, baron Tupinier, replied—in what amounted to a rather abrupt refusal—that the best means of obtaining information on the subject was from the fiercely proslavery newspaper L'Outre-mer (Paris), "if its tendencies do not render it suspect in Mr. de Gasparin's eyes."[11] Still, by the late 1830s the government's reliance on British or French newspaper accounts for insight into the British emancipation system had declined markedly.

A parallel source of news, which soon superseded journalistic sources, had already been established by the mid-1830s with the dispatch of direct observers to British territories. It is revelatory that the navy and colonial department's detailed effort to index articles on English abolition ended in January, 1836. Obviously, by this time information was being obtained by more direct procedures. It appears, in fact, that this new means of intelligence gathering might have originated with French colonial authorities rather than as a result of directives from Paris. The first move along these lines seems to have been taken in 1833 by the governor of Martinique, Dupotet, who, upon receiving Rigny's request of May 24 for all possible data on British dependencies, dispatched a naval

9. Minister of the Navy and Colonies to Minister of Foreign Affairs, September 16, 1839, in Mémoires et documents, Afrique 28, Traite des Noirs 14, Archives des Affaires Etrangères, Paris, hereinafter cited as AAE.
    10. Minister to Commander of West Indian Naval Station, October 30, 1839, in Corr. Gén. 191, Minister to Direction des Fonds, October 16, 1840, in Corr. Gén. 194, ANSOM.
    11. Minister to Gasparin, April 11, 1839, in Gén. 171 (1376), ANSOM.

lieutenant, Pardeilhan, and his vessel to Saint Lucia.[12] Other French colonial officials followed suit, and by the summer of 1835 the navy and colonial ministry under Duperré had sanctioned these procedures and adopted them as its own principal method of obtaining information on developments relating to British slave liberation. A register in the French colonial archives lists thirty-nine reports that resulted from these measures between 1833 and July, 1841, and several additional assessments came in after 1841.[13] The French navy and colonial department had stumbled on, and then developed, what it believed to be a more reliable and efficient means than press accounts for fathoming the British emancipation record.

Although the new method of intelligence gathering provided considerable material, the aptitude and objectivity of the observers, and thus their reliability, should be questioned. The choice of the men sent out on mission to the British colonies apparently was often made at random, depending at first almost entirely on the personnel and vessels available at any given moment to colonial administrators. Pardeilhan, for example, was the commander of a small customs cutter in port at the time Dupotet made his decision to send out a ship. Similarly, Dupotet informed the French government that he would dispatch a naval officer and his vessel to British Guiana as soon as one became free for such a mission; and Dupotet's successor, Halgan, indicated that he had hoped to obtain more data on British possessions but that no ship had been at hand to send to Jamaica.[14]

The element of chance in the selection of emissaries also entered the picture in another fashion. After sending in several reports, Pardeilhan and his crew disappeared in a hurricane in February, 1838; and another officer on a similar mission, Captain Halley, perished in rough seas off Cayenne in 1839. The Ministry of the Navy and Colonies instructed the West Indian naval commander to replace Pardeilhan with Captain Monay of the *Victorieuse*, but Admiral Arnous replied that this officer was on duty elsewhere and

12. Governor of Martinique to Minister, August 2, 1833, in Gén. 156 (1302), ANSOM.
13. Gén. 144 (1225), ANSOM.
14. Dupotet to Minister, October 28, 1833, in Gén. 178 (1420), Halgan to Minister, September 5, 1835, in Gén. 144 (1225), ANSOM.

that Captain Marie Jean François Layrle of the *Hussard* would be equal to Monay for the task.[15] Apparently, even when officials in Paris designated individuals for observation service, they permitted local naval authorities to exercise considerable freedom in executing the orders. Moreover, it seems that certain well-known or influential personalities could impose themselves on the government as observers. In the late 1830s Jules Lechevalier, an author, journalist, and Saint-Simonian theorist who appears to have had the respect of the navy and colonial ministry and connections with the plantocracy, wrote from Martinique requesting a mission to the British West Indies. He explained that he was intending to visit the British dependencies to write articles for the Parisian daily *La Presse*—incidentally, an organ sympathetic to slavery— but that most of his salary for this appointment would go to pay off debts incurred with his former newspaper, the proslavery *Journal de Paris*. He added that if the administration would agree to grant him an additional sum he would write some items for *La Presse* and other, confidential ones for the navy and colonial department. Although he had the support of Admiral Alphonse Louis Théodore Moges, governor of Martinique, navy administrators in Paris refused to provide him with funds, much to his chagrin.[16] Nevertheless, Lechevalier submitted to the navy and colonial ministry a report on his trip that eventually found its place among official material, thus receiving governmental sanction ex post facto. It seems, then, that the entire process of selecting candidates for missions to the British colonies was quite unspecific and uncoordinated, with functionaries receiving appointments for reasons other than particular abilities or aptitudes.

The research methods of French commissioners proved as arbitrary at times as the means by which they had been selected. Captain Halley, on mission in 1838 to study Jamaica, admitted that he had spent only twelve days on the island before making his report. Likewise, Pardeilhan, who was supposed to visit Jamaica in 1837, wrote his account of conditions there while his ship was quarantined in a Jamaican port because of smallpox. As he had

15. Layrle to Minister, September 13, 1842, in Gén. 169 (1374), Arnous to Minister, December 30, 1839, in Gén. 144 (1225), ANSOM.
16. Lechevalier to Filleau de Saint Hilaire, Director of the Colonies, December 28, 1838, September 4, 1839, both in Gén. 169 (1373), ANSOM.

been unable to land on the island himself, he had obtained the information upon which he based his observations from two "reliable" people.[17] Even when French assessors gave the appearance of being thorough in their investigations, their procedures could be questioned. A French abolitionist, writing from Guadeloupe, suggested that Attorney General Bernard of that island, entrusted with a mission to British territories, had made superficial evaluations because of his "incurable laziness."[18] Indeed, it seems that while on Barbados, Bernard investigated almost entirely through contacts with the British planter class or colonial officials.[19] As Jules Lechevalier—who, by the way, was himself quite thorough in his research methods—remarked, it was particularly difficult for French observers to be impartial, because, on Jamaica for example, they often made their initial contacts with former *colons* of Saint Domingue, who associated the entire emancipation process with the terror of their previous experience.[20] Still more important, all of the French personnel sent on mission to British holdings were either naval officers or local functionaries, strata known for their connections with and sympathy for the French colonial establishment and its essential structure, slavery. In fact, at times these assessors themselves were directly associated with the institution of slavery. Bernard of Guadeloupe, for instance, was not only attorney general of that colony, but the owner—through his wife, apparently—of one of the largest plantations on that island.[21] One of the most astute of the French emissaries, Jean Marie Eugène d'Arvoy of Mauritius, also seems to have possessed sugar plantations or to have been personally involved with enterprises that used slaves before he assumed observer status.[22] As the British

17. Halley, report of December 3, 1838, Pardeilhan to Minister, April 18, 1837, both in Gén. 178 (1418), ANSOM.
18. Société française pour l'abolition de l'esclavage, *No. 8. Année 1838* (Paris, June, 1838), 29, report from Guadeloupe dated February 26. For an English edition of Bernard's assessment of Barbados, see David L. Gobert and Jerome S. Handler (eds. and trans.), "Barbados in the Apprenticeship Period: The Report of a French Colonial Official," *Journal of the Barbados Museum and Historical Society*, XXXVI (1980), 108–28.
19. Gobert and Handler, "Barbados in the Apprenticeship Period," 109.
20. Lechevalier, *Rapport*, II, vi. For Lechevalier's methods, see Hayward, "From Utopian Socialism."
21. *La Réforme*, May 15, 1844; Victor Schoelcher, *Colonies étrangères et Haïti. Résultats de l'émancipation anglaise* (2 vols.; Paris, 1842–43), II, 436.
22. Personnel dossier, d'Arvoy, in AAE.

abolitionist periodical the *British and Foreign Anti-Slavery Reporter* remarked, the direct ties French commissioners had with the colonial system made their testimony inconclusive and unsatisfactory to "any impartial person."[23]

Not only did French observers harbor sociocultural bias toward the British emancipation process, but the instructions they received prior to undertaking their duties often tended to prejudice their findings further. These directives, which varied considerably, at times were clear and forthright pleas for well-informed evaluations. Pardeilhan, for example, was enjoined to "gather all information capable of enlightening" the government on the slavery question. However, the general instructions sent by the navy and colonial minister to the colonial governments insisted that officials on mission examine in particular the maintenance of "production and colonial staples."[24] Injunctions of this kind tended to stress a negative aspect of British emancipation—declining production—rather than positive or ethical ones, such as the preservation of order, the improvement in freedmen's living standards, or the recovery of human dignity. Furthermore, these orders often gained additional nuance or bias when paraphrased by colonial governors. When charging Attorney General Bernard with his assignment, Admiral Arnous, then the governor of Guadeloupe, admonished him to be objective but at the same time told him that "reliable documents no longer permit us to doubt" that on nearby English islands "emancipation has exercised the most baneful influence on work and production and has considerably weakened the value of property, while also placing the black population in a flagrant state of vagabondage." In the colony of Bourbon the highly prejudiced Governor de Hell sent an influential member of the Colonial Council, the slave-owning Dejean de la Batie, on a mission to Mauritius. Hell encouraged his representative to operate with "the most complete impartiality" but then suggested that abolitionists were unrealistic and that slave liberation was Utopian.[25] Laden with backgrounds and instructions like these, French assessors of British emancipation were likely to operate

23. *BFAS Reporter*, April 17, 1844.

24. Minister to Pardeilhan, June 17, 1836, in Gén. 144 (1225), Minister to Governors, July 4, 1835, in Corr. Gén. 187, ANSOM.

25. Arnous to Minister, September 7, 1835, in Gén. 144 (1225), Hell to de la Batie, October 15, 1839, in Gén. 164 (1333), ANSOM.

with as much partiality—though of a negative rather than positive nature—as the French government believed the British press displayed.

A close examination of the most significant and representative reports made by French observers of England's colonies shows the extent to which they stressed the negative facets of the British experiment. One of the earliest and most influential scrutinizers of the British colonial scene was the ill-fated Pardeilhan, who issued a preliminary statement in October, 1835, a report on British Guiana in March, 1837, and three long letters on Jamaica in 1837 and 1838. In his document on British Guiana, Pardeilhan insisted that the British Emancipation Act was "a narrow and shabby work," drawn up "without knowledge of reality" and leading to "a future of misery and barbarity" for the colony. Whites in British Guiana, he testified, despaired for the attitude of the blacks; apprenticeship had exacerbated relationships between field hands and planters, something that augured poorly for the future and might lead to a return to barbarism. Citing the "well-known laziness of the Negro," he noted that few blacks worked voluntarily under the new regime and doubted whether they would toil at all after apprenticeship ended. Pardeilhan also charged that British Protestant ministers, by preaching equality before God, were actually issuing "a call for violence"—an accusation closely resembling those of British opponents of emancipation. Moreover, he asserted, there was a growing tendency to thievery among apprentices, who did not know how to save or economize and simply tended to live by laboring as little as possible. At times Pardeilhan could make apparently discerning remarks, as when he contrasted, though without drawing the necessary conclusions, the wealth of the whites, brought on by rising sugar prices and the indemnity they had received, with the nudity of the ex-slaves or when he added as an aside that for the freedmen labor was "the most odious sign of slavery." Nevertheless, despite these glimpses of reality and his assurances that his observations were "disinterested," Pardeilhan's early reports not only grossly exaggerated and totally misrepresented the facts by displaying all the prejudices of the planter class but echoed the nineteenth-century work ethic so prevalent among established July Monarchy notables.[26]

26. Report on Demerara, March 1, 1837, in Gén. 165 (1336), ANSOM.

Pardeilhan's tendencies to see developments from the plantocratic point of view continued in his later submissions. In a letter written in 1837, while his ship was in quarantine for smallpox off Jamaica, Pardeilhan did not hesitate to emphasize that production was down in England's colonies, that colonists were profoundly discouraged, that churches were spreading subversive ideas, and that the situation would be totally hopeless following the termination of apprenticeship. The gist of his contention was that by 1840 British freedmen would be worse off than French slaves; therefore, France should proceed only gradually with emancipation. The following year Pardeilhan wrote from Kingston that British Caribbean society was dying, that it might be replaced by "an agglomeration of little barbarous tribes living miserably on the debris" of former colonial wealth. According to the French naval lieutenant, who reemphasized his "impartiality," the English had tried to make a new people before they had made men out of their slaves and, "with the thoughtless application of philanthropic dreaming, only had known how to destroy, while founding nothing." Referring again to the British emancipationists, he added that "the unfortunate Negroes have no greater enemies than these fanatics who dare pretend to be their saviors." Finally, writing from Jamaica in February and August, 1838, Pardeilhan charged that the abolitionist axiom about free labor being cheaper than slave had been put to the lie, for, while wages had doubled, work had generally been abandoned since the end of apprenticeship on August 1.[27] Basing his later reports on Jamaica, the British possession that suffered the most from the effects of slave liberation, Pardeilhan had managed to enumerate all of the most negative aspects of Britain's achievement.

Needless to say, Pardeilhan's assessments received a mixed reception in Europe. Accurately analyzing the essence of his dispatches, the French parliamentary commission studying Passy's emancipation proposal in 1838 concluded that they were "written in somewhat exaggerated terms" and "in the sense of the maintenance or prolongation of [French] slavery." The French abolitionist society was less kind in its appraisal when it insisted that the

27. Pardeilhan to Minister, April 18, 1837, February 1, August 14, 1838, all in Gén. 178 (1418), ANSOM.

lieutenant's statements were "foolish rantings."[28] Officials in Paris, though, saw Pardeilhan's evaluations in a different light. In 1838 the minister of the navy and colonies attempted to insert Pardeilhan's jaundiced note of February, 1838, on Jamaica in the French press. The minister also expressed his desire to bring this document to the attention of the head of the French Cabinet, the president of the Council of Ministers, Count Louis Mathieu Molé.[29] A British colonial newspaper, the Jamaica *Despatch*, was undoubtedly correct when it surmised that Pardeilhan's accounts had influenced—at least to some extent—the French government not to liberate the slaves. Indeed, a functionary in the French navy and colonial department gave credence to this supposition by making a marginal note stating "that's perfect" (*parfait*) on this British press report.[30] British disgust with the attitude of this earliest French observer was clear. As a result of the unfair tone of Pardeilhan's writings, the British Colonial Office ordered its administrators in the colonies, who had provided the French naval officer with numerous official documents, henceforth to be much more reticent and reserved with visiting French commissioners.[31] Ironically, these restrictions probably limited the source material available to future French emissaries and obliged them to become more reliant on the British plantocracy for information.

Not all of the observations made by Frenchmen on Britain's Caribbean colonies were as distorted as those of Pardeilhan. Attorney General Bernard's three reports, issued in 1835, were, in fact, among some of the most reasonable ones made by French investigators, despite abolitionist denunciations of them as superficial. They were largely factual accounts of the political, economic, and social structures of Antigua, Barbados, and Jamaica. The reports were not entirely free of bias or misconceptions, however. For example, Bernard tended to associate himself with the planter class and to emphasize the pitfalls rather than the accomplishments of emancipation. At one point he even exclaimed that

28. Rémusat Commission, Minutes, March 20, 1838; Société française pour l'abolition de l'esclavage, *No. 19* (Paris, April, 1842), 58, session of March 10, 1841.
29. Internal navy and colonial department memo, in Gén. 178 (1418), ANSOM.
30. Marginal note on the translation of an article from the British Guiana *Royal Gazette* of April 18, 1839, which cited a Jamaica *Despatch* article of January 18, 1839, in Gén. 144 (1225), ANSOM.
31. Minister to Commander of West Indian naval station, October 30, 1839, in Gen. 144 (1225), ANSOM.

Barbadian blacks must be given "the tastes and aptitudes of civilized life."[32] An evaluation of British Guiana written in 1838 by the colonial delegate of French Guiana, Vidal de Lingendes, a person who could be suspected of incarnating all the prejudices of an official colonial spokesman, was also much more balanced and fair than might be expected. He pointed out both the achievements and difficulties of British apprenticeship, though insisting that production had declined under this system and that Negroes had a natural penchant for laziness. Indeed, Lingendes' somewhat moderate tone was perhaps motivated by his desire to point out that British slaves had been better prepared for freedom than French ones and that French abolition should be postponed.[33]

In contrast with these more objective assessments, the director of finances of French Guiana, Guillet, issued a report on British Guiana in 1839 couched in terms similar to those Pardeilhan used. He depicted British missionaries disrupting work by spreading "their dangerous maxims" among blacks, whose "laziness, wavering, and insouciance" made planters despair. Guillet also insisted on a theme common to other French commissioners: that British colonial blacks were better off than "the mass of the laboring population of Europe." Similarly, Captain Legretier, who delivered a brief account of the situation on Antigua in the early 1840s, repeated clichés about blacks being "indolent by nature."[34]

Although most of the evaluations received by the French navy and colonial department contained considerable bias and misrepresentation of fact, undoubtedly the least reliable and most blatantly prejudiced of all observers was Dejean de la Batie, a member of the colonial council of Bourbon, who submitted a note on the neighboring British territory of Mauritius in 1840. De la Batie admitted that he had previously spoken out against emancipation but claimed that he had now stripped himself of all personal sentiment, arriving at "a sort of virginity of thought." However, these claims of objectiveness were not borne out by the tenor of his work. In his submission he purported that blacks were not working, that

32. Bernard, report on all three islands, April 10, 1836, in Gén. 178 (1418), ANSOM.
33. Vidal de Lingendes, report of December 28, 1838, in Gén. 165 (1356), ANSOM.
34. Guillet, report of March 16, 1839, Legretier, report of January 1, 1841, both in Gén. 144 (1225), ANSOM.

they had a "natural aversion" for "laborious and orderly" lives. This led him to stress the progressive deprivation of freedmen since the end of apprenticeship: crime was increasing, moral attitudes acquired during slavery were disappearing, and blacks were ceasing to be grateful, loyal, and affectionate, while becoming increasingly prone to "insubordination, laziness, and drunkenness." De la Batie revealed the extent to which he idealized servitude by proclaiming that slaves lived in a state of "infantile joy" from the "cradle to the tomb" but that British abolition had silenced "such gay and so rarely interrupted songs of the blacks and Negresses."[35]

De la Batie's partiality was clearly evident to more open-minded contemporaries. A significant British abolitionist, George W. Alexander, was categorical in denouncing de la Batie's study as "marked by the most inveterate prejudice against emancipation." The Parisian newspaper *Le Temps*, in one of its more liberal moments, gave an identical judgment when it called de la Batie's work an example of "colonial dissoluteness."[36] Governor Hell of Bourbon, however, praised the report as a "remarkable memoir" and its author as "a person of great intelligence, gifted with a quite strong sense of observation."[37] The Ministry of the Navy and Colonies was apparently divided in its opinion of de la Batie's account. One unidentified official remarked that it was "much too expurgated" and that it amounted to an "apology of the French *colon*"; but the minister himself, Admiral Albin Reine, baron Roussin, believed that his observer had "displayed a rare spirit of investigation." Interestingly enough, the ministry decided to publish de la Batie's findings, the minister justifying this decision with the spurious argument that it was the only report available on Mauritius.[38] Obviously, high-placed French administrators shared de la Batie's attitudes and wished to see them publicized.

One of the most serious and professional of all the French assessors of the British colonial scene was Jean Marię Eugène d'Arvoy, who, during a nine-year period from 1835 to 1844, sent in

35. De la Batie, report, undated but identifiable from corroborative evidence as 1840, in Gén. 164 (1333), ANSOM.
36. Alexander, report from Paris, dated March 22, in April 17, 1844, issue of *BFAS Reporter*; *Le Temps*, January 11, 1842.
37. Hell to Minister, November 15, 1839, April 14, 1840, both in Gén. 164 (1333), ANSOM.
38. Internal department note, April 5, 1841, Minister to Governor of Bourbon, September 4, 1840, both in Gén. 164 (1330), ANSOM.

twelve evaluations of the situation on Mauritius.[39] D'Arvoy had
been a merchant captain from Bordeaux before becoming a resi-
dent of Mauritius, where he eventually served as honorary French
consul. As a witness of the postemancipation period on that island
he drew up reports that, at the beginning of his career at least, were
noteworthy for their analytical approach and their effort at objectivity. Although d'Arvoy claimed to have "always been an enemy
of slavery," he, like the other French observers, shared the attitudes
of the planter class in whose circles he gravitated; as mentioned
earlier, he had probably even possessed or employed slaves. Still,
d'Arvoy stood out among his peers for his effort to analyze in depth
the mutations that were occurring in the socioeconomic structure
of the British colonial establishment. He tried, for example, to
understand the situation from the blacks' point of view, noting that
slaves had tended to associate work with bondage and that "for
them 'being free' means the right to live without working." He
remarked that freedmen were "vane, lazy, over-particular, and un-
disciplined," having "all the vices of civilization, and only the
vices"; but he attempted to explain this state as "the result of the
debasement in which they have been so long held." While contend-
ing that many apprentices were not working effectively, he was
also quick to point out that Mauritius was prospering nevertheless
because of the indemnity paid former slave owners and the maintenance of staple production through the importation of laborers
from nearby India.[40] D'Arvoy's early evaluations, then, differ considerably from those of most of his colleagues in their attempt to
assess the situation fairly both from the planters' and blacks' point
of view.

Only after the termination of apprenticeship accelerated the
movement of blacks away from praedial tasks did d'Arvoy begin to
become obsessed with the problem of the cost and efficiency of free
labor. This tendency is reflected in the reports he wrote after the
apprentice system ended in Mauritius on April 1, 1839, eight

39. For a more detailed discussion of d'Arvoy and his reports, see Lawrence C.
Jennings, "Réflexions d'un observateur sur l'émancipation des esclaves britanniques à l'île Maurice," *Revue d'histoire moderne et contemporaine*, XXIX (1982),
462–70.
40. D'Arvoy to Hell, March 24, 1835, d'Arvoy, "Historical account and observations on the emancipation of blacks on Mauritius," September 14, 1837, both in
Gén. 164 (1332), ANSOM.

months later than in the other British holdings. He now remarked that British emancipation, "the most impressive monument of English philanthropy," had perhaps brought happiness to former slaves but that it appeared likely to ruin "most Whites and others who are now proprietors in the colonies." Shortly thereafter he denounced the fact that freedmen were quitting the plantations and that those who did consent to labor were demanding exorbitant salaries. D'Arvoy's disquietude and disapprobation were apparent when he noted that "the future is alarming for everyone," since black Mauritians had "definitely decided not to cooperate with work on the sugar plantations." His dispatches were taking on a somber and sinister tone as he observed that "thousands of unfortunates have no idea of our social obligations."[41] By 1840 d'Arvoy's reports resembled those of his less disinterested counterparts. Blacks, he said, had retained their "savage manners and vicious tendencies"; the English had liberated them "without civilizing them." Like most middle- and upper-class nineteenth-century Europeans imbued with the work ethic for the poor, d'Arvoy proved unable to accept or understand the changing patterns of labor accompanying such an important structural mutation as the suppression of slavery. Like other French observers of the British experience, he now used this precedent to advocate a gradual and cautious approach to slave liberation in France's possessions.[42] D'Arvoy's concern with what he saw as the disastrous socioeconomic results of the British process had obviously altered his view on the British emancipation process. In the early years of d'Arvoy's mission the navy and colonial minister had thanked him for the "care," "intelligence," and "clearness" of his communications, but by 1843 a high official in this department found them "suspect in my eyes of great partiality."[43] Even one of the most astute French evaluators of the British colonial scene had come to assess emancipation in a decidedly negative vein.

An evolution similar to d'Arvoy's can be discerned in the case of

41. D'Arvoy to Minister, April 9, May 1, July 1, August 1, 1839, all in Gén. 164 (1329), ANSOM.

42. D'Arvoy to Minister, August 24, 1840, in Gén. 164 (1329), ANSOM.

43. Minister to d'Arvoy, February 6, 1838, in Gén. 164 (1332), note in the hand of Henri Joseph Mestro, head of the Political and Commercial Bureau in the navy and colonial department and right-hand man of the director of the colonies, Filleau de Saint Hilaire, January 17, 1843, in Gén. 171 (1379), ANSOM.

Marie Jean François Layrle, a navy captain who issued a series of reports on Britain's Caribbean dependencies from 1840 through 1842.[44] Although he acceded to his position largely by chance, when Pardeilhan was lost at sea and his designated successor proved unavailable for service, Layrle undertook his task with determination and energy, traveling aboard his brig the *Hussard* to virtually all of the major British West Indian holdings and discharging his duties with distinction. Layrle, perhaps even more than d'Arvoy, stood out among his peers for the thoroughness, perceptiveness, objectiveness, and accuracy of his analyses. In fact, his accounts were more highly praised and more influential than those of any other French observer of British colonial developments.[45]

Some aspects of Layrle's reports are indeed laudable, even when viewed with historical hindsight. The emphasis he placed on the diversity that marked the extinction of slavery in the different British possessions is noteworthy, the essence of his findings on this matter being corroborated by modern scholarly accounts.[46] Layrle stressed, for instance, that "the results of this social transformation vary according to the area that one examines."[47] He pointed out that enormous differences prevailed between, on the one hand, islands such as Barbados, Saint Christopher, and Antigua, where high population density and little untilled soil obliged freedmen to remain on plantations and work for their former owners, and, on the other hand, the remaining British Caribbean dependencies, where the quantity of virgin land permitted blacks to flee the estates and set themselves up as marginally productive small independent farmers.[48] Layrle also emphasized the varied effects of slave liberation on the general wealth and well-being of

44. For more detail on Layrle and his evaluations, see Lawrence C. Jennings, "French Perceptions of British Slave Emancipation: A French Observer's Views of the Post-Emancipation British Caribbean," *French Colonial Studies*, III (1979), 72–85.

45. Personnel dossier, Layrle, in Service historique de la Marine, Vincennes, France.

46. See, for example, the studies by Green, *British Slave Emancipation*, and Burn, *Emancipation and Apprenticeship*.

47. Layrle to Minister, September 13, 1842, in Gén. 169 (1374), ANSOM.

48. Report on Saint Lucia, Saint Vincent, and Grenada, April, 1840, report on Barbados and Antigua, May 13, 1841, both in Gén. 144 (1225), ANSOM. Layrle's report on Barbados has been translated and annotated by David L. Gobert and Jerome S. Handler, "Barbados in the Post-Apprenticeship Period: The Observations of a French Naval Officer," *Journal of the Barbados Museum and Historical Society*, XXXV (1978), 243–66, XXXVI (1979), 4–15.

the postemancipation colonies. As he remarked, "alongside work and wealth one finds indolence and ruin." British Guiana and Trinidad, he explained, were experiencing prosperity because of their rich lands; the situation on Barbados and Antigua was stable as a result of the availability of inexpensive labor; Saint Vincent and Saint Christopher, though suffering, were better off than Grenada and Saint Lucia, while all four of these were less wretched than Jamaica, "an area lagging behind all the others." As a whole, he suggested, wherever blacks had abandoned the plantations, "there is impoverishment and decadence."[49]

In describing the position of the plantocracy, Layrle proved once again to be a keen analyst. His reports indicated that emancipation had not affected all planters in the same way. In some locations, such as British Guiana, where estate owners had not been deeply in debt prior to abolition, much of the indemnity had gone directly to the masters and had brought them considerable wealth. The situation was different on the islands of Saint Vincent, Grenada, and Jamaica, where many estates had operated with huge deficits that had absorbed the indemnity, the funds being siphoned off to creditors in Europe. Large landowners on these islands tended to be "disgusted" and "discouraged," seeing "the future painted in the most somber colors." While conceding that colonial grumblings might be enhanced by much exaggeration, Layrle believed that many complaints were justified. Still, he could not share the feeling prevalent among some owners that all was lost. In general, Layrle maintained, most proprietors had been able to cope with the situation and even make profits as long as staple prices remained high; but planters, with the exception of those on Antigua and Barbados, found themselves at a disadvantage when sugar values fell.[50]

Although he was objective in many ways, Layrle, like other French commissioners, showed himself to be particularly sensitive to the problems of the planter class. In discussing the alterations that had occurred in the relationship between proprietors and

49. Report on Barbados and Antigua, May 13, 1841, in Gén. 144 (1225), report on Jamaica, January 9, 1842, in Gén. 178 (1418), report on British colonies, September 1842, in Gén. 169 (1374), ANSOM.

50. Report on Saint Lucia, Saint Vincent, and Grenada, April, 1840, in Gén. 144 (1225), Layrle to Minister, September 24, 1841, September 13, 1842, both in Gén. 169 (1374), ANSOM.

freedmen, Layrle remarked on more than one occasion that estate owners were at a disadvantage, for they desperately needed manpower and their competition with each other for laborers inflated the wage scale. Thus, he indicated that "the roles are inverted. . . . [I]t is now the masters who are dependent upon the good or bad graces of the former slaves"; it was "no longer the planters who lay down the law, but the Blacks."[51] Perhaps statements such as these partially reflected the reality of the situation in the early 1840s, when laborers were receiving premium wages and landowners had not yet taken effective concerted action to lower remuneration levels. Nevertheless, the exaggeration in Layrle's assertions reveals a clear procolonist bias in this most detached observer of the postemancipation British Caribbean.

At times Layrle's concern for the welfare of the British plantocracy obviously influenced his analysis of the freedman's position in the 1840s. While avowing that blacks in the English colonies had been "wretched under slavery," when "work was incessant," he still remained convinced that "the situation of blacks is a far cry today from what it had been just a few years ago under servitude." To be sure, the French naval captain was astute enough to admit that not all former slaves had benefited materially from abolition. He indicated, for example, that in Antigua "the Black is still badly off," and in Jamaica "Blacks live as they did under slavery." Elsewhere, though, he found them to be living on a more comfortable level. In "contrast with their former huts," he claimed, they now lived in "beautiful houses of wood," "charming houses" that were decently furnished. Blacks were "well dressed, their women even better outfitted"; sometimes "the women push their elegance to the point of ridicule." Furthermore, their tables were "ornamented with English china" and laden with white bread, "fresh meat and ham." Layrle concluded that freedmen "lacked nothing" from a "physical point of view." Indeed, he maintained that "the material well-being that the Blacks have acquired is the best thing that can be said about British emancipation."

51. Report on Saint Lucia, Saint Vincent, and Grenada, April, 1840, in Gén. 144 (1225), report on Jamaica, July 1, 1840, in Gén. 178 (1418), report on British colonies, September, 1842, in Gén. 169 (1374), ANSOM. It is interesting to note that Layrle had married a French *colon* and obviously gravitated in the same colonial circles as the other French commissioners (Personnel dossier, Service historique de la Marine).

Exclaiming, "what happy Blacks," he proceeded to explain that they were paid high wages, worked only when they wished, and were certainly "happier than most peasants of Europe."[52] The importance Layrle placed on the massive benefits former slaves had reaped from abolition had some basis in fact, for modern historians have also noted an increase in their living standards in the late 1830s and early 1840s.[53] Still, there is little doubt that, by contrasting the difficulties planters faced with the material well-being of the former slaves, Layrle was offering an apologia for British colonial interests while begrudging freedmen their modest gains.

Layrle did not reproach blacks for their infatuation with what he referred to as "civilization," for he believed that their tendency to imitate whites and purchase expensive items might "assure work" by obliging them to return to plantation toil.[54] Throughout his correspondence, Layrle, like d'Arvoy and other French emissaries, displayed a keen interest in the labor problem facing the British Caribbean, although his attitude toward this issue varied somewhat in his different dispatches. At times he affirmed that work habits had improved from the 1830s to the 1840s, while at others he gave credence to the colonial dictum that blacks were afflicted with a "natural laziness" that led them to avoid all praedial tasks, especially because former slaves associated field work with bondage. Still, his overall assessment of the labor question stressed that "the failure of free labor on large estates" was the counterpoint of the "material well-being that Blacks" had acquired. Most field hands were active, but they were tilling their own small holdings, producing garden crops while refraining from toiling on sugar and coffee plantations. In other words, "work had not been abandoned," it had simply "taken a different direction" and had "diminished on the large domains." This development, Layrle was quick to point out, might be agreeable to former slaves, who could live independently off their own plots and work occasionally on estates

52. Report on British colonies, September, 1842, Layrle to Minister, September 13, 1842, in Gén. 169 (1374), report on British Guiana, November 15, 1841, in Gén. 165 (1336), ANSOM.
53. See in particular Green, *British Slave Emancipation*, William Law Mathieson, *British Slave Emancipation, 1838–1849* (1932; rpr. New York, 1967), and George R. Mellor, *British Imperial Trusteeship, 1783–1850* (London, 1951).
54. Layrle to Minister, September 24, 1841, report on British Guiana, November 15, 1841, both in Gén. 165 (1336), ANSOM.

at high wage rates. Still, he felt, these changing labor patterns dealt a "mortal blow to large plantations" and could lead to the ruin of colonies such as Jamaica, which might "cease to exist as a producing colony."[55]

Layrle also linked "the shrinking of exportable products, which are the only source of wealth to the colonies," to a diminution of work. He emphasized that all of Britain's tropical establishments, with the exception of Antigua, Barbados, and Trinidad, "had experienced considerable reductions in their crops" from preemancipation levels, with Jamaican harvests "decreased by more than half" and those in the British Caribbean as a whole down by one-half to two-thirds—a clear exaggeration, for the actual decline was approximately one-third. There was no doubt in Layrle's mind that planters were suffering from "the inconsistency and ill will of workers," and that "the diminution of work" was a serious blemish on British slave liberation. Layrle was adamant in affirming that "from the point of view of work, emancipation has not succeeded in the colonies; this is an incontestable fact."[56] This led him to generalize further by insisting on several occasions that British abolitionists, following the credo of economic liberalism, had been wrong in assuming that freeing the slaves would increase productivity, for "in no part of the globe could free labor produce as much" as coerced labor.[57] In reality, when the reports Layrle and his fellow observers submitted to their government are viewed with historical hindsight, they stand out particularly for the manner in which they reflect the overriding concern of the British and French plantocracy with the economic consequences of emancipation. Quite clearly, production problems in the British Caribbean had led even the most detached French commissioner to issue statements that could easily be interpreted as indictments of the entire abolition process.

Layrle disclaimed any affinity with "those erroneous theories which purport to demonstrate that the black race is beneath other

55. Report on Jamaica, July 1, 1840, in Gén. 178 (1418), Layrle to Minister, September 13, 1842, in Gén. 169 (1374), ANSOM.
56. Layrle to Minister, September 13, 1842, report on British colonies, September, 1842, in Gén. 169 (1374), Layrle to Minister, June 8, 1840, in Gén. 144 (1225), report on Jamaica, January 9, 1842, in Gén. 178 (1418), ANSOM.
57. Report on Jamaica, July 1, 1840, in Gén. 178 (1418), report on British Guiana, November 15, 1841, in Gén. 165 (1336), report on British colonies, September, 1842, in Gén. 169 (1374), ANSOM.

races." He also rejected "the possession of man by man" as "unjust and immoral" and expressed the wish that slavery would "disappear forever from the earth." Professing to be "an abolitionist at heart," he affirmed that he would "be happy to participate in some manner in the cessation of slavery and attach [his] name to this great act of humanity and justice."[58] At other times, however, he adopted a line of reasoning employed by many opponents of emancipation, demonstrating that the British experience had definitely altered his thoughts on the issue. He became convinced that the British move had been "hasty," "unjust," and "unfortunate," precipitating British possessions into "decadence and ruin" and sacrificing "both colonial and metropolitan interests." In fact, he contended, British actions had resulted in "the abandoning of the colonial future to the hazards of colonial reform."[59]

Layrle followed up his bleak assessment of the British initiative with suggestions that France should profit from the errors of her neighbor. Proclaiming that French islands in the West Indies shared the same topographical and demographic characteristics as Jamaica, he predicted that after emancipation they would "be faced with the same damage caused to plantation production." He added that it was "necessary to be just to all," that improving the position of slaves should not be a "reason to ruin the masters, the colonies, our commercial ports and our navy." While desiring "the cessation of slavery," Layrle at the same time wished to see France's "colonies prosper." Thus, he proposed that his country be generous with her dependencies and grant them a "six to ten year" reprieve from abolition so that planters could take contingency measures to protect themselves as much as possible "from this great disaster."[60] In effect, the most astute and objective of French observers had ended up adopting a stance on slave liberation similar to that of many shrewd defenders of French colonial interests, who by the 1840s were prepared to recognize the necessity of emancipation in principle but who wished to delay its implementation.

58. Layrle to Minister, November 15, 1841, in Gén. 165 (1336), report on British colonies, September, 1842, in Gén. 169 (1374), Layrle to Director of Colonies, August 1, 1840, in Gén. 144 (1225), ANSOM.
59. Report on Saint Lucia, Saint Vincent, and Grenada, April, 1840, in Gén. 144 (1225), Layrle to Minister, November 15, 1841, in Gén. 165 (1336), ANSOM.
60. Report on Jamaica, January 9, 1842, in Gén. 178 (1418), report on British colonies, September, 1842, in Gén. 169 (1374), Layrle to Director of Colonies, August 1, 1840, in Gén. 144 (1225), ANSOM.

When Layrle's reports were made public in Europe they were, as might be expected, poorly received in antislavery circles. The British abolitionist Alexander, writing from Paris, insisted that Layrle displayed "an evident antipathy to emancipation, and sympathy with the planters." Layrle had viewed "productiveness and riches for the planters" as "of far greater importance than the rights and happiness of the negro." In Alexander's view, Layrle's prejudices led him to "see the darkest side of every feature in negro emancipation." Alexander also charged that Layrle's studies were "intended to induce the French government to withhold" liberty from French slaves.[61] The moderate Société française pour l'abolition de l'esclavage tended to be more charitable in its evaluation of Layrle's work. While it showed no enthusiasm for his submissions, it noted that they "contain numerous, and for the most part very satisfactory, facts."[62] However, a more radical French abolitionist, Victor Schoelcher, was much more critical in his analysis. In an influential book published in the early 1840s Schoelcher categorized Layrle as "a decided adversary of emancipation."[63]

The French government, for its part, held a much more favorable opinion of Layrle's mission. His work was lauded in 1840 by the minister of the navy and colonies, Admiral Roussin, for its "care," "zeal," and intelligence. The following year Roussin's successor, Admiral Duperré, remarked that Layrle's reports "are of a nature to shed much light on the examination of the question of slave abolition." The minister later recommended that they be made available to the public.[64] As a result, they were published by the French government, as a three-hundred-page book.[65] Layrle's studies also appeared, along with those of several other French observers, as parts of the last two volumes of a five-volume series of documents concerning British emancipation produced by the navy and colonial department between 1840 and 1843.[66] Perhaps the greatest

61. Statements from Alexander dated March 22 and 25, respectively, in April 17 and May 1, 1844, issues of *BFAS Reporter.*
62. Société française pour l'abolition de l'esclavage, *No. 19,* session of March 10, 1841.
63. Schoelcher, *Colonies étrangères et Haïti,* I, 211.
64. Minister to Arnous, commander of West Indian naval station, May 29, September 27, 1840, Minister to Director of Naval Personnel, May 11, 1841, all in Gén. 144 (1225), ANSOM.
65. Capitaine de vaisseau Marie Jean François Layrle, *Abolition de l'esclavage dans les colonies anglaises* (Paris, 1842).
66. Volumes I and II of the series were published by the official government press

compliment paid Layrle, though, was his appointment as governor of French Guiana in 1842, a move that launched the former naval captain on a long and distinguished career as a high administrator in the navy and colonial ministry.[67] No other French assessor of the British abolition process was rewarded so splendidly for his services. All of this tends to indicate the extent to which Layrle's superiors seemed to approve of, and undoubtedly agree with, his analysis of British emancipation and its possible negative implications for France's slave establishments. Indeed, when Admiral Mackau, minister from 1843 to 1847, spoke on slavery as a member of the Broglie Commission in the early 1840s, he exploited the negative aspects of Layrle's dispatches, quoting especially the captain's statement that the British act had been "a hasty and unjust measure."[68] In the 1840s, then, even the French emissary most favorable to the British course of action was cited by French officials for his statements criticizing the process of slave liberation. In the 1830s, when the French navy and colonial ministry was formulating its policy toward British abolition on the basis of contradictory newspaper accounts or the even more deprecatory reports of earlier French observers, such as Pardeilhan, it is understandable that it chose to adopt a highly cautious approach toward the British model.

Facing the eventuality of British emancipation, the French navy and colonial minister warned his colonial governors on May 24, 1833, of the possibility of negative repercussions in France's colonies and requested all available information on developments concerning British dependencies. At the same time he notified the governors that he intended to consult the Colonial Councils on

---

under the name of the navy and colonial department functionary who compiled them: F. Chasseriau, *Précis de l'abolition de l'esclavage dans les colonies anglaises: Imprimé par l'ordre de M. l'Amiral Baron Duperré* (Paris, 1840–41). Volumes III through V appeared simply under the title of the navy and colonial department series: *Abolition de l'esclavage dans les colonies anglaises* (Paris, 1841–43).

67. After serving as governor of Guiana (1842–45), Layrle became governor of Guadeloupe (1845–48). He was recalled from his post by the abolitionist-dominated provisional government of the Second Republic after the Revolution of 1848 had toppled the Orleanist regime; but in 1849, after the election of Louis Napoleon Bonaparte to the presidency, he was appointed director of personnel in the navy and colonial department, a position that he apparently held until his retirement in 1863 (Personnel dossier, Layrle, in Service historique de la Marine).

68. Broglie Commission, Minutes, March 14, 1842.

possible decrees to improve the position of French slaves.[69] Rigny reiterated this policy in a new circular to his colonial administrators on August 25, 1833, when there was no longer any doubt that the British reform would be implemented. His government, he explained, wished "to remain a peaceful spectator to the grave measures that England has decided to take for the abolition of slavery in her colonies; but in order to be able to preserve such an attitude, and in order to protect the French colonies from the perils of assimilation, it is necessary, in its opinion, to enter frankly and broadly into the path of ameliorations."[70] In an attempt to deflect the possible dangers that British actions posed for the French colonial establishment, the French government had decided to accelerate the ameliorative program for the slaves adopted after the July Revolution and at the same time closely observe British developments concerning slavery.

A French navy and colonial department internal memo, dated December 27, 1833, and drawn up for the director of the colonies, Edmé Jean Filleau de Saint Hilaire, by an assistant in the ministry—perhaps the influential Henri Joseph Mestro—provides further insight into the French government's stance toward British emancipation, and indeed toward slave liberation in general at this time. The note suggested that since England had increased her public debt by the equivalent of 500 million francs (£20 million) for the freeing of her slaves, some Frenchmen might think that France should do the same. The position paper indicated, though, that in England religious movements favorable to abolition had so moved public opinion that the British government "had been forced to yield," while "in France, where the great mass of the population is little concerned about the colonial regime, protests against slavery only have reverberations within the circle of philosophical discussions, and our government remains, in the area of what is called public opinion, almost free in its resolutions." For the moment,

69. Minister to Governors, May 24, 1833, in Corr. Gén., Colonies françaises, 1833, ANSOM.

70. This dispatch is cited in an internal note to the navy and colonial minister by Saint Hilaire, dated June 5, 1835 (in Gén. 156 [1299]), in a circular from the minister to his governors, August 1, 1835 (in Corr. Gén. 187), and in subsequent correspondence and internal memos of the navy and colonial department, but the original dispatch no longer seems to exist in ANSOM.

therefore, it was "very doubtful that the legislature would be eager to impose on the State a heavy pecuniary burden to satisfy a few publicists," especially since the peaceful situation in the French colonies permitted "the real friends of humanity to wait for time to bring about the most durable improvements in the condition of blacks." Moreover, the memo contended that the British apprentice system would be unsuitable for French dependencies. Thus, the French government, while awaiting the results of events in the British West Indies, should act to "prevent not provoke catastrophes"; for in France no "popular force" had thrown the administration "outside the path of prudence." Many French colonial slaves had already been manumitted by their masters since 1830, and perhaps the introduction of *rachat* (the formal right of bondsmen to purchase their freedom) would suffice to extinguish French slavery slowly. The memo concluded by stating that "everything tends to coincide in determining the French government to persevere in the line of conduct it has adopted for the last three years . . . and await, as a simple spectator, but with the necessary precautions for the preservation of public order, the result of the great experience that is taking place in the English colonies." Interestingly enough, in the very first internal note on the British emancipation process, an influential French functionary had given credence to the British abolitionists' claim that their movement had obliged a reluctant government in London to act, a belief that would be shared by most Frenchmen—be they functionaries, abolitionists, or apostles of slavery—for much of the remainder of the July Monarchy.

An addendum to the memo agreed that it was doubtful France would be willing to pay an indemnity proportional to the English one, or 180 million francs, to free France's 285,000 slaves: "In France, where very few people know what the colonies are, or concern themselves with the fate of the slaves, they would not decide to increase the public debt in favor of the *colons*, for whom, it must be said, the country has very little sympathy, only to satisfy morally a few philanthropists."[71] Faced with the British example of granting generous compensation to the colonists, the first reaction of high officials in the navy department was to reject humanitarian

---

71. Memo for Director of the Colonies and attached note, December 27, 1833, in Gén. 206 (1513), ANSOM.

considerations for practical ones and deduce that there was no compelling reason for France to alter her wait-and-see attitude toward British emancipation.

After slave liberation had been effected in British territories, the French government made a public pronouncement of its policy toward the move, which, though couched in more diplomatic terms, clearly indicated that it had not wavered from the position stated in the 1833 memo. The occasion was offered by French abolitionists when they interpellated the government on the slavery question in the Chamber of Deputies on April 22, 1835. French emancipationists obviously thought the moment propitious for such an intervention, for a Cabinet change had just brought to power as president of the Council of Ministers the abolitionist duc de Broglie, who had spoken out against slavery and the slave trade on numerous occasions and had been one of the founders of the Société française pour l'abolition de l'esclavage in late 1834.

If the abolitionists had been counting on this change to alter French policy, though, they were sadly mistaken. Individual ministers could have some influence on policy, as could the King, the Council of Ministers, and the president of this body; but it appears that throughout much of the July Monarchy, French government attitudes toward slavery and emancipation were primarily formulated by the upper echelons of the bureaucracy within the navy and colonial department. The most important functionary in this ministry was the director of the colonies—Filleau de Saint Hilaire from 1830 to 1842 and Joseph Henri Galos from 1842 to 1848. Their chief assistants were Mestro and Gerbidon, with Mestro actually drawing up many memos and drafts. These position papers often seem to have spelled out the government's plans, which individual ministers and heads of government approved of and complied with to a large extent. The continuity this practice imprinted on the French stance toward abolition, despite frequent changes in governments and navy and colonial ministers in the 1830s, became quite apparent with Broglie's response to the abolitionists.

Broglie's remarks as head of government contrasted singularly with statements he had made as an individual before assuming office. As the moderate republican newspaper Le National (Paris) indicated shortly after his statements to the abolitionists, France was unlike England in that the first minister was "above all servant to the royal will" and could not impose his own program on the administration.[72] Such an assertion might have exaggerated the direct influence of the king, but it showed to what extent knowledgeable observers were aware of the inherent continuity of French administrative policies. Broglie's comments in the Chambers definitely echoed the position set forth in the internal navy and colonial department memos drawn up earlier. Broglie made reference to "the great and perilous endeavor being carried on in the colonies of Great Britain" and reminded his interlocutors that "the trial is not yet concluded, the result is not as yet known." Although he said he firmly hoped the endeavor would succeed, he suggested that "everyone will understand that at such a time, any government which possesses slaves must be preoccupied with calming tempers rather than agitating them." It was Broglie's opinion regarding "this question that the government must impose upon itself the greatest reserve; that its task at the moment, its natural role, is to wait, to observe, to gather facts, information, and meditate upon them." He ended by assuring his audience "that the government will gather all information" possible, "that it will reflect," that "it will make decisions only with full knowledge of the facts." The following day the minister of the navy and colonies, Admiral Duperré, spoke in the same vein, though his call for a cautious approach made reference to English emancipation being accompanied by "tremors" and "perturbations."[73] These assurances, which seemed to satisfy the abolitionist interpellators, were in effect the first public affirmations of a program which had evolved out of the circumstances of 1833, which had been ruminated on within the navy and colonial ministry, and which had now been formally espoused by the government. While sanctioning the ministry's quest for more data on British developments, Broglie's pronouncements about seeking "full knowledge of the facts" also gave his administration ample time to refine its policy on the issue.

Internal navy and colonial department memos presented by Saint Hilaire to Duperré during 1835 shed further light on the factors motivating official French attitudes toward British slave

72. *Le National*, June 15, 1835.
73. *Le Moniteur universel*, April 23, 24, 1835.

liberation. In a note dated March 18, Saint Hilaire argued that France's slaves were far more backward than those of England, for the slave trade to Britain's dependencies had ceased years ago, while it had continued to France's until 1830. In French territories, according to the director of the colonies, "everything remains to be done in the way of civilization." Here Saint Hilaire was reiterating an old French and English concept currently being revived in French colonial circles, that the civilization of slaves increased with the number of years since the slave trade had ended and uncivilized elements had stopped arriving in their midst. He suggested, too, that the Colonial Councils be questioned on the best means to arrive at emancipation, a statement which shows that administrators in Paris, like those in London in 1823, hesitated to take action without the advice or approval of the colonists themselves.[74]

Saint Hilaire was still more explicit in a memo dated June 5. Stating that French policy had been clear since 1833, he added: "One understands the wish of the Government to remain in observation" of the British accomplishment "not only throughout the entire period of apprenticeship . . . but undoubtedly during the time immediately following its termination." Only then would it be possible "to know the conduct of the Black" no longer under the "restraints of this intermediary state." Another reason for "precautionary measures by the Government and caution by the *colons*" was the presence in France "of British sectarians whose mission is to achieve the universal extinction of slavery," a clear indication of official French concern about British abolitionists destabilizing the French political scene. Moreover, Saint Hilaire continued, even French emancipationists estimated the cost of indemnifying slave owners at 180 to 200 million francs; and an "elective Chamber, in which mention of the least expense invokes" protests about "the taxpayer's interest," would "probably refuse to follow, at the price of such a burden, the example of England." It would be wise for the government to wait not only until August, 1840, to make a decision, "but until the end of 1841 at least in order to know . . . what [could] be expected of the liberated apprentice in terms of work and

74. Saint Hilaire, note on emancipation, March 18, 1835, in Gén. 156 (1299), ANSOM.

civilization."[75] Still, he advocated the drawing up of contingency plans for earlier emancipation in case either French public opinion or developments in the colonies required it. Because of this, it was necessary to consult the colonists, who, under the "rights of common law," could not be "deprived of their property" without indemnity.[76] Obviously, if French officials were willing to equate slaves with property and await the approval of the *colons* before proceeding with eradicating slavery, little could be accomplished in the near future.

In a note of October 1, Saint Hilaire repeated his contention that France's slaves were not as well prepared for freedom as England's had been, adding that early information from British dependencies indicated that apprenticeship was unsuitable for French possessions. He reiterated, too, his conviction that the French legislatures would never agree to burden the treasury with a large compensatory sum. "Thus," Saint Hilaire believed, "it would be absolutely impossible to apply to our colonies the English system of emancipation."[77] In this memo, as in the memo of June 5, the most influential bureaucrat in the navy and colonial department revealed himself to be highly solicitous of colonial interests, extremely wary of British "sectarians," thoroughly imbued with a legalistic approach to abolition, and fully persuaded that the cost of emancipation was prohibitive—in short, he was totally uncommitted to slave liberation. Given the influence of men such as Saint Hilaire and of the negative reports on British developments provided by French observers, it is perfectly understandable that Paris should espouse a policy of cautiously awaiting the final outcome of British events. Moreover, such a course of action had still another advantage in the eyes of at least one unidentified official in the navy and colonial ministry, who seemed to suggest that France's tropical dependencies could only stand to benefit from the emancipation-induced decline into which Great Britain's colonies

75. Although English apprenticeship actually ended in August, 1838 (April 1, 1839, for Mauritius), it had originally been projected to endure until August 1, 1840, for praedial workers.
76. Saint Hilaire, note for the minister, June 5, 1835, in Gén. 156 (1299), ANSOM.
77. Saint Hilaire, note on emancipation for "Mr. the Duc" (undoubtedly referring to Guizot's friend and collaborator, the duc de Broglie), October 1, 1835, in Guizot Papers, 42AP40, Archives Nationales, Paris.

seemed to be gravitating.[78] At this point, it appeared to many that France had much to gain and nothing to lose in adopting an attitude of watchful waiting.

The minister of the navy and colonies, Duperré, evidently agreed with the suggestions made by his subordinates. On August 1, 1835, he reminded his colonial governors of the policy toward British emancipation set forth in 1833 and still followed by his government. He added, though, that as a result of discussions within the Chambers, the government could no longer simply observe but had decided both to act to bring about improvements for the slaves and to question the Colonial Councils about the possibility of abolition. In effect, he was asking the colonies how far they wished to conform to England's initiative.[79] On another occasion, too, Duperré admitted that his administration, faced with interpellations by French abolitionists, had thoroughly examined the issues of British and French emancipation and concluded that it must persevere in its ameliorative program.[80]

Following up on these matters, the government duly introduced an ordonnance on April 29, 1836, to regularize procedures for manumitting individual slaves. At the same time, it passed legislation to enforce the old ancien régime principle that disembarkment of any slave for metropolitan France constituted automatic liberation. Paris soon learned, however—as it must have suspected all along—that the colonists, like their British colonial brethren in the 1820s, could not be counted on to support the liberalization process envisaged by metropolitan authorities. When the Colonial Councils replied to Duperré's queries, they rejected outright not only the idea of emancipation but also the proposed introduction of two reforms, *rachat* and *pécule* (the right of slaves to save and own assets), that the navy and colonial department had suggested to them. The French government, meanwhile, continued its policy of awaiting the results of British abolition before committing itself

78. This is apparent from a marginal note on a report by Lieutenant Dagorne, a naval officer whose visit to Saint Christopher had convinced him that the decline in the British colonies was to the benefit of those colonial powers, such as France, that retained slavery. An official in the navy and colonial department remarked concerning this opinion: "This is true" (Lieutenant Dagorne, report of December 21, 1835, in Gén. 144 [1225], ANSOM).

79. Minister to Governors, August 1, 1835, in Corr. Gén. 187 and Gén. 156 (1299), ANSOM.

80. Minister to Governor of Senegal, October 23, 1835, ANSOM.

to any explicit slave liberation project. When questioned in the lower house on May 25, 1836, about the Cabinet's sentiments on the matter, Duperré replied that his administration intended to arrive at emancipation by "successive improvements of the slaves' condition" but that abolition "requires time, and information which we do not yet possess. The experience being carried out in the [English] colonies next to ours can furnish us" with these insights: "Is it therefore wise, even possible, to hasten things in any way concerning such an issue?"[81] Duperré was simply repeating the government's previously determined stance on the emancipation question.

The same approach was pursued by Duperré's successor, Admiral Rosamel. In the Chamber of Deputies on June 6, 1837, under interrogation by French abolitionists, Rosamel replied that it would be best for France to await further information on both the English and French colonies before acting on slave liberation. Count Molé, then president of the Council of Ministers, supported Rosamel by stressing that the English example was obliging France to take a stance on slavery but that the French must proceed "slowly, gradually, with great prudence and discernment" so as to harm none of the interests involved in the issue.[82] In 1838 the minister of the navy and colonies spoke in the lower house to invoke again the necessity of awaiting the outcome of the English precedent, which he now categorized as causing a "precarious situation" in the British West Indies. This time, Rosamel was seconded, not only by Molé, but by the minister of finance, Jean Pierre Joseph Lacave-Laplagne. The latter insisted that the British experience had not yet been concluded, that it would be three or four years before its results were known, and that it was indispensable for his nation to proceed slowly and prudently.[83] The argument that it was necessary to wait until the outcome of British colonial events could be judged was a useful device for a government pressed for action by abolitionists but determined to follow a dilatory approach to emancipation.

A memo dated December 21, 1836, and sent by Saint Hilaire to Rosamel shows that as time progressed and information began to

81. *Le Moniteur universel*, May 26, 1836.
82. *Ibid.*, June 7, 1837.
83. *Ibid.*, February 16, 1838.

filter in from the English colonies it had the effect of confirming the French government's doubts about British actions and reinforcing its own position. After conceding that eventual French abolition was "only a question of time and money," Saint Hilaire reiterated his assertions that the French—unlike the English—government was "almost free" from the pressure of "public opinion," and that France was "not disposed" to make the required pecuniary sacrifices for the payment of an indemnity. He added, though, a new charge: that immediate slave liberation would constitute a "death blow" that would destroy the French planter class, "put an end to cultivation," and ruin metropolitan creditors of the colonists. Significantly, in support of this argument he cited "what is happening in the English colonies." Saint Hilaire insisted that reports by the early emissaries to the British Caribbean—Bernard, Laplace (a naval captain sent to Barbados), and Pardeilhan—demonstrated "that generally ties of obedience are loosened in labor units, work is languishing, and the produce of agriculture has notably diminished." Moreover, he noted, British settlers were dreading the day when apprenticeship would end and all restraints would be removed from freedmen. "In the midst of such circumstances," the director of the colonies hoped that the French government would abide by Rigny's policy of remaining "peaceful spectators of the effects of British emancipation," at least until 1840, "before submitting the state of slaves in France's colonies to any sort of change." If his nation did not follow this option, he predicted, French slaves might return to a "state of barbarism."[84] The negative tone apparent in the evaluations of most French observers was clearly being echoed by the navy and colonial department in Paris. These assessments were also justifying the French government's inaction in the field of emancipation and at the same time reinforcing its policy of awaiting further British developments.

Faced with the British decision to abolish slavery, the French government had steadily transformed its initial cautious attitude toward the British experiment into a settled policy of deliberation and prudence in everything concerning slave liberation. Although

84. Saint Hilaire, note for Rosamel, December 1, 1836, in Guizot Papers, 42AP40, Archives Nationales. This document was sent to Guizot—a member of the Cabinet at that time—on December 24 prior to its discussion in the Council of Ministers.

such a stance had part of its basis in purely French considerations, such as the lack of popular support for abolitionism, there is no doubt that the negative perceptions French decision makers received from their sources of intelligence on the British colonial scene highly influenced their attitudes. Moreover, while some liberal organs might insinuate that the French navy and colonial minister was demonstrating bad faith by doing no more than observing the British situation,[85] the French government was fully aware that public opinion in general condoned such a policy. Awaiting further results of British proceedings while bringing about minor colonial reforms had become a pattern that the different French administrations followed steadfastly until the premature end of British apprenticeship in 1838 and, with variations, thereafter. Instead of provoking France to free her own slaves, the British example had elicited a policy of caution and temporization from the July Monarchy in the mid-1830s. The British precedent provided a means of postponing emancipation and justifying such a decision. In this sense, the position of the French government had much in common with that of French colonial defenders of slavery.

85. Concerning the government's slavery policy, Le Courrier français exclaimed on November 6, 1836: "It's a comedy that is being played."

THREE

FRENCH COLONIAL VIEWS ON BRITISH EMANCIPATION

Those elements within colonial and metropolitan France that wished to prolong, if not openly defend, slavery could be expected to react negatively to British emancipation. In almost every way the British precedent constituted a threat to the French slave system. During the early 1830s, at least, French *colons* had feared that the British example would cause unrest or even revolt within the French slave community. The passage of time showed that French slaves were remaining relatively calm, and fears of a British-inspired slave revolt receded, but the continuation of evasions to neighboring British possessions did not permit French colonial fears to subside entirely. Although colonialist claims that British abolition was causing marked economic decline in the French Caribbean were certainly exaggerated, there is little doubt that the spirit of freedom spreading from the nearby British dependencies contributed to the uneasiness—primarily inspired by the possibility of French slave liberation—that had gripped French tropical colonies by the mid-1830s and created in them an atmosphere of anticipation, uncertainty, and economic stagnation that lasted throughout the remainder of the July Monarchy. Moreover, Britain's decision to free its slaves removed a major cog from the system of states still permitting bondage, thus weakening indirectly the position of French defenders of slavery. Finally, not only abolitionists on both sides of the Channel, but even many apologists for French slavery, came to believe that the British move encouraged, indeed presaged, emancipation by France. Under these circumstances, French proslavery spokesmen reacted predictably by denouncing Great Britain, questioning her motives in eliminating servitude, and uttering highly critical remarks about the British experience.

Evidence suggests that French colonial advocates operated in a quite synchronized manner. No sooner had British abolition been decided on than they began to muster arguments against it. Their phraseology varied considerably, but they all tended to agree on its negative consequences and pass over or minimize its successes. Clearly, they had become preoccupied with its possible repercussions on France and her colonial establishment. As a result, when French apostles of slavery cited the British example, they used it as a means of warning against similar actions by France, something they were convinced would prove disastrous to their interests. In this sense, Britain's slave liberation program had the effect of awakening and crystallizing French plantocratic protests against both British emancipation and any French proclivities to follow in Britain's footsteps.

Given their profound opposition to freeing the slaves, proponents of the colonial status quo were eager to espouse, defend, and encourage the French government's intention of deferring abolition while awaiting the results of the British experiment. The colonial delegates played a major part in this campaign, usually coordinating their attack through their Council of Delegates, which met regularly in Paris and kept in close touch with the delegates' employers, the Colonial Councils of the individual colonies. The delegates were well prepared for their role. As of 1833 each of the four leading French dependencies regularly elected one or two delegates to represent them in mainland France. As the colonies had no right to elect their own deputies to the lower house, the men selected as delegates were often deputies of metropolitan ridings who had known sympathies for the colonial cause or whose loyalties could be influenced by the ample salaries paid the delegates for their services. Furthermore, these representatives administered and dispersed large slush funds provided by the Colonial Councils for use in propagandizing the colonial cause in metropolitan France. These funds permitted the delegates not only to subsidize the press, but to influence votes in the legislative bodies, making the delegates formidable and effective defenders of colonial interests.

Thus, when Admiral Duperré on May 25, 1836, spelled out before the Chamber of Deputies his plans for improving slave conditions while examining Britain's actions, the deputy-delegates gave him their full-fledged support. Charles Dupin, representing Martinique, immediately spoke up to second Duperré's policy. Employing words strikingly similar to those of Saint Hilaire—an indication, among many others, that delegates had close contact with navy and colonial department officials or access to ministry documents—Dupin suggested that by 1841 it would be possible to judge "the great experiment attempted by the Parliament of England." He followed this with the exhortation: "May French impatience deign wait five years."[1] As the influential doctrinaire newspaper *Le Journal des débats* remarked concerning Dupin's intervention, colonial advocates had previously cried out against any attempt even to discuss slavery, but now Dupin had changed tactics and was simply requesting a delay.[2] Unlike a few of their diehard compatriots and the standard proslavery advocates in the United States, most responsible French colonial spokesmen appear to have decided after the British initiative that their best strategy was to espouse their government's cautious policy and attempt to prolong slavery ad infinitum rather than defend it openly.

In the Chamber of Deputies debate, Dupin was joined by his cohort, Mauguin, then president of the Council of Delegates, who insisted that French slaves must be sufficiently prepared for liberty, as England's had been. At the same time, Mauguin, who had recently purchased *Le Journal du commerce*—probably with the assistance of colonial capital—and rebaptized it *Le Commerce*, repeated in his newspaper the contention that it was necessary for France to profit from and improve on the English example of slave liberation.[3] In the summer of 1836 two other delegates, E. Sully-Brunet of Bourbon and Jabrun of Guadeloupe, the latter an owner of more than one plantation, reiterated the same theme. They wrote a letter to the General Councils (*Conseils généraux*), or departmental councils, the consultative bodies of the metropolitan French departments, to counter a note to them from French abolitionists

---

1. *Le Moniteur universel,* May 26, 1836.
2. *Le Journal des débats,* May 26, 1836.
3. *Le Moniteur universel,* May 26, 1836; *Le Commerce,* May 26, 1836.

that had encouraged them to issue a call for emancipation. In their missive the two delegates again emphasized the need to wait until 1841 to assess fully the results "of this grave and costly experiment" undertaken by England.[4]

Favard, delegate of French Guiana, chose a different medium to put forth his message. He authored a brochure in 1838 whose central thesis was that the British precedent proved slave liberation could only be successful if carefully planned and preceded by a slow transitional phase.[5] In the same year Mauguin, supported by the proslavery legitimist leader representing Marseille, Pierre Antoine Berryer, intervened in a Chamber of Deputies debate to stress again that England had prepared her slaves far in advance for freedom and that, besides, the final results of the English initiative were not yet known. As Count Adolphe d'Angeville, a champion of the colonial cause who maintained that French slaves were well treated, exclaimed in the same session, the British process would be concluded only in 1840, and Frenchmen should have "the patience to wait that term" before compromising the fate of their territories.[6] Dupin, too, spoke up again on the issue in 1838, obviously out of fear that the July Monarchy might be seriously considering freeing the slaves at this time. Having replaced Mauguin as president of the Council of Delegates, he wrote to the navy and colonial minister in late 1838 to suggest that news from the British Caribbean was alarming enough to warrant awaiting the "enlightenment of experience." He exhorted the minister: "Before all else, wait for the end of the English experience; this is what the voice of wisdom recommends."[7] As British apprenticeship had been terminated in 1838 and additional information was becoming available on the state of blacks under complete freedom, Duprin was now being purposefully vague about when the British experience would actually end, thus postponing further any evaluation of it.

That the delegates and their supporters were procrastinating became clear when Sully-Brunet published a pamphlet in 1840

4. Sully-Brunet and Jabron to General Councils, August 25, 1836, in Gén. 156 (1301), ANSOM.
5. M. Favard, De l'abolition de l'esclavage dans les colonies françaises (N.p., [1838]). It seems certain that this booklet was published in 1838, for it was reviewed by Le Temps on June 6 of that year.
6. Le Moniteur universel, February 16, 1838.
7. Dupin to Minister, October 10, 1838, in Gén. 161 (1323), ANSOM.

advising that French slaves not be freed until 1860. According to this new brochure, England's Negroes had been much better prepared for liberty than France's; moreover, emancipation was a mere scheme of the British to advance their own interests. Sully-Brunet contended that England's dubious objectives should induce France to act prudently and take careful preparatory measures before eradicating bondage.[8] In reviewing Sully-Brunet's study, Mauguin's organ fully supported these views. In fact, Mauguin went beyond Sully-Brunet in declaring in the lower house in 1843 that France should imitate England's example by taking thirty years to prepare for emancipation. If this thirty-year period was to have begun with the end of the French slave trade, emancipation would take place in the early 1860s.[9] Another leading spokesman for the colonies, Thomas Marie Adolphe Jollivet, a deputy from Brittany who as of 1841 also served as delegate for Martinique, produced a volume in 1842 which insisted, too, that France must postpone abolition until her slaves were as well prepared for liberty as England's had been in 1833.[10] Colonial advocates were obviously prepared to avail themselves of any argument apt to delay the freeing of French slaves. Their contentions that these slaves were less fit for freedom than those of the British colonies had been and that the outcome of the British emancipation process was still totally uncertain were crude but apparently effective devices permitting them to press for the indefinite postponement of abolition.

The delegates' employers, the Colonial Councils, were as eager as their appointees in Paris to defer emancipation and block any moves perceived as constituting even oblique blows to the structure of slavery. When the colonial governors carried out their instructions and questioned these bodies on slave liberation in general and the improvement of slaves' status through the implementation of *pécule* and *rachat* in particular, the councils were quick to invoke against these measures objections identical to those put forth by their delegates. The colonial council of Guadeloupe rejected both *pécule* and *rachat* on May 24, 1836, because of the supposed need to gather information on the English

8. E. Sully-Brunet, *Considérations sur le système colonial et plan d'abolition de l'esclavage* (Paris, 1840), 17–25.

9. *Le Commerce*, February 13, 1840; *Le Moniteur universel*, June 29, 1843.

10. Thomas Marie Adolphe Jollivet, *Parallèle entre les colonies françaises et les colonies anglaises* (Paris, 1842), 6–7, 13–18.

colonies before considering such important changes; moreover, it pointed out that awaiting the results of the English initiative would afford additional time to prepare blacks for freedom. Other colonial legislatures reacted similarly. Bourbon's council replied to the navy and colonial ministry's entreaties by asserting that the problem of abolition could only be resolved by "time and the wisdom furnished by the results of the English experiment." While the Colonial Council of Martinique cited the "perturbations" in British dependencies as one of its reasons for rejecting emancipation, that of Guiana repeated the more orthodox colonial line, that it was imperative to wait and study the English system.[11] The liberal *Courrier français* accurately perceived colonial aims when it remarked some time later that the Colonial Councils, rather than openly attacking the principle of emancipation, were proposing that no action be considered until the British experiment had been completed.[12]

Other, less official—and at times newly converted—proponents of the colonial cause echoed the councils' sentiments in the mid-1830s and the early 1840s. In a brochure against abolition published in 1836, André de Lacharière, a member of the Guadeloupe Colonial Council, expressed the desire that France scrutinize the British procedure, "await the results" of it, take "note especially of the errors" it entailed, and "avoid" its "dangers."[13] In the debate of May 23, 1836, in the Chamber of Deputies, Claude Charles Etienne Hernoux, acting as reporter of the commission examining the yearly colonial budget, recommended that France carefully investigate the British example and proceed "gradually and without upheaval" in its own colonial possessions.[14] Some elements of the procolonial press were quick to adopt the same stance. *Le Temps*, a daily that wavered on the issue but usually condoned slavery, argued that the English experience had hardly begun and that it was natural enough to await its results. *Le Sémaphore de Marseille*, a newspaper that earlier had

11. Governor of Guadeloupe to Minister, September, 1836, Colonial Council of Bourbon, February, 1836, Colonial Council of Martinique, 1836, Colonial Council of Guiana, June 22, 1836, all in Gén. 156 (1299), ANSOM. See also Sociéte française pour l'abolition de l'esclavage, *4e publication* (Paris, [1836]), 53–54.

12. *Le Courrier français*, October 4, 1839.

13. André de Lacharière, *De l'affranchissement des esclaves dans les colonies françaises* (Paris, 1836), 69–70.

14. *Le Moniteur universel*, May 23–24, 1836.

been favorable to British slave liberation, now borrowed the theme that it behooved France to work for cautious rather than instant emancipation and to follow England's lead in advancing slowly toward its objective. *Le Mémorial bordelais*, an organ that had become ardently proslavery after an editorial change in the mid-1830s, adopted a slightly different tactic. According to *Le Mémorial*, the English had moved too rapidly in freeing their slaves; the Paris government should "proceed with wisdom and slowness."[15] Although *Sémaphore* and *Mémorial* were diametrically opposed in their assessments of Britain's approach, they were on common ground in rallying to the French government's policy of procrastination.

The most vociferous journalistic supporters of the plantocracy were especially eager to espouse a governmental policy that served their own ends. A short-lived Parisian newspaper probably in the pay of the *colons, La Paix*, viewed the English precedent as unsuccessful and approved of the decision not to follow it.[16] Two other procolonial publications, *La Revue du dix-neuvième siècle* (Paris), which received direct financial support from the colonists of French Guiana, and its supplement, *Le Bulletin colonial*, constantly seconded the government's position. Indeed, many of their articles on slavery were written by Adolphe Granier de Cassagnac, an inveterate opponent of abolition. Citing the "disastrous and inhuman effects" of British emancipation, *La Revue* contended that it would be unreasonable for France to follow England's example when the results were still uncertain; and it lauded the minister of the navy and colonies, Rosamel, for deciding to wait until the British experience had been consummated. On another occasion an article by Granier de Cassagnac supported the Colonial Council of Guiana's stance that it was essential to delay abolition for "a series of years," as England had, until "material and moral improvements" could bring "civilization" to the slaves. *Le Bulletin colonial* also maintained the necessity of delaying slave liberation, as it claimed the British had.[17] The recently founded, highly influ-

15. *Le Temps*, March 1, July 4, 1840; *Le Sémaphore de Marseille*, March 7, October 5, 1838; *Le Mémorial bordelais*, June 25, 1839.
16. *La Paix*, June 7, 1837.
17. *La Revue du dix-neuvième siècle*, November 13, 1836, January 29, 1837; *Le Bulletin colonial*, February 15, March 15, 1840.

ential, and rapidly growing *La Presse* of Emile de Girardin, which often published articles by Granier de Cassagnac—and which may have received stipends from the planters—also asserted that emancipation must be deferred because French slaves were much less educated and prepared than their British counterparts. Mauguin's *Le Commerce* was as insistent as its fellow procolonial organs that it was imperative for France to observe developments in the British Caribbean and move "slowly, with mature consideration, progressively," letting time take its course. Referring to the supposed difficulties facing Britain's territories, the daily repeated the need for "prudence" and "'slowness" in policy, combined with "preparatory instruction" for the slaves. *Le Commerce*, in fact, overtly admonished French colonial advocates to use the results of the English system, not to uphold slavery in principle, but to encourage the adjournment of its extinction, indicating once again that the colonial lobby was making a concerted effort to organize and coordinate the defense of slavery.[18]

That highly placed French colonial administrators should accept, explain, and implement their government's position of awaiting the outcome of British emancipation before introducing its own abolition plan is understandable. That a governor should constantly admonish his superiors in Paris to follow such a policy, however, shows the extent to which some authorities in the colonies identified with the plantocrats on this issue. Admiral Moges, governor of Martinique from 1838 to 1840 and commander of Caribbean naval forces in the 1840s, proved to be one of the French officials most solicitous for colonial interests. He began his interventions on the question in early October, 1838, by purporting that the British program was not operating effectively and that France should await its results before judging it. Two weeks later he suggested that the only posture "compatible with reason and prudence" was to take no action until the English record could be better evaluated in 1840. On November 6 he elaborated on his stance by exhorting Paris "to declare clearly to the Chambers that in the presence of the English experience, which is far from being concluded, we are determined not to touch colonial questions be-

18. *La Presse*, August 10, 1838; *Le Commerce*, February 15, September 3, October 1, 1838, March 20, 1839.

fore the results are in; and that there is a truce or adjournment [on these issues] at least until January 1, 1840."[19] In 1839, though, with 1840 approaching, he altered his position. He now advocated waiting two or three additional years, until the English situation "will have spoken for itself." It was not possible, he held, to have a specific plan of preparing French slaves for freedom until the definitive results of the British process were known. In the meantime, French slaves should be educated and made ready for liberation. Early in 1840 Moges insisted that news from British territories was still contradictory, that at least eighteen more months were required to judge the situation in the West Indies.[20]

Later in 1840 Moges received word that he had been appointed a member of the royal commission presided over by the duc de Broglie, a nomination that in itself undoubtedly testified to the approbation his dispatches were receiving in Paris. Moreover, in acknowledging his appointment to the commission, Moges again seized the opportunity to remark that the situation in the British Caribbean was "all clouds and confusion."[21] In 1842, after returning to the West Indies as naval commander, Moges still perceived "a somber veil of anxiety and sadness hovering over the future" of England's dependencies. France's best strategy, he reemphasized, would be to wait until all the evidence was in on the British holdings.[22] Moges was as constant as other advocates of the colonial status quo in using a whole panoply of arguments based on the British example to postpone French emancipation. The July Monarchy's policy of remaining relatively inactive while observing the British abolition process had solid support and encouragement, not only from overt colonial promoters of slavery, but also from important figures in the French colonial administration.

Besides attempting to use British developments to delay the freeing of French slaves, defenders of colonial interests stressed repeatedly the economic argument against abolition.[23] This tactic of the

19. Moges to Minister, October 11, November 6, 1838, both in Gén. 161 (1223), October 25, 1838, in Gén. 144 (1225), ANSOM.
20. Moges to Minister, May 16, 1839, in Gén. 171 (1376), July 27, 1839, in Gén. 161 (1323), March 20, 1840, in Gén. 144 (1225), ANSOM.
21. Moges to Minister, August 20, 1840, in Gén. 171 (1376), ANSOM.
22. Moges to Minister, January 15, February 6, 1842, both in Gén. 144 (1225), ANSOM.
23. Interestingly, in South Carolina the planter class employed a similar discourse, underlining the economic shortcomings of British slave liberation. See Joe

French plantocracy reflected to some extent the notion of its British counterpart that emancipation was simply part of a long-term process of economic transition that would only be completed when adequate production was reestablished. Nevertheless, it is apparent that French proslavery elements saw this device primarily as one of the most effective means of advancing their cause. By emphasizing the point that British emancipation had resulted in a diminution of work and staple output, the French colonial establishment could denigrate not only the British initiative but the practicality of slave liberation as a whole. The economic approach was extremely appropriate in a society whose upper echelons shared the dogmatic conviction prevalent in all of nineteenth-century Europe that industriousness was necessary and beneficial for its poorer social strata. It was effective, too, because most French officials, from the commissioners who were visiting the British territories to high functionaries in the navy and colonial department and the ministers themselves, had become convinced that abolition had proved calamitous for British colonial productivity. Finally, this point of view was easy to expound and develop because it could be given a firm foundation in fact.

Not only did British emancipation cause short-term disruptions as blacks celebrated their newfound freedom, but it also brought about conjunctural mutations in production patterns. As mentioned previously, many freedmen fled plantation tasks, which they identified with all the constraints and cruelties of slavery, for the cities or made the decision to live primarily off their own plots, working only occasionally, and at high wages, for their former masters. The result was a severe labor shortage that could not be overcome even by the practice of importing Indian or "free African" laborers. The shortage in turn brought about high salaries and decreased profits, causing some bankruptcies among the less efficient plantations, and a reduction in the output of colonial staples: coffee, cocoa, and especially sugar. The results varied both temporally and spatially—some areas, such as Mauritius and Barbados, actually increased their sugar crops, while others, such as Antigua, held steady—and marked declines came only after the

Wilkins, "Window on Freedom: South Carolina's Response to British West Indian Slave Emancipation, 1833–1834," *South Carolina Historical Magazine,* LXXV (1984), 135–44.

end of apprenticeship in 1838; however, there is no doubt that the foremost of all colonial commodities, sugar, experienced a serious drop in production. Jamaica, the leading British Caribbean colony, particulary suffered decreases in sugar output. During the decade 1824 through 1833 the British West Indies produced an annual average of 204,699 tons of sugar, while in the period 1839 through 1846 they accounted for only an average of 131,177 tons, a fall of 35.9 percent.[24] Although some of this loss might have been offset by gains in Mauritius and India, the overall decline was nevertheless severe. This slide in production was reflected in official British import-export statistics and admitted in time, more or less grudgingly, even by many British abolitionists, though they might disagree on the percentage of reduction. It was also reported by all the official French observers of the British colonial scene and covered by the French press. As they became increasingly aware of these developments, French colonial spokesmen found in them the ammunition they needed to launch a frontal attack against the entire British emancipation process.

French journals devoted to the colonies were quick to pick up reports about diminution of work and production in the British Caribbean following the end of servitude. *Le Moniteur de commerce*, which had emphasized the uncooperative and insubordinate nature of British freedmen during the early stages of emancipation, by 1836 was placing most importance on the precipitous fall in production in the British West Indies: "nothing can ward off the storm which menaces production." The newspaper added that output was plummeting primarily because blacks were not working sufficiently; and it snidely remarked that it was to be hoped that at least some rural laborers would remain in the fields by 1840. *Le Breton* (Nantes) agreed that former slaves had refrained from most excesses but were refusing to work. Girardin's *La Presse* also underlined the fact that Negroes had stopped toiling.[25] *Le Bulletin colonial*, influenced by Granier de Cassagnac, dwelt with apparent delight on the decreased productivity in the West Indian archipelago. Mauguin's *Le Commerce*, for its part, charged that

24. Philip D. Curtin, "The British Sugar Duties and West Indian Prosperity," *Journal of Economic History*, XIV (1954), 161–62; Noel Deerr, *The History of Sugar* (2 vols.; London, 1949–50), II, 376.
25. *Le Moniteur du commerce*, May 5, September 20, 29, October 19, 1836; *Le Breton*, October 3, 1838; *La Presse*, July 23, 1840.

British sugar imports from the Caribbean had fallen by one-fourth from 1838 to 1839 (after the end of apprenticeship), while *Le Journal du Havre* insisted that production in Jamaica had plunged by one-third.[26] *Le Courrier du Havre* (Le Havre), a daily directly subsidized by the Colonial Councils, referred to Jamaica as a place where freedmen were neglecting praedial tasks, proving that "the English system is radically defective [*vicieux*]."[27] The frequent citation of Jamaica by colonially oriented organs is noteworthy, for that island was not only by far the largest British sugar colony but also the one whose staple output, and economy in general, had suffered the most following abolition. This indicates the extent to which French journalistic defenders of slavery were being selective in their choice of evidence in an attempt to tarnish the British accomplishment as much as possible.

Throughout the 1840s French newspapers sympathetic to the colonies continued to underscore the economic failures of British emancipation. *L'Outre-mer*, a colonial advocate par excellence, implied that any journal that denied the fall in British staple production was deluding the public. According to *Le Bulletin colonial*, the diminution in crops was caused by the laziness of blacks.[28] *Le Courrier de la Gironde* (Bordeaux) affirmed that official British documents indicated that the decline in production was caused by the preference of freedmen to work their own plots and do no more than the minimum required of them on the estates, even in exchange for high wages. The results were so dramatic, *Le Courrier* suggested, that it would take the British colonies fifty years to recover from the disaster. A fellow Bordeaux daily, *Le Mémorial bordelais*, stated in 1843 that English abolition had brought an exorbitant increase in the price of sugar, an excessive salary rate for workers, and a drop in output, problems that meant ruin for the planters and demoralization for the former slaves themselves, who had become impertinent and slothful. It declared, too, that even Lord Edward Stanley, the British colonial secretary, had admitted before the Commons in 1842 "the unfortunate ef-

26. *Le Bulletin colonial*, November 30, 1836, April 20, December 3, 1838; *Le Commerce*, October 14, 1839; *Le Journal du Havre*, July 21, 1840.
27. *Le Courrier du Havre*, June 5, 1840. For evidence of direct colonial influence on this publication, see Jennings, "La presse havraise et l'esclavage," 65.
28. *L'Outre-mer*, July 17–19, 1840; *Le Bulletin colonial*, August 2, 1840.

fect" slave liberation had had on production. All this led *Le Mémorial* to warn: "One sees, therefore, to what point England has come with her emancipation. Let her example serve as a lesson for us." The following year the journal returned to the charge by insisting that the British move had brought "indolence, and all the vices that accompany it." Obviously overemphasizing its point, it purported that British colonial production had practically ceased, that blacks were going fishing rather than toiling in the fields. *L'Armoricain* of Brest was only slightly more accurate when it maintained in 1845 that British staple output had decreased by one-half since the termination of slavery.[29] Apologists for the colonies among the French press were quite prepared to misrepresent the facts in order to enhance the effectiveness of their attack on the economic shortcomings of the postemancipation British colonial structure.

Similar criticism of the most vulnerable aspect of the British abolition record came directly from French observers of the scene. As was noted previously, even those official French representatives sent to the British dependencies who were most favorable to the results of British abolition, d'Arvoy and Layrle, had stressed the economic tailspin concomitant with it. This same tendency, albeit less objectively expressed, can be seen in comments sent in by nonofficial assessors. Thus, Captain Pelletier, a merchantman from Bordeaux who had visited Mauritius, stated in his sea report that the ending of slavery had dealt a "terrible blow" to agriculture on that British island, resulting in one-third of the cane remaining uncut despite the importation of laborers from India. Similarly, Bellegarrigue, a Frenchman living in Jamaica, wrote to a member of the Guadeloupe colonial council that "plantation culture is nearly abandoned," with colonial settlements being depopulated as blacks went off to found their own villages. An influential member of the Colonial Council of Martinique, J. B. Le Pelletier du Clary, employed almost identical terminology in declaring that British West Indian staple production had decreased so much from 1838 to 1839 that if the same pattern prevailed for the next four years total output would be reduced to "nothing."[30]

29. *Le Courrier de la Gironde,* December 21, 25, 1842; *Le Mémorial bordelais,* November 30, 1843, March 24, 1844; *L'Armoricain,* June 7, 1845.

30. Pelletier, report of January, 1840, in Gén. 164 (1331), Bellegarrigue to

French colonial governors rendered equally bleak judgments on the economic situation in British tropical holdings. Early evaluations by these officials in the mid-1830s reflected, not only their anxiety about social instability in British possessions, but also their concern about the lack of sustained labor. Jubelin, when governor of Guiana, related how production and work had plummeted in British Demerara. The governor of Martinique, Halgan, though admitting that he had little information on Jamaica, alleged that the dearth of labor on this island augured poorly for its future. Reports of these kinds continued to flow in from administrators in the late 1830s and 1840s. In 1843 the governor of Martinique, Admiral du Valdailly, insisted that "the English experience confirms each day" that work could not be continued after emancipation.[31] After he had become governor of Guadeloupe, Jubelin reiterated his contention that in the British colonies "work is being obtained only with great difficulty." In fact, he claimed, the situation might deteriorate even further because young blacks had become accustomed to laziness. As time went on, Jubelin was "more and more confirmed in the opinion that work" was still diminishing in England's dependencies, something which, he believed, should make the French hesitant to follow in their neighbor's footsteps.[32] Admiral Moges agreed with Jubelin's analyses. One of the arguments that Moges used in counseling a cautious French approach to abolition was that work in the British colonies was capricious, uncertain, and reduced. He affirmed that Jamaica's future was somber because of the lack of industry among freedmen and that English documents, combined with Layrle's evaluations, had convinced him that work continued to decline steadily in the British West Indies. According to this official, the reliability of noncoerced labor was "the entire question concerning emancipation and the colonial future."[33]

Cicéron, September 10, 1840, in Gén. 170 (1375), Le Pelletier du Clary, report for Colonial Council, 1839, in Gén. 171 (1376), ANSOM.

31. Jubelin to Minister, April 6, 1835, in Gén. 165 (1337), Halgan to Minister, October 19, 1835, in Gén. 144 (1225), du Valdailly to Minister, November 25, 1843, in Gén. 171 (1379), ANSOM.

32. Jubelin to Minister, April 26, 1838, in Corr. Gén., Guadeloupe 85, December 7, 1839, in Gén. 171 (1376), April 17, 1840, in Corr. Gén., Guadeloupe 86, ANSOM.

33. Moges to Minister, July 27, 1839, in Gén. 161 (1323), December 3, 1838, February 10, 1840, both in Gén. 144 (1225), ANSOM.

Excerpts gathered by the navy and colonial ministry from news-papers published in the French colonies showed, quite understand-ably, their preoccupation with the same problem. *Le Courrier de la Guadeloupe* cited a declaration by the governor of Jamaica certify-ing that the sugar crop had decreased considerably in 1834. Noting the same statement, *La Feuille hebdomadaire de l'île de Bourbon* concluded: "One can judge from this what Negro labor will be like" after the termination of apprenticeship.[34] Another Bourbon newspaper, *Le Conservateur*, asserted in 1838 that abolition had "delivered a mortal blow to [British] colonial output" as a whole, because the Negro had "returned to his natural laziness." *La Feuille hebdomadaire*, writing again in 1840, agreed with other colonial journals that "the great inconvenience of emancipation" was the reduction of work. Five years later the paper insisted once more that British slave liberation had caused a considerable de-cline in crops.[35] *L'Avenir de Pointe-à-Pitre* was as categorical as other colonial publications in proclaiming that "the great afflic-tion of English emancipation" was "the tendency of freedmen to desert large-scale cultivation."[36]

The colonial press was joined by other influential spokesmen for the plantocratic cause in underscoring the economic difficulties facing the British West Indies. Baron de Cools, colonial delegate for Martinique, was emphasizing this point when he presented to the French navy and colonial department British documents indicat-ing that Jamaican sugar exports had dropped by 12 percent in 1835.[37] Some time later Favard, future delegate of Guiana, submit-ted a letter to *Le Temps*—edited as of 1839 by Conil, former dele-gate of Bourbon—in which he claimed that events in the Carib-bean proved "slave abolition must necessarily entail the ruin of all colonial property." This was the case, he explained, because aboli-tion had removed from the "Black race" all restraints on "its natu-ral propensity for laziness and antisocial life." As far as Favard was concerned, "economically" English emancipation had "com-

34. Article in *Le Courrier de la Guadeloupe* cited by *Le Journal des débats*, November 26, 1835; *La Feuille hebdomadaire de l'île de Bourbon*, February 24, 1836, in Gén. 178 (1418), ANSOM.
35. *Le Conservateur*, May 10, 1838, in Gén. 164 (1331), *La Feuille hebdomadaire de l'île de Bourbon*, February 12, 1840, January 22, 1845, in Gén. 171 (1376) and Gén. 197 (1489), respectively, ANSOM.
36. *L'Avenir*, November 6, 1846, in Gén. 197 (1489), ANSOM.
37. Cools to Minister, April 16, 1836, in Gén. 178 (1418), ANSOM.

pletely failed."[38] Chambers of commerce of French port cities were also highly solicitous of colonial welfare and prone to concentrate on the economic aspects of the British experiment. Thus, in 1838 the Chamber of Commerce of Nantes wrote to François Guizot, then president of the legislative commission investigating the Passy proposal for emancipation, to remind him that English possessions provided an ample demonstration that as soon as blacks were freed, colonial production diminished.[39] A French diplomatic observer was even more pessimistic in his evaluation. According to the French consul in New Orleans, Etienne David, production had fallen dramatically in the British West Indies, causing many planters to abandon their lands.[40] A similar claim was made by Charles Dupin, president of the Council of Delegates in 1844. Supporting his assertions with official British documents, Dupin issued a booklet in which he stressed "the rapid, frightful decrease of intertropical products," the "deplorable decline of crops" in England's dependencies.[41] In late 1847 and early 1848 French *colons* were still decrying the "ruin and misery," the "economic demise" of the postemancipation British Caribbean.[42] French colonial advocates had clearly learned that the multitude of documentation furnished by London could be exploited selectively as powerful evidence against the economic feasibility of slave liberation.

The same debate was carried over into the French legislative bodies. Already in 1835 Mauguin remarked categorically that West Indian events demonstrated "that Negroes cannot be brought to work voluntarily." A year later he again noted the "bad effects" of decreased productivity caused by English abolition. By the 1840s other legislators had taken up the economic theme. The deputy Dominique Augustin Affrican Stourm, speaking in 1843, brought the lesson home to France by predicting that French sugar output

38. *Le Temps*, July 8, 1840; M. Favard, *Examen des résultats produits par l'émancipation des noirs dans les colonies anglaises* (Paris, 1842), 12, 26.

39. Nantes Chamber of Commerce to Guizot, May 2, 1838, in Archives de la Chambre de Commerce de Nantes, Archives départementales de la Loire-Atlantique, Nantes.

40. Consul to Minister of Foreign Affairs, May 27, 1840, in Correspondance politique, Etats-Unis 96, AAE.

41. Baron Charles Dupin, *Second mémoire. Situation comparée des colonies françaises et des colonies anglaises* (Paris, 1844), 15–18.

42. Guadeloupe Colonial Council, session of July 9, 1847, in Corr. Gén., Guadeloupe 237, Colonial Council of Martinique, session of January 7, 1848, in Corr. Gén., Martinique 122, ANSOM.

would decline as England's had if Paris eliminated colonial slavery. The following year Amaranthe Alphonse Dougommier Denis, acting as reporter on abolitionist petitions presented to the Chamber of Deputies, fiercely attacked British emancipation for having brought about a drop of more than one-third in sugar production. The English example, Denis asserted, confirmed the rule that granting freedom to slaves would inevitably lead to the abandonment of tropical cultivation.[43] A year later General Amédée Louis Despans-Cubières, former minister of war, spoke out in the Chamber of Peers on the diminution of work in British territories, which, he predicted, would soon reduce production "to zero." He was supported by Joseph Napoléon Ney, prince de la Moskowa, Marshal Ney's eldest son, who insisted "that production in the English West Indies has fallen by more than a third," that slave liberation had "completely ruined" these islands.[44] The repetition of these charges, and indeed the similarity of terminology employed in this discourse, provides further evidence indicating that colonial sympathizers had joined their efforts against the British antislavery process.

By the 1840s the deputy and delegate Jollivet had emerged as a leader in the attempt to disparage the economic facets of the British experience. While addressing the lower house, Jollivet, like other colonial apologists, cited Lord Stanley's statement in the Commons in 1842 to show that British emancipation had had "unfortunate results" for production.[45] Jollivet was even more effective outside the legislature, employing his talented pen to turn out a series of booklets, pamphlets, and letters which were widely propagated and cited in colonial circles and which served as standard-bearers for the attack on the British record. In a booklet published in 1841 he countered abolitionist claims about increased production in the British colonies by quoting admissions to the contrary made in the Commons by Sir T. F. Baring, the chancellor of the exchequer, and Lord John Russell, the colonial secretary. The following year he produced a similar pamphlet in which he referred to Russell's declaration of May 7, 1841; in this same publication

43. *Le Moniteur universel,* April 23, 1835, May 26, 1836, May 13, 1843, May 5, 1844.
44. *Ibid.,* April 5, 6, 1845.
45. *Ibid.,* May 5, 1844.

Jollivet quoted Layrle on the unproductiveness of free labor and cited a letter by Charles Metcalfe, governor of Jamaica, about the impossibility of procuring a large enough working force.[46] In another booklet that appeared in 1842 Jollivet provided a list of speakers in British Parliament who, he claimed, had made public utterances indicating or implying a decline in sugar production. A third short book published by Jollivet that year employed selected passages from British documents appearing in the French navy and colonial department's five-volume series to illustrate the precipitous decline in output and work caused by slave liberation in the British Caribbean. By so doing he hoped to show "the disastrous results of the abolition of slavery in the English colonies" and prove that "emancipation in [France's] colonies would have even more immediate and calamitous results than in the English [ones]."[47]

Jollivet repeated what he termed the "incontestable fact" that British abolition had brought a "considerable reduction" of colonial products in a letter that he addressed to American slave owners in Louisiana on February 25, 1843. Again he cited excerpts from British statesmen to prove his point.[48] Commenting on Jollivet's methods, the French antislavery organ *L'Abolitioniste français* pointed out that he had systematically quoted out of context negative aspects of statements largely favorable to emancipation;[49] but such a rectification was unlikely to sway Jollivet's colonial audience. The fiercely proslavery *Le Globe* (Paris) proudly repeated Jollivet's demonstration that slave liberation had ruined

46. T. M. A. Jollivet, *Des missions en France de la Société abolitioniste* [sic] *anglaise et étrangère* (Paris, 1841), 2–3; *Parallèle entre les colonies*, 30–32.

47. Jollivet, *De la philanthropie anglaise* (Paris, 1842), 7–11; *L'émancipation anglaise jugée par ses résultats. Analyse des documents officiels imprimés par l'ordre de M. le Ministre de la marine et des colonies* (Paris, 1842), 5, 104.

48. Jollivet, *A MM. les habitants de la Louisianne* [sic] (Paris, 1843). For a discussion of the proslavery attitude of French citizens and officials residing in mid-nineteenth-century Louisiana, see Lawrence C. Jennings, "L'abolition de l'esclavage par la IIe République et ses effets en Louisiane, 1848–1858," *Revue française d'histoire d'outre-mer*, LVI (1969), 375–97. It is noteworthy, too, that Jollivet had probably made contact with Duff Green, an apostle of American slavery, when the latter was in Paris in 1842 and that he cited the slavery apologist John C. Calhoun in his writings, suggesting a community of interests between the French and American plantocracies. See Frederick Merk, *Slavery and the Annexation of Texas* (New York, 1972), 111, 115.

49. *L'Abolitioniste français*, May–June, 1844. In the mid-nineteenth century *abolitionniste* was still not spelled with two *n*'s.

English tropical dependencies, while *Le Mémorial bordelais* praised his work for proving the "deplorable results" of Britain's actions. The latter organ proceeded to draw from Jollivet's analyses what it believed to be their logical conclusion: no one wanted slavery, but it was an economic necessity.[50] Jollivet's ably written, factual-appearing, and oft-repeated contentions fortified French colonial claims about the nefarious effects of British slave liberation on colonial productivity. They also strengthened the French antiabolitionist cause as a whole.

French colonial denunciations of the economic outcome of British emancipation were all the more significant because they tended to coincide with, and perhaps reinforce, similar judgments prevalent within the French navy and colonial ministry by the 1840s. Evidence from a variety of sources indicates that at this time the French government, like the *colons*, was especially preoccupied with the economic consequences of the British accomplishment. Officials within the Ministry of the Navy and Colonies had the practice of setting off with dark pencil or ink marks in the margins sections of received dispatches that they deemed to be of greatest interest or importance. During the 1830s the most frequently underlined parts of documents had tended to be those dealing with unrest in British territories, though even then questions relating to interruptions in labor patterns had often attracted attention. By the 1840s, however, the most marked-off portions of documents relating to British abolition were invariably those touching on the reduction in colonial output.[51] In one instance, when Moges sent in a report in 1843 qualifying the British antislavery measure as "ruinous" and "menacing for the fortune of the white proprietor," a functionary in Paris set off these phrases with black ink and added: "There is the truth!"[52] On other occasions, too, French government leaders uttered words indicating their anxiety over these matters. Speaking in the Chamber of Deputies in 1840, Adolphe Thiers, president of the Council of Ministers, emphasized "that emancipation has considerably diminished

50. *Le Globe*, December 10, 1842; *Le Mémorial bordelais*, December 14, 1842.
51. See, for example, dossiers, in Gén. 178 (1419) and Gén. 178 (1421), covering 1840–43, ANSOM.
52. Notation on Moges to Minister, November 21, 1843, in Gén. 171 (1379), ANSOM.

work and production" in the English colonies.[53] In 1842 Duperré, then navy and colonial minister, made a telltale communication to Guizot, foreign minister and de facto head of government as of October, 1840. According to Duperré, "the effects of [British] emancipation are very satisfactory as concerns moral issues and public order, but as for colonial holdings, and notably the production of sugar, the consequences of abolition are generally poor, and the large colonies are advancing toward their ruin if prompt measures are not taken to remedy their distress."[54] Decision makers in Paris were echoing the same concerns about productivity as the colonial lobby.

Interestingly enough, Duperré professed to be basing his conclusions partially on information drawn from a report presented to the Commons in 1842 by a British parliamentary committee investigating the state of the postemancipation West Indies. In reality, though, while this British document had mentioned some economic shortcomings, the overall picture it had painted of the British Caribbean had been a decidedly positive one. For high French officials to focus only on its detrimental remarks concerning economic performance shows to what extent they, like the plantocracy, made short shrift of moral, social, or racial considerations and placed importance only on work and productivity. In this sense, the abolitionist Victor Destutt de Tracy was quite perspicacious when he posed the rhetorical question: "why is it that every time the example of England is cited, only its negative aspects are stressed?"[55] His reflection, made in the course of a legislative debate in 1837, applies equally well to the attitude that important French officials displayed toward questions related to British slave liberation throughout most of the July Monarchy.

Another indication of this attitude by French government leaders comes from statements uttered by Mackau and Jubelin as members of the Broglie Commission studying the French emancipation option in the early 1840s. As indicated previously, prior to their appointments as commission members both had served as colonial governors. Following their service on the commission,

53. *Le Moniteur universel*, May 9, 1840.
54. Duperré to Guizot, October 28, 1842, in Mémoires et documents, Afrique 28, AAE.
55. *Le Moniteur universel*, June 7, 1837.

Mackau became minister of the navy and colonies (July 27, 1843, to May 7, 1847), while Jubelin was appointed his undersecretary of state (August 10, 1844, to February 25, 1848). The sentiments they expressed in the commission give some indication of the policy they were apt to adopt or implement while in control of colonial affairs during the latter years of the July Monarchy. A detailed examination of the minutes of the Broglie Commission shows the degree to which both men were obsessed with the issue of the insufficiency of work and production in the postemancipation British colonies. Their negative attitude toward both slave liberation in general and the British precedent in particular were noted by the *BFAS Reporter* when it referred to Mackau's "almost implacable enmity to abolition, which is shared, as might be expected, by Jubelin, Saint Hilaire, Audiffret, and Wustemberg"—other commission members.[56]

Mackau set the tone for his interventions within the commission in one of its earliest sessions, on June 7, 1840, when all of the questions or comments he made about the British situation touched on economic matters. He emphasized that work had decreased by one-fourth to one-third after the end of apprenticeship; asked whether small-scale farming might not replace large-scale sugar cultivation; cited one report from the governor of Martinique to the effect that blacks were abandoning praedial tasks; and referred to another indicating that production in Demerara had fallen by one-half. When the royal investigative body met again in 1842 after a recess of a year and a half, Mackau's position remained unchanged. In reply to a positive statement by Broglie about the overall consequences of British emancipation, Mackau insisted that proprietors in Demerara had suffered considerably. He also affirmed that, because French dependencies were less prepared for abolition than English ones had been, liberated blacks would refuse to work, and colonial staple output would fall precipitously. According to Mackau, "the application of the British method would therefore be a veritable calamity for [France's] colonies."[57]

During the session of February 14, 1842, Jubelin testified in the same vein. The British example, he asserted, had shown that a

56. *BFAS Reporter*, February 21, 1844.
57. Broglie Commission, Minutes, June 7, 1840, January 31, 1842.

decline in production was inevitable after the termination of slavery; therefore, if the British system were to be applied to France's possessions, sugar cultivation, "the essence of our colonial establishments" and one of the sources of metropolitan prosperity, would be greatly compromised. When an abolitionist member of the body, Tracy, interceded in an attempt to minimize the economic disadvantages of slave liberation, Mackau interjected in support of Jubelin that general French emancipation would result in indolence on the part of the freedmen, greatly perturbing France's colonial interests.[58] Whenever Mackau spoke up within the commission concerning the British experience it was invariably to emphasize its detrimental effects.

In late February, 1842, Mackau invoked Layrle's reports to show that work had been abandoned in postemancipation British colonies. On March 14 he again cited Layrle's observations, this time quoting his assertion that British abolition was unjust because it had ruined colonial holdings. Moreover, Mackau claimed, Layrle had shown, not only that production had declined in Jamaica, but that if it continued to diminish the island "would cease to exist as a productive colony." Furthermore, Mackau drew from Layrle's submissions the rather dubious conclusion that what had occurred in Jamaica was the best possible lesson for France's West Indian territories.[59] When Jubelin on May 23 stressed that slave liberation had "gravely compromised" British planters, proving "entirely disastrous" for them, he was supported by two other members of the commission. The deputy Jacques Henri Wustemberg, representing Bordeaux, where he had been president of the tribunal of commerce, developed the line of reasoning introduced earlier by Mackau and Jubelin. England's precedent, he insisted, would ruin "large-scale cultivation" and "the production of sugar." More significant still was the intervention of Joseph Henri Galos, also a deputy of the Gironde department, who replaced Saint Hilaire in 1842 as director of the colonies, a position he would retain for the duration of the July Monarchy, making him Mackau's chief assistant in the navy and colonial ministry. Galos made a deposition that closely resembled the wording of the dispatch Duperré was to send to Guizot later in 1842, showing once again the unity of

58. *Ibid.*, February 14, 1842.
59. *Ibid.*, February 28, March 14, 1842.

feeling about British actions within the navy and colonial department. Concerning the British precedent, Galos exclaimed: "one is forced to admit that, alongside the favorable results on moral and social issues, it offers disastrous ones for work and production; in a word, from the economic point of view, England's act is an unfortunate operation."[60] Statements like these, made by procolonial elements of the Broglie Commission who also held—or were to hold—high positions within the navy and colonial department, were as negative about the economic outcome of British abolition as the statements of the *colons* themselves. Evidently, the ethical and social results of the British experience were discounted by many Frenchmen preoccupied with its economic aspects. Arguments about decreased British staple production, joined to those about the need to await the final outcome of Britain's initiative, proved to be highly effective means by which French procolonial spokesmen worked to influence a similar-thinking government to postpone emancipation of France's own slaves.

French apostles of slavery proved extremely adroit in underscoring those elements of the British record that served their own ends. In this sense it is noteworthy that not all aspects of the British model were criticized by French colonial supporters. As was suggested earlier, some Frenchmen who wished to defer abolition indirectly praised the amount of effort Britain had put into civilizing its slaves before freeing them. This, of course, was an essential corollary to the contention that French blacks were not as ready for liberty as their British brethren. Mackau clearly gave voice to these sentiments on one instance when he invoked "the example of England" during debates in the Broglie Commission. During the last twenty years of English colonial slavery, he claimed, England had striven with "assiduous care" to bring about "important ameliorations" for those in bondage. It was indispensable for France to take the time, not only to match England's procedures, but to improve on them.[61] In the eyes of French colonial proponents, Great Britain's actions were not entirely negative when they could be used as a means to postpone further the liberation of French slaves.

French colonial exponents also viewed another aspect of British

60. *Ibid.*, May 23, 1842.
61. *Ibid.*, March 21, 1842.

emancipation as a positive factor meriting imitation by the July
Monarchy. Already in 1834 Halgan, then governor of Martinique,
suggested that perhaps the most salient point about the British
initiative was the indemnity the Whig government had given slave
proprietors. In 1835 *Le Journal du Havre* reminded the government
in Paris that if France wished to follow in England's footsteps it
would have to compensate its slave owners.[62] In the Chamber of
Deputies, Delegate Dupin, who usually had little good to say about
the British experience, joined in praising British legislators for having granted an indemnity.[63] In like manner, Jollivet presented the
Chamber's commission of 1838 investigating slavery with a statement asserting that "emancipation can only take place with the
conditions adopted by the British Parliament, that is, with an indemnity of around 750 francs per slave head, seven years of apprenticeship," and adequate preparation for freedom.[64] Mauguin was
even more demanding during a speech in the lower house when he
insisted that any indemnity given French masters should be higher
than the British one. He followed this up with a formal letter to the
minister of the navy and colonies in which he affirmed that French
slaves could not be freed without "the conditions already admitted
by England," the foremost of which was indemnification.[65] Besides using the British precedent to reinforce the colonial contention that the granting of sufficient compensation was a necessary
prerequisite to French emancipation, Mauguin was obviously acting with another motive in mind. *Le Constitutionnel* was undoubtedly correct when it surmised that Mauguin was insistent
about the need for a generous indemnity because he realized that
this itself was an effective ploy to adjourn French slave liberation.
Le Courrier français agreed that colonial defenders were resorting
to this device as a means to divert Frenchmen from any antislavery
program.[66] Even when colonial advocates gave their approbation
to an aspect of the British system, they were doing so with the aim
of prolonging servitude.

62. Halgan to Minister, August 9, 1834, in Gén. 156 (1299), ANSOM; *Le Journal
du Havre*, April 24, 1835.
63. *Le Moniteur universel*, May 26, 1836.
64. Rémusat Commission, Minutes, March 28, 1838.
65. *Le Moniteur universel*, April 23, 1835; Mauguin to Minister, June 18, 1835,
in Gén. 156 (1299), ANSOM.
66. *Le Constitutionnel*, April 23, 1835; *Le Courrier français*, May 26, 1836.

The French government, itself committed to a legalistic approach and not eager to emancipate, assured the *colons* in 1835 that it would not act without granting them a just indemnity.[67] Still, plantocratic spokesmen repeatedly returned to this issue, perhaps because, as Moges suggested in one of his notes, a fear existed in colonial circles that the administration in Paris might not follow the British indemnity procedure.[68] Thus, in 1838 both *Le Temps* and *Le Bulletin colonial* admonished French settlers to require more than adequate compensation, as British slave owners had, for any slave liberation act the government might implement.[69] Similarly, Jules Lechevalier, with his ties in both governmental and colonial camps, insisted in all of his writings on the need for a liberal indemnity, following the British model.[70] During the sessions of the Broglie Commission in the early 1840s Jubelin pronounced the principle of compensation to be inviolable, while Mackau intimated that even the British grant had been inadequate.[71] As late as 1847 the governor of Guiana, Pariset, cited the British example while stressing the necessity for ample reimbursement in any French abolition legislation.[72] The British precedents of granting an indemnity and of slowly preparing slaves for freedom were viewed positively by French colonial elements only inasmuch as they coincided with colonial interests.

With these exceptions aside, French procolonial organs depicted all other aspects of the British abolition process in somber tones. This is quite clear from the disparaging attitude they often displayed when commenting on the overall significance of the British experience. *Le Journal du Havre* launched an oblique attack on the British record when it pointed out that high sugar prices resulting from the decline in English staple production were causing more slaves to be imported into Cuba and Brazil from Africa, stimulating the slave trade. Thus, the newspaper queried, "what has humanity gained from the emancipation of slaves in the English colonies?" *Le Bulletin colonial*, for its part, belittled the attempts by

67. Minister to Governors, August 1, 1835, in Corr. Gén. 187, ANSOM.
68. Moges to Minister, July 20, 1840, in Gén. 171 (1376), ANSOM.
69. *Le Temps*, February 16, 1838; *Le Bulletin colonial*, April 22, May 6, 1838.
70. See, for example, Lechevalier, report to Governor of Martinique, November 15, 1838, in Gén. 169 (1373), ANSOM.
71. Broglie Commission, Minutes, February 14, 28, 1842.
72. Pariset to Minister, September 25, 1847, in Gén. 173 (1388), ANSOM.

French abolitionists to defend the British initiative. It insinuated that humanitarians believed the British experience had been satisfactory simply because "as of now the planters of Jamaica are not exterminated by the blacks," or because "arson and murder" had not yet obliged all plantation owners to flee the island.[73] The indomitable *Revue du dix-neuvième siècle* employed bitter irony to mock Britain's achievement. The *Revue* depicted British abolitionists as former slave traders and planters who had profited from bondage as long as it existed, had made fortunes by selling their slaves before emancipation, and were now hypocritical enough to read the Bible and refuse to eat slave-grown sugar. In a subsequent article the journal changed its approach but retained its sarcasm by asserting that English philanthropists would be willing to condone servitude if they themselves owned slaves.[74] Crude indictments of this kind, prevalent in the antiabolitionist lexicon of the eighteenth century, had not entirely disappeared by the late 1830s in France.

Although some journalistic opponents of British antislavery measures resorted to unveiled criticism or sardonic accounts to disparage them, other newspapers adopted more sophisticated tactics. Two port city dailies, *Le Mémorial bordelais* and *Le Sémaphore de Marseille*, implied that England had proceeded with resolve and premeditation, that behind her "philanthropic effort" she was nurturing her own surreptitious designs.[75] *Le Commerce* was more explicit when it predicted that England would exploit her move in an attempt to instigate slave revolts in the American South: "Thus, while England has been praised for emancipating her slaves and lauded for her supposed sentimentalism, she was acting . . . in egotistical ways." In a later article *Le Commerce* elaborated on its stance. English slave liberation, it declared, "this pretense of philanthropy," was really "a trap for the maritime powers" to "ruin the output of the West Indies and substitute for it the production of India."[76] *Le Commerce* contended that emancipation was just "a means" for England to satisfy its own interests and better exploit India. According to this organ, English states-

73. *Le Journal du Havre*, July 2, 1840; *Le Bulletin colonial*, March 15, 1840.
74. *La Revue du dix-neuvième siècle*, December, 1836, January 24, 1837.
75. *Le Mémorial bordelais*, March 4, 1838; *Le Sémaphore de Marseille*, September 20, 1842.
76. *Le Commerce*, April 18, 1838, October 14, 1839.

men were hoping that their country "would draw along by her example all other nations" and thereby destroy the West Indian sugar industry to the advantage of the East Indian one.[77]

Mauguin's *Le Commerce* was not the first colonial sympathizer to employ this argument. Such criticism of Britain's aims predated the July Monarchy, being prevalent in some circles during the Restoration. Similar statements had also been made in the Chamber of Deputies in the mid-1830s. Mauguin had suggested at this time that an underlying factor behind British slave liberation was the desire to sacrifice the West Indies for the benefit of India. During the same session his like-minded colleague, Louis Estancelin, had declared that since England could no longer provision its Caribbean holdings with blacks via the slave trade it was determined to obtain the monopoly of colonial products for the Asian subcontinent.[78] By the early 1840s Jollivet was developing this same concept in his proslavery pamphlets. In *Question des sucres dans la Chambre des Communes d'Angleterre* he stated categorically that Britain hoped to make the rest of the world dependent on India for colonial staples. In another booklet published the same year he repeated his assertion that there was "a purely political calculation" behind Britain's apparent philanthropy in abolishing slavery: England was encouraging other nations to follow its lead in order to compromise their West Indian colonies and enhance the position of British India.[79]

That some British believed India had brighter prospects at this time than the Caribbean area is beyond doubt. In the 1840s even a handful of free-market advocates among the British abolitionists, such as George Thompson, believed that the West Indies had little future as a staple producer and the East Indian sugar would flourish under noncoerced labor.[80] However, claims that Britain was consciously sacrificing the West Indies to India had scant basis in fact, as French emancipationists tried in vain to point out. No evidence indicates that any British statesman ever seriously calculated or

77. *Ibid.*, February 13, 1840, June 8, 1841.
78. *Le Moniteur universel*, April 23, 1835.
79. T. M. A. Jollivet, *Question des sucres dans la Chambre des Communes d'Angleterre. Du travail libre et du travail forcé, leur influence sur la production coloniale* (Paris, 1841), 20; *Des missions en France*, 4–5.
80. David Eltis, "Abolitionist Perceptions of Society After Slavery," in Walvin (ed.), *Slavery and British Society*, 207–208.

planned along these lines. To be sure, British expectations about East Indian sugar production were high at first. Still, while Indian sugar output increased considerably in the 1830s, this trend was reversed by the late 1840s, never permitting the subcontinent to corner the sugar market as some Frenchmen surmised it would. After the lowering of the tariff on Indian sugar in 1835 the value of this exported commodity increased from £134,000 that year to £1,690,000 in 1847; but the long-range results of East Indian production were highly disappointing. Indian output tumbled drastically after the mid-1840s, when the British market was opened to foreign sugar. By the 1860s it had become apparent that India's future lay more in growing cotton than in producing sugar.[81] Nonetheless, attacks in the 1830s and early 1840s on the intentions of British emancipationists were astute attempts by French colonial elements to besmirch the British experience. Such efforts became even more prevalent after the right-of-search controversy stirred up French resentment of Great Britain in 1842. Finally, because of the close connections between French and British abolitionists, criticisms of this kind were an effective means by which French defenders of slavery could try to discredit the French anti-slavery movement.

When examining British emancipation, French colonial spokesmen steadily discounted or denied the benefits it had brought blacks, its underlying humanitarian motivation, and its overriding justice. Instead, they systematically sought out its every weak point or accepted only those tangential aspects of the British record that coincided with French colonial interests. Their arguments about the necessity of awaiting the final outcome of the British experiment proved to be an adroit means of advocating the postponement of French slave liberation; their insistence on the economic failure of the British move had the effect of denying the benefits of abolition. Both of these points were skillfully put forth by all elements of the colonial lobby, giving this group the appearance of unity and enhancing the weight of its arguments. The effectiveness of the colonial campaign against British emancipation was further advanced by the fact that its line of reasoning

81. Mathieson, *British Slave Emancipation*, 239; Burn, *Emancipation and Apprenticeship*, 87; Temperley, *British Antislavery*, 102, 106; Curtin, "The British Sugar Duties," 159–60; Deerr, *The History of Sugar*, I, 56–57.

struck a sympathetic chord with a French government dubious about the effects of the British initiative and favorable to the interests of its colonial establishment. Colonial injunctions about the desirability of waiting were welcome encouragement for a French government that had already adopted such a policy. Colonial warnings about the dire economic consequences of British slave liberation appeared to be borne out by the reports of official observers and other corroborative evidence. In sum, the plantocracy and the French government shared many of the same doubts and hesitations about the British emancipation process and the wisdom of applying it to France. Both of them saw the British model in largely negative terms. In this sense, French colonial proponents had much more success in reinforcing and encouraging the policies of their government than French abolitionists had in trying to convince the July Monarchy to follow the British example.

FOUR

FRENCH ABOLITIONIST VIEWS ON BRITISH EMANCIPATION

French abolitionists could naturally be expected to have as much sympathy for British slave liberation as their opponents had antipathy for it.[1] The British, after all, had set an example that Frenchmen opposed to slavery were quick to praise and anxious to imitate. For French emancipationists, Great Britain, the leading colonial power of the time, had proved that the eradication of bondage was possible even when nearly 800,000 slaves and a substantial indemnity were involved. France had less to sacrifice than Britain, as French slaves were fewer, the French colonial establishment less dynamic, and the French economy less dependent on slave-produced sugar—indeed, Northern France was harvesting a rapidly increasing volume of beet sugar by the 1830s and 1840s.[2] It

---

1. Although a plethora of works examine all aspects of the British and American emancipation processes, no detailed study of their French equivalent exists. The best available modern treatments devoting a few pages to the French scene are the following, listed in order of appearance: Gaston Martin, *Histoire de l'esclavage dans les colonies françaises* (Paris, 1948), 280–92; André-Jean Tudesq, *Les grands notables en France: Etude historique d'une psychologie sociale* (2 vols.; Paris, 1964), II, 834–52; Antoine Gisler, *L'esclavage aux Antilles françaises (XVIIe–XIXe siècle)* (1965; rpr. Paris, 1981), 128–45; Seymour Drescher, *Dilemmas of Democracy: Tocqueville and Modernization* (Pittsburgh, 1968), 151–95; William B. Cohen, *The French Encounter with Africans: White Response to Blacks, 1530–1880* (Bloomington, Ind., 1980), 192–204; Schnakenbourg, *La crise du système esclavagiste*, 92–136, 185–92; and Seymour Drescher, "Two Variants of Anti-Slavery: Religious Organization and Social Mobilization in Britain and France, 1780–1870," in Bolt and Drescher (eds.), *Anti-Slavery, Religion and Reform*, 43–63.

2. For a contrast between the relatively stagnant French colonial establishment of the 1830s and 1840s and the prosperous state of British tropical dependencies prior to 1833, compare the conclusions of Schnakenbourg, *La crise du système esclavagiste*, with those of Roger Anstey, *The Atlantic Slave Trade and British Abolition, 1760–1810* (Atlantic Heights, N.J., 1975), and Drescher, *Econocide*.

is revealing that on the eve of abolition colonial trade amounted to 18 percent of the British gross national product but only 7 percent of the French.[3] Material factors notwithstanding, in the eyes of liberal Frenchmen, Great Britain's accomplishment posed a question of honor, for they were determined that their nation should not permit itself to fall behind Britain in such a notable humanitarian action. Britain's precedent proved so attractive to Frenchmen opposed to servitude that it constituted the prime factor leading to the formation of the Société française pour l'abolition de l'esclavage, the only significant abolitionist organization under the July Monarchy. The British not only inspired but assisted their French counterparts. Just as French opponents of the slave trade or slavery during the Revolutionary and Restoration periods had received encouragement and support from the British Saints, during the July Monarchy French and British abolitionists wove close ties as the latter attempted to help and influence their brethren across the Channel. In every way, then, French emancipationists were so marked by the British achievement that it is essential to focus in detail on their attitude toward the whole range of issues raised by the British model.

Whereas French procolonial forces censured British slave liberation, elements favorable to French emancipation often tended to be effusive in their praise of the British antislavery process, especially during the 1830s. Such sentiments were clearly expressed at an early date in the abolitionist-leaning press. The organ of the Société de la morale chrétienne, precursor of the French abolitionist society, hailed August 1, 1834, as "the loftiest triumph a people has ever experienced" and "the most noble sacrifice that egotism ever made to justice and humanity." Similarly, *La Revue des colonies* (Paris), published by Cyrille Charles Auguste Bissette, a free man of color who had been active in the struggle against slavery since 1824, saluted "this act more generous than history has ever recorded."[4] Another of the earliest journals to acclaim Britain's decision, ironically, was *Le Journal du commerce*, liberal until its purchase by Mauguin in 1836. In 1834 and 1835 it referred to "this

3. Seymour Drescher, "Public Opinion and the Destruction of British Colonial Slavery," in Walvin (ed.), *Slavery and British Society*, 44.
4. *Journal de la Société de la morale chrétienne*, 2nd ser., VI (July–December, 1834), 46; *La Revue des colonies*, no. 4, October, 1834.

great work of civilization and humanity," "an event which has not been duplicated in the history of the world," an act of "admirable generosity" whereby England, the nation that had "most sinned against the Negro race," had redeemed itself. A more influential left-of-center daily, Le Constitutionnel, lauded British emancipation throughout the 1830s, referring to England's "great measure," her "great act" of a "high moral and philanthropic character," which would mark the century, her "noble initiative," and her "eternally honorable solution."[5] The equally liberal Courrier français applauded the "glorious" British accomplishment. Moreover, it attempted to refute colonial charges against Britain's achievement by insisting that nothing in official English documents provided any evidence of long-range political machinations motivating the British decision. The doctrinaire Journal des débats also extolled the "inevitable and desirable emancipation triumphing peacefully" in England's dependencies. The republican Le National, for its part, remained constant in its judgment from the mid-1830s to the early 1840s, citing British slave liberation as "this debt to humanity and national honor," "this noble example," "this great idea."[6]

Within French legislative bodies, too, abolitionists were quick to stand up and applaud the ending of bondage in British tropical territories. In the Chamber of Deputies in 1835 Tracy eulogized the British decision as "this honorable monument for England, this monument worthy of posterity's recognition," while Alphonse de Lamartine exclaimed that England had just "honored herself by one of the most incredible acts ever accomplished by man." During the same session, a leading abolitionist, François André Isambert, praised Britain's move as "a measure unique in the annals of the world," one "which will be mentioned in future times as an exalted and good political act."[7] In the more conservative Chamber of Peers, which unlike the lower house never developed a majority favorable to abolition, a Protestant leader, Vice Admiral Carel Henrik Verhuel, spoke out in 1835 to vouch for England's "great act of justice," which "honors her government." The following year

5. Le Journal du commerce, October 9, 1834, April 24, March 7, 1835; Le Constitutionnel, July 9, August 17, 1833, February 6, 1835, February 16, 1838.

6. Le Courrier français, February 7, 1835, June 21, 1838, July 16, 1840; Le Journal des débats, November 11, 1835; Le National, August 12, 1834, March 7, 1841.

7. Le Moniteur universel, April 23, 1835.

Tracy made himself heard once again on the subject among the deputies. While asserting that England should be esteemed for her actions, he took on a more defensive tone in exclaiming: "I do not understand this narrow patriotism which wishes to besmirch the act of a neighboring nation by imposing upon it the label of self-interest."[8] As a whole, abolitionist response within the French legislature to British slave liberation was highly positive in the period immediately following the passage of the Emancipation Act, much more so than it would be a decade later.

The French abolitionist community displayed a similar attitude in its writings and public pronouncements. In a booklet published in 1835, Montrol, one of the most important early emancipationists, qualified England's destruction of slavery as a "magnificent and solemn" act of principle, "an imposing signal given to all civilized nations," and "the first step which will lead to the abolition of slavery in the entire world."[9] As late as 1840, during a February abolitionist meeting in Paris attended by a prestigious British delegation, French philanthropists were exceedingly laudatory of the British precedent. Toasting his British guests, Odilon Barrot, a leader of the dynastic opposition, declared the British achievement to be "the most noble, the most holy thought that has ever preoccupied men." Lamartine joined him, proclaiming his British associates to be "these apostles . . . these Christian missionaries" whose deeds would "shine in the history of mankind." The great poet-politician declared that the moment which brought liberty to British slaves had been "a beautiful day in the eyes of God and men." England, he asserted, had been "shamefully calumniated" for "her very virtue" by those who said that her "generous efforts" were nothing but "an infamous trap covered by perfidious philanthropy" to destroy France's colonies by obliging her to follow Britain's lead. "Yes," he exclaimed, "that has been said, that has been believed; absurdity is infinite in its inventions, as foolishness is infinite in its credulity." In Lamartine's eyes, all accusations against the British accomplishment were pure "aberrations."[10] Closely identifying themselves with British emancipa-

8. *Ibid.*, June 16, 1835, May 26, 1836.
9. Montrol, *Des colonies anglaises*, 1, 4.
10. Sociéte française pour l'abolition de l'esclavage, *No. 16. Banquet offert à la députation de la Société centrale britannique pour l'abolition universelle de l'esclavage, 10 février 1840* (Paris, March, 1840), 3–9.

tion and its architects, French abolitionists were not only extolling the British experience but attempting to defend it from the colonial lobby's nationalistic barbs.

One of the major factors explaining the respect and admiration of French abolitionists for their British cohorts was the closeness of relations between the two groups. Indeed, in the mid-1830s the ties between French and British antislavery elements resembled those of a filial-paternal relationship. The liberation of British slaves revived the slavery question in France and stimulated a cluster of French humanitarians, most of them members of the Chambers, to form the Société française pour l'abolition de l'esclavage in 1834. The Société, founded in a preliminary fashion at the very moment when British slaves achieved their freedom (late July or early August, 1834) but only endowed with its definitive form in December, openly proclaimed that its aim was to "consider measures to imitate the example of England in achieving the general emancipation of slaves."[11] An examination of the prospectus published by the new organization shows the stimulus it had received from the British model and reveals the deep respect the French had for their colleagues across the Channel. For instance, this document cited the "great example" of the dedicated men who had brought about the end of servitude in Britain's holdings. Besides inspiring the formation of the French abolition society, British emancipationists exerted a strong influence within the nascent group during the first few months of its existence. The outline of the Société's first official meeting in Paris on December 3, 1834, included as part of the prospectus, indicates that this entire session was devoted to listening to a delegation of British abolitionists, made up of Zachary Macaulay, John Scoble, and Joseph Cooper, recount the English emancipationist experience since 1833. The presence of an English deputation at the first major meeting of the new society suggests that the British might actually have played a direct role in the formal foundation of the French body. In fact, the three British emissaries had been present in Paris prior to the December meeting, attending on November 22 with a number of French abolitionists an appeals court hearing on a purported slave conspiracy in Martinique. Then, in the session of March 30, 1835,

11. *Journal de la Société de la morale chrétienne*, 2nd ser., VI (July–December, 1834), 49, 294.

Macaulay, one of the most important British abolitionists and a man who had seen slavery firsthand in the West Indies, again addressed the Paris group; and on June 1 an eminent French member, Gustave de Beaumont, reported on his attendance at a large anti-slavery assembly in Britain.[12] One of the founding fathers of British abolitionism, Thomas Clarkson, had made several trips to France in 1789 to urge on the first French abolitionist formation, the ill-fated and short-lived Société des amis des noirs.[13] British emancipationists of the mid-1830s seem to have made an even greater effort to send members to France to spur on the fledgling French organization. What is certain is that the early months of the French abolitionist society's existence were marked by reciprocal visits and close cooperation between the London and Paris associations.

During the infancy of the Société française pour l'abolition de l'esclavage Macaulay appears to have played a principal role as British delegate to the French body and as liaison between the two movements. As the Société was made up mostly of deputies, it tended to meet only during sessions of the French legislature, which usually were held in the first half of each year; thus, the Société adjourned every summer, to reassemble in December or January. After having attended at least two of the Société's meetings during the first months of its existence, Macaulay was even more active in its second operational year, January through June, 1836. During the sessions of January 11 and 25 he presented the French with copies of his latest works, providing official documents on the British abolition process. On May 30 he intervened in a meeting to refute a claim made by Dupin in the Chambers that British production had declined after emancipation. Then, on June 6, when the French group suspended its meetings for the remainder of the year, the Société charged Macaulay and eight other of its most influential members with handling its correspondence and publications over the summer-through-autumn recess. In the spring of 1836 Macaulay received the ultimate accolade from the French organization when it named him its honorary president.[14]

12. Société française pour l'abolition de l'esclavage, *No. 1. Prospectus* (Paris, 1835), 14–16; *La Revue des colonies*, no. 6, December, 1834.
13. See especially Resnick, "The Société des amis des noirs," 560–69.
14. Société française pour l'abolition de l'esclavage, *4e publication*, iii, 42–44, 51, 53.

The close cooperation between Macaulay and his French colleagues might have continued if he had not returned to London and been confined to his home by illness in the winter of 1836. When he died in 1838, the Société read a solemn eulogy in his honor.[15]

During the years 1835 and 1836, besides participating in the Société's meetings in Paris, Macaulay published in that city five books in French on slave liberation.[16] Two of these studies were based on official British documents, and all of the books stressed the positive aspects of the British process. Moreover, these works strove to combat the idea that France's colonies were different from Britain's, thus challenging the planters' maxim to the contrary and reassuring Frenchmen that they, too, could rapidly achieve the destruction of servitude without danger. These volumes, aimed at the French audience, were a carefully executed part of the British effort to encourage Frenchmen to free their slaves. If British emancipationists operated during the mid-1830s as they did in the 1840s, it seems highly likely that they directly financed the publication of these French works.

It is somewhat difficult to trace the exact course of Franco-British abolitionist interaction in the years 1837 and 1838, for at this time the publications of the Société française pour l'abolition de l'esclavage changed format briefly and no longer gave minutes of its meetings or summaries of its activities. It appears probable, however, that, following Macaulay's departure from France, relations between the London and Paris groups slackened temporarily while French emancipationists took their battle into the Chambers and their British counterparts tended to believe that France would soon implement slave liberation. Already during the London abolitionist assembly that Gustave de Beaumont had attended in the spring of 1835, Lord Henry Brougham had expressed the

15. Société française pour l'abolition de l'esclavage, *No. 8*, pp. 44–48, meeting of June 20, 1838.
16. Zachary Macaulay, *Faits et rensiegnements prouvant les avantages du travail libre sur le travail forcé, et indiquant les moyens les plus propres à hâter l'abolition de l'esclavage dans les colonies européennes* (Paris, 1835); *Haïti, ou renseignements authentiques sur l'abolition de l'esclavage et de ses résultats, à Saint-Domingue et à la Guadeloupe* (Paris, 1835); *Tableau de l'esclavage tel qu'il existe dans les colonies françaises* (Paris, 1835); *Détails sur l'émancipation des esclaves dans les colonies anglaises, pendant les années 1834 et 1835* (Paris, 1836); *Suite des détails sur l'émancipation des esclaves dans les colonies anglaises pendant les années 1835 et 1836* (Paris, 1836).

conviction that, with the duc de Broglie as president of the Council of Ministers (Broglie served as first minister from March 12, 1835, to February 5, 1836), the French government would not let three additional months go by before proposing abolition.[17] This current of optimism on the part of British abolitionists, though tempered at times by expressions of disillusionment or exasperation, would prove constant for most of the duration of the July Monarchy. For the years 1837 and 1838 this sentiment, combined with the preoccupation of most English emancipationists with their struggle to terminate apprenticeship as soon as possible in British dependencies, might have deflected British philanthropic interest from French affairs to some extent. It does seem, though, that Brougham, who wintered regularly at Cannes, made at least one trip to Paris in 1838. Moreover, at an abolitionist gathering held on August 31, 1838, at Token House Yard in London, the Agency Committee, the leading British antislavery organization since 1831, promised its support and cooperation to its French friends and encouraged them to strive for general and immediate freeing of the slaves.[18] The Société reciprocated in late September by writing to congratulate its London associate on having brought an early end to apprenticeship. Concurrently, the Paris body promised to follow the British in their great work of eradicating servitude.[19] Still, it was not until the years 1839 and 1840 that Franco-British emancipationist interaction reached another high point.

The formation in 1839 of a new English abolitionist organization dedicated to campaigning actively for universal slave liberation, the British and Foreign Anti-Slavery Society (BFASS), apparently stimulated closer relations between English and French opponents of slavery. Joseph Sturge of Birmingham, an animator of this new society, which believed in the necessity of exporting emancipation to other countries, set the tone for the new group when he expressed his conviction in January, 1839, that "both France and America are already feeling the powerful effects of our example."[20]

17. Société française pour l'abolition de l'esclavage, *No. 1*, p. 16, meeting of June 1, 1835.
18. Société française pour l'abolition de l'esclavage, *No. 12* (Paris, February, 1839), 9.
19. *Le Siècle*, September 29, 1838.
20. Quoted in Temperley, *British Antislavery*, 65. Temperley's book provides the best analysis until now of Franco-British abolitionist cooperation, though the re-

The implication was that an additional effort by the British could ensure the success of the cause in nations such as France. Following through in this spirit, the BFASS agreed in its first meeting on April 17, 1839, to "open an active correspondence" with French and American abolitionists "to encourage them by every means in [Britain's] power" to work for the destruction of slavery. Two days later the society decided to form delegations to visit both the French embassy in London and France itself to promote its objectives.[21]

The BFASS's actions were probably encouraged by a statement made to Chief Justice Reddie of Saint Lucia by Jules Lechevalier when the latter visited the island as part of a fact-finding mission on British emancipation. Passing himself off as an official commissioner of the French government, Lechevalier informed Reddie that he intended to propose a plan for slave liberation in the French colonies and suggested that, if possible, British abolitionists pressure French authorities to back his endeavor. It is likely that Lechevalier was seeking support for his concept of emancipation, which included a generous indemnity for plantation owners combined with effective guarantees that blacks would continue to toil after liberation, a position that identifies him with the moderate French procolonial forces. However, Reddie, interpreting Lechevalier's move as a genuine commitment to abolition by a significant French official, wrote to Sturge, who brought the matter up in the BFASS meeting of June 3, 1839. The London group responded forthwith by writing to one of its members, W. T. Blair, in France at the time, to request him to use any influence he might have in supporting "the views of the French commissioner." Two weeks later it formally appointed Blair and an associate already in France, Josiah Forster, to intervene with the French administration in favor of abolition. On July 26 the BFASS also drafted a letter to the French abolitionists, inviting them to send a delegation to attend the proposed World Anti-Slavery Convention, to be held in London in June, 1840. Simultaneously, it re-

---

search for his short account of this question is largely limited to British primary sources.

21. British and Foreign Anti-Slavery Society Minute Books, April 17, 19, 1839, Rhodes House Anti-Slavery Papers, Bodleian Library, Oxford, hereinafter cited as BFASS Minute Books.

quested them to enter into correspondence with the Société, to send copies of their works, and to inform the BFASS of any way in which it could help the French cause.[22] In October the British group wrote again, suggesting that representatives of the organization visit France and requesting a copy of the recently published Tocqueville Commission report on emancipation. In late 1839, the BFASS appointed a deputation of Blair, Scoble, Alexander, and James Whitehorne to discuss with the French the best means of promoting the eradication of slavery, though the delegation did not actually set out for France until January 23, 1840.[23]

By late 1839 and early 1840 French abolitionists were once again fully reciprocating British overtures. In November, 1839, the secretary of the Société française pour l'abolition de l'esclavage, Isambert, sent a copy of the Tocqueville report to London and followed it on December 31 with a letter requesting information on English colonies for the period 1830 through 1839.[24] On the arrival of the British representatives in Paris in late January, 1840, personal contacts were renewed between the British and French, this process culminating in the attendance of the British group at two Paris meetings of the Société in early February. During a business session on February 5, Scoble, Alexander, and Whitehorne testified to the positive effects of emancipation on Britain's dependencies.[25] On February 10 a less formal dinner reception for the British received considerable publicity and French press coverage.

During this gathering the British deputation was feted and toasted by all the notables of the French abolition society. In the process each side flattered the accomplishments of the other. Lamartine encouraged the British to inform their London colleagues that "France is ready to accomplish her part in the regenerative work that she first signaled to the world and of which you have had the honor of giving the most illustrious example." He assured the delegates that within three years not a slave would exist in French tropical territories, for already Frenchmen had rejected the idea of slavery; they were now simply debating the

22. *Ibid.*, June 3, 17, July 26, 1839.
23. *Ibid.*, October 25, December 27, 1839, January 31, 1840.
24. *Ibid.*, November 29, 1839, January 4, 1840.
25. Société française pour l'abolition de l'esclavage, *No. 17* (Paris, April, 1840), 39.

means of accomplishing abolition. Scoble replied by applauding "the progress" that emancipationism had made in France. At the same time, he evoked the memory of Macaulay to attempt to spur the French on to rapid action and expressed the hope that the venerable Clarkson would live long enough to see bondage eliminated from France's dependencies. Scoble also expressed his desire that "the ties of fraternal relations and international friendship become tighter between France and England, that Frenchmen and Englishmen, united in denouncing servitude, never be divided by jealousies or national animosities."[26] This phrase was an obvious appeal for Anglo-French abolitionist unity in the face of the strain in relations that the so-called Eastern Crisis, or Egyptian Crisis, of 1840 was already exerting between the governments in London and Paris. The overall tone of the meeting was one of close friendship; and the British must have left Paris with more confidence than ever in the imminence of French emancipation. Nevertheless, the threat of diplomatic storms that would menace Anglo-French abolitionist cooperation was already looming on the horizon.

On May 8, 1840, a new British delegation, comprising David Turnbull, the Reverend D. Wright, and J. H. Tredgold, secretary of the BFASS from 1839 to 1842, had an audience in the French Royal Palace with King Louis Philippe to encourage him to take prompt and effective measures to end French colonial slavery.[27] In the meantime, the London organization had resolved to draft an address to be presented to Adolphe Thiers—who had just formed the new Cabinet in France—by Forster, Scoble, Alexander, and Cooper. In so doing the BFASS intended to express its "earnest hope and desire" that an abolition measure would be effected by the new administration. Then, with the London abolitionist assemblage of mid-June approaching, the BFASS appointed a special reception committee of Alexander, Forster, and Turnbull to meet the French deputation, headed by Isambert, on its arrival in England.[28]

It seems that the French, for their part, had had some difficulty assembling a prestigious delegation to send to London. Many of the more influential members of the Société française pour l'abolition de l'esclavage, such as Broglie, Tocqueville, Passy, Tracy and

26. Société française pour l'abolition de l'esclavage, No. 16, pp. 2–16.
27. Société française pour l'abolition de l'esclavage, No. 17, pp. 79–80.
28. BFASS Minute Books, March 30, June 11, 1840.

Count Xavier de Sade, had been obliged to decline the invitation because their presence was required on the recently formed Broglie Commission in Paris. Others, such as Gustave de Beaumont, were tied up by legislative duties, while Lamartine felt it necessary to take the waters in the Pyrenees for his health. Fortunately, Isambert was able to tear himself away from his legislative and legal functions to head a six-man group. In either a self-righteous assertion or an attempt to compensate for the lack of illustrious representatives from his organization, Isambert declared to his British associates: "I would rather immolate myself than leave my country unrepresented at your solemn abolitionist convention."[29] In the end, Guizot, then the French ambassador in London, attended the convention on an unofficial, personal basis, his presence lending some authority to an otherwise lackluster French deputation.

Isambert's official speech before the London assembly—delivered in French but translated by the Reverend John Bowring—was greeted with cheers when he declared that slavery was condemned in principle in France and that the July Monarchy would soon liberate colonial slaves. The British must have been particularly pleased to hear Isambert's assurances that his country would opt for "complete and mass emancipation" and that there would be no apprenticeship.[30] British confidence in the advancement of the French antislavery cause was probably also enhanced by a letter from the Société to the BFASS in which the former vouched for the "favorable progress that public opinion is making in France towards the prompt abolition of slavery."[31] Moreover, when the London meeting closed with a mass gathering at Exeter Hall on June 24, Isambert made utterances suggesting that King Louis Philippe shared the objectives of the French abolition society.[32] A similar assurance was given to Scoble by the radical French abolitionist Bissette in the autumn of 1840. The latter affirmed that he knew "certainly that the French government" was "seriously thinking of

29. Isambert to Tredgold, June 5, 7, 1840, MSS Brit. Emp. s.18, C7/133, 135, 139, Rhodes House Anti-Slavery Papers.
30. The *BFAS Reporter* published Isambert's speech on July 1, 1840, and that of his colleague Albert Crémieux on July 15. See also *Le Courrier français*, June 20, 1840, and *Le Siècle*, June 30, 1840.
31. *BFAS Reporter*, July 15, 1840.
32. *Le Courrier français*, June 27, 1840; *Le Siècle*, June 30, 1840.

the abolition of slavery" and preparing moves in that direction.[33] These declarations, combined with confidential statements from other French abolitionists that a project for emancipation would likely be proposed in 1841,[34] probably reinforced the innate optimism prevalent in British antislavery circles about the forthcoming liberation of French slaves. This French insistence on impending success also apparently indicates that many French emancipationists were either overly confident about the progress that their cause was making in France or too proud to admit any setbacks or shortcomings to their British colleagues.

As far as French abolitionists were concerned, though, their attendance at the World Anti-Slavery Convention in London appears to have had no significant short- or long-term effect on their movement. French representatives in London, unlike their Scotish, Irish, or American counterparts, seem to have had little interest in controversial issues, such as the dispute over the seating of women members, which so disrupted and influenced other delegations.[35] At least there were no subsequent repercussions from these questions in either French abolitionist society meetings or the French press. One receives the impression that French emancipationists had dispatched a delegation to London as a sign of sympathy and indebtedness toward their British brothers but that the French group as a whole remained somewhat aloof from the mainstream issues brought up at the 1840 assembly. The fact that few French abolitionists were persuaded to attend the London convention is in itself noteworthy. French opponents of slavery were obviously oriented toward the immediate situation facing them at home and little inclined to become involved in a universal abolitionist campaign.

Although undoubtedly comforted at the time about the situation across the Channel, the BFASS resumed its efforts to encour-

33. Bissette to Scoble, September 28, 1840, C13/113, Rhodes House Anti-Slavery Papers.
34. Reported by the *BFAS Reporter* on April 18, 1840.
35. See Donald R. Kennon, " 'An Apple of Discord': The Woman Question at the World's Anti-Slavery Convention of 1840," *Slavery and Abolition*, V (1984), 244–66; C. Duncan Rice, *The Scots Abolitionists, 1833–1861* (Baton Rouge, 1981), 80–114; Temperley, *British Antislavery*, 85–92; and Donald Maynard, "The World's Anti-Slavery Convention of 1840," *Mississippi Valley Historical Review*, XLVII (1960), 452–79.

age French abolitionism in late 1840 and early 1841, when the
Société française pour l'abolition de l'esclavage reopened its doors
during the new legislative session. Now that the Thiers government had fallen over the Egyptian Crisis, the BFASS resolved to
draft a letter, to be signed by the aged Clarkson, for the new Soult-
Guizot Cabinet in Paris.[36] When the Clarkson letter was sent out
to Guizot, who was de facto first minister from 1840 to 1847 and a
member of the French abolition society, it implored him "to use
your high influence with the French Cabinet to put an immediate
end to slavery in all your colonies . . . without apprenticeship."[37]
On February 26 and March 8, 1841, Isambert, in his role as secretary of the Société, replied to the entreaties from London for increased correspondence with letters in which he asked the BFASS
for further "documentary evidence of the beneficial working of
emancipation" in England's tropical holdings, an indication that
this sort of information was not flowing as freely between London
and Paris as in the days of Macaulay. At the same time, he assured
the British "that a final blow" against slavery was being delivered
in the legislative debates in Paris and that Guizot "is favorable to
us."[38] Statements of this kind led the *BFAS Reporter*, and the British emancipationists whose feelings it faithfully reflected, to believe that "slavery . . . is shortly to be abolished by law in the
French colonies." Apparently in an attempt to seal the impending
abolitionist victory across the Channel, the *Reporter* also enjoined
"every friend of the negro in France" to "petition at once for immediate and entire liberty of the negro."[39] Throughout much of the
remainder of the July Monarchy, British abolitionist spokesmen
would continue to imagine that somehow British methods of orga-
nized mass protest against slavery could be as effective in France as
they had been in the United Kingdom.

Isambert gave further assurances about the situation in France
when he wrote to Tredgold in May, 1841, that his government
would present a law banning slavery in the parliamentary session

36. BFASS Minute Books, December 2, 1840. General Nicolas Jean de Dieu Soult
was figurehead president of the Council of Ministers from 1840 to 1847, when
Guizot assumed the presidency himself for the duration of the July Monarchy.
37. *Ibid.*, March 25, 1841. A copy of Clarkson's letter, dated January 18, 1841, is
also found among the Guizot Papers, 42AP18, Archives Nationales.
38. BFASS Minute Books, January 29, 1841; *BFAS Reporter*, March 24, 1841.
39. *BFAS Reporter*, April 7, 1841.

of 1842 because "public opinion" was opposed to bondage and "the honour of France can no longer suffer its continuance."[40] In an effort to strengthen French resolve as much as possible, a British antislavery meeting in Exeter Hall adopted a motion on May 14, 1841, to make an additional appeal to the French for "complete and unconditional emancipation." Accordingly, a new delegation of Forster and Joseph Gurney was sent to Paris in late May to meet with French emancipationists and the king.[41] By the time the delegation returned home in mid-June, however, the certainty of the BFASS about impending liberty for French slaves had diminished markedly. Perhaps basing its judgment on preliminary reports sent back by the deputation in Paris, the *Reporter* printed an article on June 16 in which it openly questioned the French government's commitment to slave liberation. Stating that French "planters and their friends are found everywhere," that this "compact and wealthy body" is "the greatest obstacle to emancipation in the dependencies of France," the *Reporter* bewailed colonial influence over the French navy and colonial ministry. It concluded, not without foundation, that French statesmen were more concerned with the question of compensation for the masters than with freeing the slaves. When Isambert wrote to Tredgold—with the confidence usually displayed by French abolitionists communicating with London—on June 22 that it appeared the navy and colonial minister, Duperré, was preparing an emancipation law, the *Reporter* rather brusquely expressed its hope that it would be proposed officially "without further delay."[42] Some of the BFASS's initial optimism and patience with the situation in France was beginning to wear thin as British philanthropists became more aware of French realities.

British emancipationist impatience with French developments was also apparent in late 1841 when the *Reporter* reprinted an article from *Le Constitutionnel* suggesting that Guizot was betraying the abolitionist cause.[43] The *Reporter* now believed the French administration was definitely impeding slave liberation, but it retained its faith that French abolitionists could recuperate their

40. *Ibid.*, June 2, 1841.
41. Reported in *Le Siècle*, June 19, 1841.
42. *BFAS Reporter*, June 16, 30, 1841.
43. *Ibid.*, December 29, 1841.

position by other means "both within and without the walls of the legislative chambers." Thus, it expressed its "gratification" on learning that the French abolition society was planning a public meeting for early 1842 in an attempt to imitate the British initiative by appealing directly to French opinion. Such a course of action, the British organ believed, "if conducted with wisdom and energy, cannot fail to give a powerful impulse" to the cause of abolition.[44] Little did British humanitarians realize that the outbreak of the right-of-search dispute between France and Britain in early 1842 would abort the public assembly and do irreversible harm both to Franco-British abolitionist relations and to the antislavery movement in France.

Throughout the period 1833 to 1841 French procolonial spokesmen, whose power the British had come to recognize, followed closely the interaction between French and British emancipationists and proved ready to exploit these ties for their own ends. Long before the Egyptian Crisis and the right-of-search affair had soured Franco-British relations, French proslavery factions attempted to kindle latent Anglophobia in France in an effort to discredit French abolitionists through their British bedfellows. As early as 1834 *Le Temps* proclaimed that the English "seem to wish to draw us" into a questionable path and insisted that French abolitionists were attracted by the program of an English group that had brought about the too-precipitous eradication of bondage. The following year *La Guienne* decried the fact "that men who claimed to be Frenchmen before anything else, were always prepared to march in the tow of England." In 1838 *Le Bulletin colonial* launched a bitter frontal attack against French emancipationists in an attempt to cast doubt on their independence. It purported that Lord Brougham had set out for Paris "to urge on the strong and revive the weak" among French antislavery liberals. Already in 1834, according to this journal, "the resurrection of the French society for the abolition of slavery" had coincided with "the voyage of a few English abolitionists to Paris," where they knew they could "find docile instruments" and "pliable philanthropists."[45] Similar chords were struck by other antiabolitionist campaigners. Le Pel-

---

44. *Ibid.*, January 12, 1842.
45. *Le Temps*, January 6, August 28, 1834; *La Guienne*, February 16, 1835; *Le Bulletin colonial*, April 22, 1838.

letier du Clary of the Colonial Council of Martinique asserted that the English were supplying their French allies with "political falsehoods" in an effort to mislead French opinion about the success of the British initiative, while *Le Journal du Havre* suggested that the abolitionist Tracy's proposals reflected England's desire to destroy France's colonies.[46]

In 1840 *Le Bulletin colonial* resumed the attack when it referred to British delegates visiting Paris as "these missionaries" trying to sway the French. In its opinion, English perseverance in pressing for the destruction of French slavery should "open the eyes of the most blind and convince the most credulous" about England's intentions. It also mocked Isambert and his associate Albert Crémieux for having attended the World Anti-Slavery Convention in London, where they acted "like brothers and friends" of the English. *Le Temps,* citing the ephemeral Parisian tabloid *Le Capitol,* curtly asked its fellow Frenchmen "how men who must possess the sentiment of national dignity, could have gone [to London] to put themselves under the patronage of English abolitionists, to have the right to carry out secondhand philanthropy?"[47] Also writing during the period of the Egyptian Crisis, Jollivet, too, strove to discredit the prototype of British altruism in the eyes of his fellow Frenchmen. In one of his pamphlets he clamored: "Let them no longer speak of the philanthropy of England; let them no longer propose it as a model for us; let us receive her examples and advice with mistrust, and as dangerous and self-seeking."[48] By playing on the supposed complicity of French abolitionists with their British confederates, especially as of 1840, when Anglo-French relations cooled considerably, proslavery elements in France were able to question the motives and patriotism of the French antislavery movement. This ploy would prove even more effective when the right-of-search controversy broke out in 1842.

French abolitionists, under attack from the colonial lobby for their connivance with Great Britain, also faced the difficult task of defending the British record from the economic point of view. One of the major indictments French *colons* had laid against British

46. Le Pelletier du Clary, report of 1839, in Gén. 171 (1376), ANSOM; *Le Journal du Havre,* October 16, 1839.

47. *Le Bulletin colonial,* February 16, June 28, 1840; *Le Temps,* June 22, 1840.

48. Jollivet, *Des missions en France,* 15.

slave liberation was that it had led to the lessening of work and production in Britain's possessions. If the French emancipationists were to present the British experience as a successful one worthy of French emulation, it behooved them to disprove, or at least explain away, the colonists' charges. French abolitionists did make a concerted effort along these lines during the first decade after the destruction of British slavery, but in many ways their endeavors fell short or miscarried.

In the years immediately following the Emancipation Act, several French abolitionist spokesmen took their cue from British proponents of slave liberation and denied that freeing the slaves had had any real effect on work or productivity. In one of the booklets Macaulay published in France he affirmed the classical laissez-faire thesis that free labor could be more efficient than the coerced variety.[49] As late as 1841, in Clarkson's letter to Guizot, the BFASS was still claiming that blacks did twice as much work when free as when in bondage.[50] Many French emancipationists tended simply to repeat these points of the humanitarian and economic liberal credo. For example, Montrol, when referring to the British achievement, declared it to be a well-established fact that freely contracted labor was more productive than bound labor.[51] Passy, speaking in the Chamber of Deputies in 1835, predicted that by 1840 England's former slave dependencies would be "more flourishing" under nonconstrained labor than ever before. During the same session his eloquent colleague Lamartine also declaimed that "free labor is more productive than forced labor." A year later in the Chamber Marquis Frédéric Gaetan de La Rochefoucauld-Laincourt cited British documents to show that British Guiana had exported more sugar in 1835 than in an average previous year, concluding from this that noncoerced labor was more effective than that performed by slaves.[52] In 1838 Passy used the identical tactic of quoting export statistics from specific British territories to prove that sugar output in Antigua had increased between 1834 and 1838. Two years earlier Tracy had taken a slightly different

---

49. Macaulay, *Faits et renseignements prouvant les avantages du travail libre.*
50. Clarkson to Guizot, January 28, 1841, in Guizot Papers, 42AP218, Archives Nationales.
51. Montrol, *Des colonies anglaises*, 2.
52. *Le Moniteur universel*, April 23, 1835, May 23–24, 1836.

stance when he suggested in the lower house that production had not suffered after all in Britain's holdings and that those who said it had were simply trying to denigrate emancipation.[53] *Le Courrier français* also strove to dispute the contention that the British initiative had resulted in a decline in staple output by quoting British documents which showed that "the effects of emancipation had been very satisfactory" during 1834 and 1835, that production per working hour had nearly doubled since the end of servitude.[54] The Rémusat Report, made to the Chamber of Deputies in 1838, employed similar arguments. Rémusat, a moderate abolitionist, cited a statement by Brougham to the effect that on the whole colonial production had not diminished. He concluded from this that the British record showed nonslave labor could be productive.[55] Clearly, as Jules Lechevalier remarked in his report on the Caribbean, the English experience had been so varied and the evidence drawn from it so contradictory that planters could find declines where abolitionists could detect increases in productivity.[56]

In the 1840s a few French emancipationist sympathizers maintained their position on the positive economic consequences of British slave liberation. A resolution submitted by the Société française pour l'abolition de l'esclavage to the Broglie Commission referred to the official document series published by the navy and colonial department to demonstrate that in Antigua during the five years following 1834, crops had been more abundant than in the preceding half-decade. In 1843 *Le Journal des débats* printed a long article in which it tried to show that British abolition had not hurt production or colonial trade.[57] An advocate of immediatism, Guillaume de Félice, was still convinced in 1846 that the English experience had proven correct "the old axiom of social economics" that the freedman was necessarily more active and productive than the slave. A brief increase in sugar output in some British Caribbean holdings in the mid-1840s permitted Schoelcher as late as 1847 to assert that sustained work was "perfectly compatible with

53. *Ibid.*, February 16, 1838, May 26, 1836.
54. *Le Courrier français*, May 28, 1836.
55. Rémusat Commission, *Rapport*, 45–46.
56. Lechevalier, *Rapport*, I, 17, 42. See also excerpts in *Le Moniteur universel*, January 31, 1840.
57. Société française pour l'abolition de l'esclavage, *No. 19*, p. 60, session of May 5, 1842; *Le Journal des débats*, January 1, 1843.

liberty in the West Indies."[58] However, arguments of this kind were becoming rare among French abolitionists by this time. As indubitable evidence began to flow into France indicating that British sugar harvests had indeed diminished by one-fourth to one-third in the late 1830s, French emancipationists had to face the reality of the situation.

For most French antislavery advocates the moment of truth began to approach when a noticeable drop in production occurred following the end of apprenticeship in British tropical dependencies in 1838. As late as 1837 an important abolitionist organ, *Le Constitutionnel*, was still uncertain about the effect the termination of the apprentice system would have in Britain's possessions. Perhaps in an attempt to prepare its readers for the worst, it surmised that staple output would decline, because freedmen would cease to work after the last constraints on them had been removed.[59] By 1839, any doubts that might have subsisted about the production question were being dispelled. The Tocqueville Report on slavery, which came out in mid-1838, was much less roseate than Rémusat's had been. Although in one part of his account the abolitionist Tocqueville repeated the dictum that free labor could be more efficient than slave labor, elsewhere he conceded that there had been some difficulties with work in British territories. He noted that results varied among the West Indian islands, with decreases in some and increases in others; he also admitted that blacks were working less well in Jamaica, where sugar crops were threatened, though he failed to point out that Jamaica was by far the largest and most important of the British plantation colonies and sugar producers.[60] Commenting on Tocqueville's conclusions, *Le Constitutionnel* agreed that harvests had diminished in certain colonies; it added, though, in an article published the following year, that where work had been troubled the fault had almost always lain in actions of British planters rather than of former slaves, a standard justification used by British abolitionists to explain any adverse effects of slave liberation. Other reasons for these developments were elaborated on by *Le Courrier français* when it

58. Félice, *Emancipation immédiate et complète des esclaves*, 93; Schoelcher, *Histoire de l'esclavage*, I, 514.

59. *Le Constitutionnel*, September 19, 1837.

60. Tocqueville Commission, *Rapport*, 21, 33, 37–40, 43–44.

intimated that any drop in sugar production was only a transitional phase and that nowhere did blacks refuse to work when well treated by planters.[61] Faced with the fact, substantiated by both French and British sources, that production of staple crops had declined in Britain's tropical holdings, French proabolitionist elements reacted like many of their British equivalents by trying to place this development in the best possible light.

This tendency became more marked in the 1840s. At the Paris abolitionist meeting of February 5, 1840, the British delegation insisted that any diminution in agricultural work had been caused by the withdrawal of women and children from the work force and by the persistence of ill feelings of former masters toward freedmen.[62] The French abolition society employed the same themes in a petition calling for eventual emancipation, which it sent to the government in early 1840, though it conceded that labor had also been somewhat adversely affected by minor perturbations in the British colonies. Likewise, Le Siècle blamed any problems concerning British staple output on the uncooperative attitude of the planters and their failure to invest their indemnities for modernization.[63] When they were willing to face the economic setbacks in British dependencies, other proponents of slave liberation, such as Schoelcher, wove still more elaborate explanations for them. In an important work published in 1843 Schoelcher wrote of the prodigious exploits of free labor in Antigua but acknowledged that this phenomenon had been balanced by a drop in production in places like Dominica. He noted, though, that property values had increased and that planters were more prosperous than before because of high sugar prices. As for Jamaica, where cultivation had declined, he held that this loss had been more than compensated for by the benefits that had accrued to blacks.[64] Sade, as an abolitionist member of the Broglie Commission, developed another explanation by positing that, if former slaves had abandoned to some

61. *Le Constitutionnel*, November 16, 1838, July 1, 1840; *Le Courrier français*, July 22, 1838, October 4, 1839.
62. Société française pour l'abolition de l'esclavage, *No. 17*, pp. 7–8.
63. Petition cited by *Le Temps*, January 2–3, 1840; *Le Siècle*, April 9, 1845.
64. Schoelcher, *Colonies étrangères et Haïti*, I, 23–32, 101–68, 227. Recent publications indicate that, contrary to French perceptions at the time, sugar prices actually declined gradually after 1839. See Francisco A. Scarano, *Sugar and Slavery in Puerto Rico: The Plantation Economy of Ponce, 1800–1850* (Madison, Wisc., 1984), 184–85.

extent work in sugar and coffee, it was to find legitimate employment more to their liking in cities or on their own small plots.[65] In explaining the extenuating circumstances behind production losses in the British Caribbean, French emancipationists were presenting a largely accurate analysis of the situation. Still, such explanations did not satisfy those procolonial elements which stressed the fact that economic decline had set in, no matter what the reasons for it might be.

Besides trying to explain the factors behind production problems in Great Britain's possessions, French abolitionist forces employed arguments aimed at minimizing the extent of the drop-off. To counter the extravagant claims of the plantocracy that cultivation had been crippled by the British action, *Le Siècle* proclaimed the injustice of the *colons'* contentions; output had actually increased on Mauritius, it explained, while elsewhere it had fallen by only one-fifth or one-sixth. *Le Journal des débats* employed the same thesis but different percentages. Despite colonial claims that British slave liberation would plunge blacks "into brutelike idleness," the newspaper insisted, under a regime of complete freedom productivity had fallen by only one-fourth. Other emancipationist spokesmen cited the same figure. The recently founded *L'Abolitioniste français* corrected the procolonial deputy Denis' assertion in the Chamber of Deputies that productivity had decreased by one-third; the actual figure, the journal maintained, was one-fourth.[66] In the same debate the abolitionist Agénor de Gasparin also insisted on a 25 percent reduction, though he indicated that recent increases in output were reversing the trend.[67] That there was little consensus even among emancipationists as to the exact extent of decline is shown by the fact that Tocqueville, when writing one of a series of articles for *Le Siècle* in late 1843, quoted from British statistics that indicated a one-fourth drop in production.[68] Then, in a speech in the Chamber of Deputies in 1845, he pointed out that Britain's dependencies were not ruined, having only expe-

65. Broglie Commission, Minutes, January 31, May 23, 1842.
66. *Le Siècle,* March 24, 1840; *Le Journal des débats,* October 3, 1844; *L'Abolitioniste français,* May–June, 1844.
67. *Le Moniteur universel,* May 5, 1844.
68. *Le Siècle,* November 9, 1843. For an English translation of these articles, see Drescher (ed.), *Tocqueville and Beaumont,* 137–73. Drescher gives the news dateline rather than the publication date for these entries.

rienced a diminution of one-third in their sugar production. When commenting on Tocqueville's discourse, L'Abolitioniste français now did a volte-face and agreed that sugar output had dropped by one-third.[69] Just prior to this the abolitionist Charles Forbes, Comte de Montalembert, had made a lengthy speech in the Chamber of Peers in which he avowed that production had fallen anywhere from one-fourth to one-half in England's colonies, though he accepted the figure of one-third as most likely.[70] Discrepancies in abolitionist estimates certainly reflected the different and incomplete sources of information available to Frenchmen about conditions in Britain's holdings. Still, one receives the impression that French emancipationists could have argued more effectively had they coordinated their efforts to a greater degree and projected more unity and certainty in their calculations.

Exponents of French abolition also affirmed that another factor would help to offset the overall production decline in Britain's territories. In the early 1840s sugar output picked up briefly in some British colonies. Le Siècle was one of the first organs to perceive this increase and use it to predict that production would soon surpass what it had been under bondage, thus proving the uselessness of slavery. Le Constitutionnel, too, admitted that declines had occurred in Jamaican sugar harvests but observed that these had been partially nullified by gains since 1841.[71] Agénor de Gasparin made the same claim in his intervention in the Chambers in 1844, as did Tocqueville in the legislative debate of 1845.[72] Such abolitionist statements had little effect on proponents of the colonial cause, who could reply that minor increases did not wipe out large-scale losses; and disagreements among emancipationists as to the percentage of the decline exposed them to ridicule by their opponents. As the Feuille hebdomadaire de l'île de Bourbon noted, it was difficult for anyone to believe in the abolitionists' statistics about the minimal extent of British colonial economic difficulties when they themselves could not agree.[73]

As the 1830s gave way to the 1840s there was a propensity in

69. Le Moniteur universel, May 31, 1845; L'Abolitioniste français, July, 1845.
70. Le Moniteur universel, April 8, 1845.
71. Le Siècle, May 24, 1841; Le Constitutionnel, August 10, 1844.
72. Le Moniteur universel, May 5, 1844, May 31, 1845.
73. Copy of Feuille hebdomadaire de l'île de Bourbon, January 22, 1845, in Gén. 197 (1489), ANSOM.

French emancipationist circles to admit openly, if begrudgingly, the economic shortcomings of the British experiment. This is apparent in the proceedings and the report of the Broglie Commission. Within this body the moderate abolitionist Broglie had tended to defend the outcome of British slave liberation. However, in the session of April 11, 1842, even he opined that British developments had clearly shown that it was inevitable for blacks to turn away from sustained praedial labor after the destruction of slavery. In his opinion this was "the great and almost only danger with general [immediate] emancipation."[74] In one of the final meetings of the commission, Broglie made a similar utterance when summing up the group's findings. Blacks, he stated, had been peaceful and civilized after obtaining their freedom but had preferred working on their own plots to laboring on plantations or had toiled on the latter only for exorbitant wages. Thus, he believed, an outstanding difficulty concerning slave liberation "is the rareness of work, or its irregularity and expensiveness."[75]

In writing the commission report, Broglie again attempted to present the British colonial situation in the best possible light. He rejoiced about the degree to which emancipation had been successful from the moral, cultural, and human points of view. Although he admitted that a decline of one-sixth to one-fourth had supervened in sugar production, he gave a series of reasons to explain this. The weather had been poor during the period 1838 through 1841; blacks had toiled hard on their own plots; planters and local administrators had been responsible for more work stoppages than the former slaves. He even went so far as to state that developments had demonstrated that, when well treated, freedmen could be brought to labor for reasonable salaries. Still, Broglie concluded, the overall economic effect of English abolition had been a decidedly negative one. Emancipation had been successful as far as the blacks were concerned, "but on the other hand, it is not less certain that so far it has turned to the notable and notorious detriment of the metropole, which wished it, and the *colons*, who have been subjected to it." Staple production had diminished by one-fourth, and British consumers were subsidizing the abolition-

---

74. Broglie Commission, Minutes, April 11, 1842.
75. *Ibid.*, May 23, 1842.

ist experiment with higher sugar prices. Former slaves were working only three-fourths as much as under bondage. Moreover, he
suggested, "the position of the *colons* has become very sad and
critical," for while mounting sugar prices had prevented their gross
revenue from plummeting, their "net revenue has diminished
rapidly" because of higher labor costs, for which the indemnity had
not sufficiently compensated them. As a result, blacks had become
"absolute masters of the [labor] market," toiling capriciously and
irregularly, working less than their praedial European counterparts. If this situation continued, he predicted, many large estates
would be abandoned, commerce would diminish, and freedmen,
too, would suffer in the long run.[76] In sum, the abolitionist Broglie,
despite efforts at a fair and understanding approach, had delivered
nearly as strong an indictment of the economic results of British
slave liberation as French apostles of slavery.

In analyzing the Broglie Report, *Le Constitutionnel* endeavored
to give it the most favorable interpretation possible. It explained
that evidence was contradictory and that any conclusion could be
drawn from it; in fact, a rise in prices had compensated for the
decrease in staple production, disproving the colonial theory that
noncoerced labor was totally ineffective. However, the daily
avowed, the report showed that a problem remained concerning
the industriousness of former slaves.[77] Two English abolitionists,
Alexander and Scoble, were less kind in their judgment. They criticized the report for its prejudice and false or incomplete ideas,
castigating it especially for not placing humanitarian interests
above colonists' rights.[78] Still, it appears that Broglie's conclusions
had a profound effect on the French abolitionist mentality in the
1840s. It clearly inspired a long speech favorable to emancipation,
which Montalembert delivered in the Chamber of Peers in 1845.
Montalembert affirmed that the liberation of British slaves had
"magnificently and splendidly succeeded" in the moral sense but
conceded that it had not had positive economic consequences.

76. Ministère de la marine et des colonies, *Commission instituée par décision
royale du 26 mai 1840 . . . Rapport* (Paris, 1843), 286–315, hereinafter cited as
Broglie Commission, *Rapport.*
77. *Le Constitutionnel*, September 17, 24, 1843.
78. George W. Alexander and John Scoble, *Liberté immédiate et absolue ou
l'esclavage. Observations sur le rapport de M. le duc de Broglie . . . adressées à
tous les Français* (Paris, 1844).

Like Broglie, he attempted to qualify his statement by pointing out that it had not been as great a failure as its critics had claimed, bringing crop reductions but not ruining British establishments. He even quoted Broglie directly to show that free blacks were working three-fourths as much as blacks under bondage. A similar approach was apparent in a report made by Jules de Lasteyrie in the Chamber of Deputies in July, 1845, on the government's plans to improve the position of French slaves. The general tone of Lasteyrie's document was favorable to British emancipation, emphasizing the fact that it had succeeded morally. He too, though, admitted that the English experience had proved to be "less successful for the maintenance of work and production."[79] In late 1847 *Le Journal des débats* also acknowledged it to be an established fact that the "almost immediate transformation from slave to free labor in the English colonies reduced more and more production there," an avowal that colonial elements noted with glee.[80] The economic shortcomings of the British achievement were becoming accepted even by French abolitionists by the mid-1840s. Prior to 1847, this realization undoubtedly had the negative effect of cooling the ardor of moderate French emancipationists for rapid liberation of France's own slaves.

A reason that might help to explain why French abolitionists were prepared to admit the reality of the economic setbacks occasioned by British emancipation is the prime importance these men, like their opponents—and indeed like most members of the nineteenth-century European middle and upper classes—placed on the work ethic for their social inferiors. This is demonstrated by several statements that French philanthropic spokesmen made concerning British colonial affairs. For example, the proemancipationist daily *Le National* showed dismay in 1839 on receiving word that former slaves in Mauritius were not working sufficiently. The newspaper exclaimed that, when freed, blacks should realize that they must work "like Whites."[81] In a meeting held the same year the Société française pour l'abolition de l'esclavage attempted to

79. *Le Moniteur universel*, April 8, 1845; Lasteyrie, report, in *L'Abolitioniste français*, July, 1845.
80. *Le Journal des débats*, November 13, 1847; Martinique Colonial Council, session of January 24, 1848, in Corr. Gén., Martinique 122, ANSOM.
81. *Le National*, December 13, 1839.

de-emphasize the production decline in Britain's dependencies but acknowledged that industriousness, "this providence of civilized man," must be encouraged among freedmen.[82] The Broglie Commission also underscored the need to remedy the failures of the British experience and adopt restrictive measures to oblige French blacks, once liberated, to toil effectively.[83] In this sense, the stance of many French emancipationists on the necessity of unfailing praedial labor was not so different from that of French colonial advocates or, indeed, from that of some British abolitionists in the late 1830s and 1840s, who were also concerned about production losses and the unreliability of noncoerced labor.[84] French proponents of antislavery, despite their attempts to explain and find extenuating circumstances for production decreases in the British colonies, not only admitted the existence of these problems, but regretted them. Perhaps this contributed to the fact that in their efforts to defend the British record, French abolitionist forces largely failed to answer effectively colonial charges about its economic deficiencies. As this was one of the primary criticisms in France of both Britain's actions and emancipation as a whole, the French colonial lobby was able to use the British example to score a notable victory over its philanthropic opponents.

French emancipationists were not much more effective in countering the other crucial axiom of proslavery forces and the French

82. *Le Siècle*, January 1, 1840; *Le Temps*, January 2–3, 1840.
83. Broglie Commission, Minutes, May 23, 1842; Broglie Commission, *Rapport*, 317–33.
84. See Davis, *Slavery and Human Progress*, 190–91, 220; Eltis, *Economic Growth and the Ending of the Transatlantic Slave Trade*, 18–28, 104–22; and Eltis, "Abolitionist Perceptions of Society After Slavery," in Walvin (ed.), *Slavery and British Society*, 195–213. These studies are just three of several recent ones that emphasize the problems of free labor versus coerced labor in the mid-nineteenth century and their moral, social, and economic implications for the immediate postemancipation period. See especially Stanley L. Engerman and David Eltis, "Economic Aspects of the Abolition Debate," in Bolt and Drescher (eds.), *Anti-Slavery, Religion and Reform*, 272–93; Stanley L. Engerman, "Economic Aspects of the Adjustment to Emancipation in the United States and the British West Indies," *Journal of Interdisciplinary History*, XIII (1982), 191–220; Engerman, "Contract Labor, Sugar, and Technology in the Nineteenth Century," *Journal of Economic History*, XLIII (1983), 635–59; Engerman, "Economic Change and Contract Labor in the British Caribbean: The End of Slavery and the Adjustment to Emancipation," *Explorations in Economic History*, XXI (1984), 133–50. Another article by Engerman, "Coerced and Free Labor: Property Rights and the Development of the Labor Force," is forthcoming shortly in French translation in *Annales: Economies, sociétés, civilisations*.

government: that it was necessary to await the final outcome of the British slave liberation process before considering a similar measure. One of the premises of this thesis was that Britain's slaves had been better prepared for freedom than France's were. Shortly after passage of the British Emancipation Act some French abolitionists were actually ready to concede this point. Montrol admitted in his booklet that French slaves had none of the civil or personal rights (the right to have savings, marry, purchase their freedom, have trial by jury) that he thought British blacks had had prior to 1833, though he averred that French slaves were often very well treated. The Rémusat Report of 1838 also appeared to accept at face value the testimony of colonial delegates and administrators that French slaves were less prepared for freedom than their English brothers had been.[85] The belief in both French abolitionist and proslavery circles that British slaves had actually been adequately prepared for freedom between 1823 and 1833, when in reality little improvement had been effected in this period, clearly shows the extent of misinformation prevailing in France concerning cardinal points of the British colonial record.

Nevertheless, as emancipationists became aware of the attempts by the French colonial party and government to postpone abolition through this device, some of them began to dispute it. Macaulay pointed out in one of his books that little had been done for British slaves before 1834, that French blacks were in the same position, and that the *colons'* claims to the contrary were "pure illusions." Shortly thereafter the Société française pour l'abolition de l'esclavage also asserted that French slaves were as advanced as England's had been in 1833.[86] During the discussions within the Broglie Commission in 1842, Tracy tried to convince his colleagues, without success, that French slaves were more ready for emancipation than English ones had been, because there was less division between the races in France's possessions. Isambert uttered similar sentiments in 1844. He argued that French slaves still had memories of freedom from their brief experience with liberty

85. Montrol, *Des colonies anglaises*, 15–16; Rémusat Commission, *Rapport*, 50–51.

86. Macaulay, *Détails sur l'émancipation*, vii–xi; Société française pour l'abolition de l'esclavage, *No. 5. Année 1837* (Paris, 1837), 5, address of August 1, 1837, to the departmental general councils.

during the Revolutionary epoch and that, besides, they were better treated than slaves in English establishments had been. Finally, in answer to charges by the deputy Denis that British blacks had been made ready for freedom for twenty-five years prior to 1833, L'Abolitioniste français pointed out that British emancipationists, such as Scoble and Alexander, themselves agreed that French slaves were more advanced than England's had been.[87] In reality, though, while arguments such as these might have fortified French abolitionists in their convictions, they appear to have had no effect on either procolonial advocates or the government.

If French abolitionists were ineffective in countering their government's cautious approach on emancipation, it is perhaps because few of them seemed willing to challenge openly its stance on slavery in the years immediately following British slave liberation. To be sure, a radical abolitionist such as Isambert might state in the Chambers that, while the French government claimed to be "awaiting the outcome of English emancipation," he personally wondered "to what time one wished to adjourn the question, since the aim of English emancipation is already partially achieved."[88] Isambert's attitude, however, was the exception to the rule in the mid-1830s. French antislavery elements might struggle to defend Britain's actions, argue that they had not had disastrous consequences, or indicate that France's slaves were as ready for freedom as Britain's had been; but few were prepared in the 1830s to suggest that their government was using the British experience to procrastinate on the issue of slave liberation. At the time, most French emancipationists themselves were committed to a policy of gradualism, and only in the 1840s would a significant faction of the French movement rally to and advocate a policy of immediatism.

Many French abolitionists were prepared to concede that the immediate eradication of servitude was neither necessary nor desirable and so were open to the idea that it was best to await the long-range outcome of the British experience. This was apparent in the first important discussion in the French legislature on the British system. The moderate abolitionist the count Louis Joseph

87. Broglie Commission, Minutes, February 21, 1842; L'Abolitioniste français, May–June, 1844.
88. Le Moniteur universel, June 7, 1837.

Alexandre de Laborde requested that his government "imitate
. . . the wise innovations of Great Britain" by ameliorating the
position of French slaves while refraining from precipitous action.
That this sentiment reflected the early attitude of the French
antislavery organization as a whole is evidenced by a policy pronouncement made by Montrol when writing for the Société française pour l'abolition de l'esclavage. He noted that the Société,
"proceeding with discretion and order," had begun by examining
English developments; its next step would be to work for emancipation with prudence and to strive for improved conditions for
French slaves.[89] It is significant that, when the colonial delegate
Dupin declared in the Chamber of Deputies in 1835 that only
Hippolyte Passy among the abolitionists appeared to believe that
French slavery could be terminated immediately without danger,
no abolitionist spoke up to contradict him or appeal for rapid
emancipation.[90] In 1838 the gradualist imprint was apparent on
the Rémusat Report, which responded to Passy's proposal for abolishing slavery. The commission for which Rémusat was the
spokesman favored freeing French slaves, but Rémusat contended
that the best procedure would be to study the difficulties and problems of the British measure first, in an attempt to avoid repeating
them. He concluded that immediate slave liberation—along British lines—would be premature, that it would be unwise to adopt
any plan before 1840, when "England will see her great experiment
draw to a close." In a book published in 1839, Agénor de Gasparin,
too, advocated gradual emancipation and at the same time expressed grave reservations about the outcome of the British process, which he believed had brought "distress" to English dependencies, the refusal of Negroes to work, and the "interruption" of
sugar harvests.[91] In the 1830s a considerable majority of the French
antislavery movement was as prepared as Dupin or Moges to observe the unfolding of the British program before moving to liberate French slaves.

Many French opponents of slavery continued to follow this cautious policy into the 1840s. For example, while speaking in the

89. *Ibid.*, April 23, 1835; Montrol, *Des colonies anglaises*, 17–18.
90. *Le Moniteur universel*, April 24, 1835.
91. Rémusat Commission, *Rapport*, 47–48, 67–69; Agénor de Gasparin, *De
l'affranchissement des esclaves et de ses rapports avec la politique actuelle* (Paris,
1839), 30.

lower house in 1840, Tocqueville proclaimed that no one in France requested immediate emancipation.[92] This same gradualist tendency was apparent among abolitionists on the Broglie Commission. As previously explained, in the course of his commission's debates on slavery, Broglie cited the economic failure of the British approach as a reason for his country to proceed slowly toward slave liberation. In the end Broglie and other supporters of abolition on the commission, such as Tracy and Sade, rallied to the proposal that slavery be eradicated from French territories only in ten years time, with five additional years of apprenticeship to follow. The reason for such a delay was to prepare slaves for liberty and avoid the economic difficulties that had befallen Britain's colonies. The commission hoped that such a course of action would reverse the British process and oblige blacks to work.[93] Such a stance by professed abolitionists on the commission led the *BFAS Reporter* to print: "it is painful to perceive how few of the members of the Commission were governed by sound principles of morals, which are never inconsistent with sound policy, or by a regard for the claims of deeply-inspired humanity."[94] However, the protests of the British abolitionist journal seem to have fallen on deaf ears in France. A noted French antislavery organ, *Le Constitutionnel*, concurred with the commission's conclusion that by taking the necessary time and precautions, France could counter the negative aspects of the British achievement. If France wished to make the transition from slavery to freedom without compromising the colonists' situation, the daily warned, it was imperative for her to profit from the English endeavor, avoid its pitfalls, and improve on it.[95] The British example had influenced many French emancipationists to be so cautious in their approach and so solicitous of colonial interests that their objectives strangely resembled those of the proslavery faction.

Four interconnecting points should be made about the French abolitionist position toward the British precedent in the first decade following its implementation. First, the attitude of French philanthropists concerning both the economic deficiencies of the

92. *Le Moniteur universel*, May 14, 1840.
93. Broglie Commission, Minutes, April 11, 1842; *Rapport*, 287, 317–22.
94. *BFAS Reporter*, February 21, 1844.
95. *Le Constitutionnel*, September 24, 1843, May 5, 1844.

British initiative and the urgency of imitating the British model was far more ambivalent than that of the opponents of slave liberation. Whereas the campaign of French apologists of slavery to prove the economic failings of British proceedings was a united and consistent one, French abolitionists were much more divided and hesitant in their defense of the British record and in their attempts to use it to advance their own cause. Second, an examination of the French antislavery movement's approach to British emancipation shows to what extent important elements of the French movement shared the concerns of their government, not to mention French apostles of slavery, about the difficulties that the British norm of slave liberation could bring to France's dependencies. In other words, significant exponents of French abolitionism were profoundly moderate in their attitude, showing as much preoccupation with such colonial problems as work and production as with the rights and welfare of the slaves, a position that approached them to their supposed antagonists, the proslavery lobby. Third, it should be noted that in many ways French emancipationists practically conceded the economic argument to their adversaries. In fact, as far as the French were concerned, the economic debate did not hinge on the ultimate value of the colonies, for everyone thought that these territories were important, if declining, mercantile appendages of France. The real debate concerned the extent to which the freeing of the slaves would work to the economic disadvantage of France and her colonies; and in this sense the British record proved a decisive one. Once both colonists and abolitionists had come to the conclusion from studying the British system that slave liberation had subtracted considerably from colonial prosperity—even though the two sides differed as to the degree of decline—the moderate French abolitionist movement suffered a major setback on the road to emancipation. Finally, by admitting the economic failure of the British experience, French abolitionists were apt to accede to the position of the government and *colons* that it was necessary to postpone the freeing of French slaves as long as possible to avoid similar reversals for France's colonial establishment. In many ways the British experiment, as viewed from across the Channel, did not further the emancipationist cause in France, as many had optimistically expected. On the contrary, it often worked to its detriment.

FIVE

FRENCH ASSESSMENTS OF BRITISH APPRENTICESHIP

Although a significant part of the French debate over British emancipation centered on the issues of economics and expediency, by the late 1830s another facet of the British question was also attracting the attention of the French colonial advocates, abolitionists, and government. The British apprenticeship system, which had been introduced by the Emancipation Act of 1833 as a transitional state between slavery and complete freedom, was intended to last until August 1, 1838, for nonpraedial slaves and until 1840 for field hands. As the date for the freeing of nonpraedial slaves approached, however, British abolitionist pressure for the curtailment of the entire system gained considerable momentum. Highly critical of a regime that they believed closely resembled slavery, British philanthropists insisted that apprenticeship be concluded for both categories of blacks as soon as possible. At the same time, British planters displayed increased apprehension about the situation, fearing that once nonpraedial workers had obtained complete freedom it would no longer be possible to retain control over agricultural laborers. In the spring of 1838 the colony of Barbados took the initiative in granting full liberty to all slaves as of August 1, setting off a movement that spread to other British possessions. Faced with both abolitionist agitation and the colonial fait accompli, the London government agreed to end apprenticeship on August 1, 1838, for all blacks, except those of Mauritius, where the change would occur on April 1, 1839.[1]

1. For recent studies on the process leading to the end of apprenticeship, see Alex Tyrrell, "The 'Moral Radical Party' and the Anglo-Jamaican Campaign for the Abo-

French officials had been closely observing the operation of British apprenticeship throughout the mid-1830s, noting the growing criticism of it and drawing their own conclusions on it. Besides the government, colonial spokesmen and abolitionists were keenly interested in the system as a possible alternative to slavery or as a process France could adopt as part of an eventual slave liberation project. The apprenticeship issue and the consequences of its premature termination developed into one of the major questions weighing on the French assessment of British emancipation in the late 1830s and early 1840s. Ultimately, the rejection of an apprentice plan like Britain's by Frenchmen on all sides of the slavery problem proved to have serious repercussions not only for French government policy but for the number of options available to Frenchmen who sought to eliminate servitude within France's tropical establishments.

It was natural for French proponents of the plantocratic cause, who wished to perpetuate slavery, to denounce an important cog in the British abolition process. One of the earliest statements by French colonial elements about apprenticeship reveals another reason why they objected to this institution. In early 1834 Governor Arnous of Guadeloupe informed the navy and colonial department that British estate owners disliked apprenticeship because of the special magistrates who had been appointed to guarantee just treatment of apprentices; evidently, French planters, like their British counterparts, would disapprove of any intermediary agency between them and their retainers. More significantly, though, the governor remarked that British proprietors would have preferred immediate and complete freedom to this intermediate process, because it would have brought them full compensation for the value of their slaves.[2] *Le Moniteur du commerce* also made its readers aware that one of the reasons why England had opted for apprenticeship was because it did not have the necessary funds to pay masters the entire value of their expropriated property.[3] In

---

lition of the Negro Apprenticeship System," *English Historical Review,* XCIX (1984), 481–502; Izhak Gross, "Parliament and the Abolition of Negro Apprenticeship, 1835–1838," *English Historical Review,* XCVI (1981), 560–76; and passages in Green, *British Slave Emancipation,* and Temperley, *British Antislavery.*
   2. Arnous to Minister, January 29, 1834, in Gén. 156 (1302), ANSOM.
   3. *Le Moniteur du commerce,* November 25, 1835.

other words, French colonial promoters were quick to note that apprenticeship had enabled the British government to reduce by half the actual compensation paid slave owners: British administrators had calculated that 50 percent of the indemnity would accrue to the planter through his use of his former slave's labor for an additional four to six years as an apprentice. Because French *colons* were especially adamant about obtaining full compensation if they were to free their slaves, they could be expected to condemn a British precedent that justified the de facto lowering of this indemnification.

Another French colonial reproach of apprenticeship derived from the labor problem. *Le Moniteur du commerce* cited English settlers and Jamaican newspapers to show that apprenticeship was causing cultivation to be abandoned in Britain's dependencies.[4] *Le Courrier de la Guadeloupe,* for its part, quoted members of the Jamaican assembly who affirmed that the British procedure was unsuccessful because it could not coerce former slaves into working.[5] Not only was apprenticeship "nothing but slavery under a different name," *Le Bulletin colonial* exclaimed, but customs figures showed it had brought a drop in production in Jamaica between 1834 and 1836. Altering its argument slightly, *Le Moniteur du commerce* returned to the charge by insisting that apprenticeship brought ruin to proprietors at the same time that it dissatisfied blacks and destroyed the authority of whites.[6] A private letter from an unidentified French planter residing in Jamaica displayed even greater exaggeration when it professed sympathy for the "poor *colons*" because apprenticeship had proved entirely to the advantage of "the Negroes."[7] Discontent with the British system was as apparent within the colonial administration as in the press. Governor Halgan of Martinique expressed apprehension about adoption by the July Monarchy of an approach similar to the English one. In the English Caribbean, Halgan remarked, apprenticeship had occasioned decreases in production and property values; moreover, if it were introduced into French colonies, the *co-*

4. *Ibid.,* August 24, 1835.
5. Clipping, undated but identifiable as 1835, in Gén. 178 (1418), ANSOM.
6. *Le Bulletin colonial,* November 16, 1836; *Le Moniteur du commerce,* November 25, 1835.
7. Letter dated July 9, 1835, in Gén. 144 (1225), ANSOM.

lons might find it necessary to employ the repressive measures that the English had been obliged to use to make blacks work at all, and that would be contrary to prevailing custom.[8] As usual, French colonial spokesmen were only ready to demonstrate concern for the welfare of the former British slave when it coincided with their own interests.

When it became apparent in 1838 that British apprenticeship was being abrogated, French colonial sympathizers paid even closer attention to developments in Britain's possessions. They now displayed uneasiness about the possible detrimental effect the ending of apprenticeship could have on peace and security. The French navy and colonial minister took note of an article in the London *Standard* which suggested that the imminence of complete emancipation had resulted in "the most vivid anxiety" in Jamaica.[9] The commander of the West Indian naval station was even more alarmist in one of his dispatches. Admiral de la Bretonnière wrote that a climate of fear reigned in Jamaica, which made him believe that "the time of crisis is not distant." Although he hoped that these "dire predictions" would not materialize, he recounted that even the governor of Jamaica had sent his family to Europe and that many planters were selling out and leaving the island. Moges, governor of Martinique, was more restrained but still apprehensive. He declared that the sudden reality of complete liberation for all categories of slaves had inspired a feeling of foreboding in the British Caribbean, where the main question was whether the free Negro would carry on sustained work.[10] The colonial-oriented metropolitan press expressed similar sentiments. *Le Bulletin colonial* indicated that British precipitation in cutting short apprenticeship presaged difficult times for English settlers. To press its point it referred to an article in a French-language newspaper on Mauritius, *Le Mauricien*, which claimed that blacks were poorly prepared for freedom, being indolent and bent on vagabondage and theft.[11] These exaggerated colonial reactions recalled the equally unfounded fear of disorder and disaster

8. Halgan to Minister, July 15, 1835, in Gén. 156 (1299), ANSOM.
9. Article dated September 5, 1838, in Gén. 178 (1418), ANSOM.
10. Commander of West Indian naval station to Minister, July 1, 1838, in Gén. 178 (1420), Governor to Minister, October 25, 1838, in Gén. 144 (1225), ANSOM.
11. *Le Bulletin colonial*, June 17, 1838.

that had accompanied the actual British decision of 1833 to free the slaves.

Even when these "dire predictions" proved groundless, French colonial advocates continued their indictment of the apprentice regime. *La Feuille hebdomadaire de l'île de Bourbon* insisted that this innovation had not been able to prevent former slaves from "abandoning themselves little by little to those habits of laziness which seem to the black the normal state in the life of free men." Thus, "the poor results of English apprenticeship only prove the inopportunity of emancipation, the folly of such a measure."[12] Apparently, now that apprenticeship had ended peacefully and could no longer be reproached as a source of disorder, colonial defenders were emphasizing its supposed impracticality in their effort to attack all aspects of slave liberation.

The advice given by French colonial authorities to the Broglie Commission in the early 1840s was clearly intended to reinforce this theme. The Commission's suggestion that France might consider adopting an abolition plan encompassing apprenticeship led the attorney general of Guadeloupe to remark that apprenticeship should not be completely discounted, for work had been better preserved under it than after its termination. The real trouble with it, he argued, was that it had not lasted long enough to prepare former slaves adequately for freedom; and in an obvious attempt to postpone French emancipation as long as possible, he insisted that apprenticeship should have lasted for fifteen rather than just four years. He was supported by the *ordonnateur* (chief financial official) of the same island, who spurned apprenticeship as having been "condemned by the English experience." Representatives of France's other colonies were even more categorical in rejecting the British approach. The director of the interior of Bourbon vouched that the results of the system had been "too baleful" to even consider it for France's establishments, while the Special Council of that colony—appointed to replace the too-uncooperative Bourbon Colonial Council—unanimously refused to consider the option "because it has demonstrated its inconveniences and dangers." The Colonial Council of Martinique agreed that apprenticeship

12. Clipping dated February 5, 1840, in Gén. 171 (1376), ANSOM.

had been "sufficiently condemned by the facts."[13] The continuity
of French colonial discourse on the issue is seen well into the
1840s by Dupin's denunciation of it as a scheme that had resulted
"only in troubles and ruin."[14] During the existence and after the
revocation of British apprenticeship, the French plantocracy steadily denounced any similar proposal that might serve French abolitionist aims by providing an alternative to slavery. In this sense,
their attacks on the apprentice process constituted an integral part
of their defense of the status quo.

Given the opposition of French colonial advocates to British
apprenticeship, one could imagine that French abolitionists would
stress its positive factors. Ironically, though, French antislavery
forces were almost as eager as their adversaries to refuse to consider this aspect of the British record. This stance by French emancipationists was undoubtedly determined by reports flowing out of
the British Isles that portrayed apprenticeship as little more than a
revised form of slavery, a system retaining all the injustices, cruelties, and inhumanities of bondage while bringing few advantages
to freedmen. Indeed, it appears that British philanthropists themselves played a crucial role in influencing their French associates
to reject this intermediate approach as totally unacceptable.

Completely disenchanted with the results of apprenticeship,
British abolitionists made numerous efforts to convince their
French allies to spurn this alternative to total and immediate slave
liberation. This was apparent already in two of Macaulay's French
booklets printed in 1836. In both works he strove to defend British
emancipation by attributing any deficiencies it might have to "the
unfortunate adoption of this system of apprenticeship."[15] British
denunciations of this option increased in 1839 and 1840, when
both the Tocqueville Commission and the Broglie Commission
considered the possibility of applying a similar process to France's
colonies. During a meeting held in early 1840, the BFASS praised
the Tocqueville Report in general but inveighed against the possible adoption by France of "partial" emancipation. The society then
went on to underline the necessity of encouraging Frenchmen to

13. Résumé of advice of colonial councils and special councils, February 7, 1841,
in Gén. 184 (1441), Colonial Council of Martinique, report, in Gén. 184 (1437),
ANSOM.
14. Dupin, *Seconde Mémoire*, 3.
15. Macaulay, *Détails sur l'émancipation*, xiii–xiv; *Suite des détails*, 81.

avoid "the pernicious example set them by the Government of Great Britain" in this matter.[16] Shortly thereafter, when the deputation from the BFASS met with French associates in Paris, Scoble launched into a critique of Lamartine's suggestion that an intermediate stage was necessary to serve as an educational period for blacks. In fact, Lamartine was venting an idea formulated by the Tocqueville Report, that there could be a preparatory period during which the state would purchase slaves from their owners and act as their overseer and tutor. Such a development, Scoble proclaimed, would mean that the government would wield the whip and chains of the master. He added that "apprenticeship can only modify the evil, and never destroy it"; France should move to give the slave "his full and complete liberty, without hesitation."[17] British abolitionists had undertaken a campaign to discourage the French from adopting what they considered to be one of the most unfortunate aspects of their own accomplishment.

The British returned to the charge in 1841 when the Broglie Commission revived the apprentice-like option proposed by Tocqueville. Guizot had come to power in France, and Clarkson sent a letter to him pleading for an immediatist program without apprenticeship.[18] Shortly thereafter the *BFAS Reporter* printed a significant article along the same lines. It expressed the belief that "slavery . . . is shortly to be abolished by law in the French colonies"; but it also displayed misgivings that France, "untaught by the lessons of experience," might adopt a course of action resembling apprenticeship, "a proved failure." It went on to explain that the proposed purchasing of slaves by the French government and "letting out their labour, differs little, if at all, from the English apprentice system." The *Reporter* beseeched Frenchmen not to proceed in this manner, to "be not content to destroy the outworks of slavery, but carry your holy warfare into its citadel."[19]

In 1842, while the Broglie Commission was still discussing different means of realizing emancipation, the British continued their efforts to dissuade Frenchmen from espousing apprenticeship. In a letter signed by Clarkson and addressed to the Société

16. BFASS Minute Books, January 21, 1840.
17. Société française pour l'abolition de l'esclavage, No. 16, pp. 13–14.
18. BFASS Minute Books, March 25, 1841.
19. *BFAS Reporter*, April 7, 1841.

française pour l'abolition de l'esclavage, the BFASS repeated its contention that slavery could not be effectively regulated, as the British had attempted to do with apprenticeship, but must be destroyed.[20] In fact, the Clarkson missive was just one of several similar documents that the British delegates brought when they came to Paris in early March, 1842, to attend the Société's scheduled public meeting. A message from the noted British emancipationist Thomas Buxton, excusing his absence from the gathering because of illness, noted that apprenticeship, "far from being a useful preparation," was "equally prejudicial to masters and apprentices." An address from the Leeds Anti-Slavery Society was even more forceful. The Leeds association insisted that for England "the intermediate state . . . was a continuation . . . of slavery in its essence, under the name of apprenticeship." The idea of a preparatory system, it reiterated, was "a well-intentioned but impracticable theory." At a banquet in Paris on March 9, which was substituted for the banned public assembly, Sturge underscored "the complete ineffectiveness" of the apprentice approach and urged Frenchmen to adopt a better emancipation plan.[21] Later on in the same year the *BFAS Reporter* expressed its "sincere regret" that the July Monarchy seemed inclined to accept the principle of freedom hindered by a sort of apprenticeship.[22] Then, in 1844, while addressing a group of abolitionists in Paris on March 29, Scoble enjoined his audience to eschew "apprenticeship, which is really a half-slavery more horrible than slavery itself."[23] Over the years the British had undertaken a well-coordinated effort to convince France to reject a transitional stage between servitude and freedom. In a sense their campaign was effective, for by 1842 French proponents of antislavery were turning away entirely from this alternative.

Influenced by reports coming out of Great Britain and pressed by their British cohorts, French emancipationists were displaying a markedly negative attitude toward apprenticeship already in the 1830s. As if embarrassed by a blemish on the British humanitarian record, which they wished to defend, certain abolitionist organs,

20. Clarkson, letter dated February 17, 1842, in Société française pour l'abolition de l'esclavage, *No. 19*, p. 17.
21. Buxton, letter dated March 3, the Leeds address, February 28, 1842, *ibid.*
22. *BFAS Reporter*, June 15, 1842.
23. Reported in *Le Lien* (Paris), April 6, 1844.

such as *Le National* and *Le Constitutionnel*, tended to shy away from commenting on the new British intermediate system. However, other newspapers reacted rapidly to its implementation. In one of its first remarks about the British situation, Bissette's *Revue des colonies* employed terms similar to those Scoble would use several years later and qualified the institution as "a sort of bastard state halfway between slavery and freedom." *Le Journal du commerce* also castigated apprenticeship as "a disguised slavery" that was ineffective in educating slaves. Five months later the same daily encouraged France to find a better means of liberating her slaves, because the British transitional approach was "nothing but the condition of slavery disguised under another name."[24]

When the British moved to abrogate the apprentice system in 1838, exponents of French abolitionism immediately congratulated their neighbors for their action. Xavier Durrieu, the republican editor of *Le Siècle*, asserted in a signed article that "Europe in its entirety" had been moved by the British decision. *Le Temps*, favorable at this point to emancipation, lauded the termination of this intermediate state as a "triumph of humanity" and suggested that France, too, should act against bondage. Breaking its earlier silence, *Le Constitutionnel* presumed that the English example might incite the French government to end its temporization and move to liberate France's slaves before 1840.[25] *Le National* also spoke up to applaud the revocation of apprenticeship as a "great and solid test which honors the English government, and will leave its mark in the history of civilization"; England was giving the signal for slave liberation in France by destroying the remnants of servitude within her own colonies. *Le Courrier français* added a word of praise for Britain's act of "humanity," which, it hoped, would show French authorities that it was wiser to free slaves than simply await the passing of events.[26] French abolitionists clearly saw apprenticeship as a remnant of slavery and its curtailment as possible encouragement to a more vigorous French antislavery policy.

As time went on and the French administration began publish-

---

24. *La Revue des colonies*, October, 1834; *Le Journal du commerce*, October 9, 1834, March 7, 1835.
25. *Le Siècle*, July 29, 1838; *Le Temps*, June 6, 1838; *Le Constitutionnel*, July 21, 1838.
26. *Le National*, August 2, June 24, 1838; *Le Courrier français*, July 20, 22, 1838.

ing official British documents on the apprenticeship period, liberal Frenchmen found more to criticize about this aspect of the British accomplishment. The appearance of the second and third volumes of the French government series in the early 1840s convinced *Le Courrier français* that blacks had been abused under the preparatory regime.[27] The moderate abolitionist Charles Joseph Dussillon noted in a booklet published in 1843 that apprenticeship had proved disappointing from the point of view of both the British *colons* and the former slaves.[28] In a volume written the previous year the radical emancipationist Schoelcher had decried this component of the British approach as an "unnecessary transition," "a false and abnormal state" that had proved "extremely detrimental" to everyone concerned.[29] Shortly after reviewing Schoelcher's book, *Le Siècle* employed similar phrases in rejecting apprenticeship, "which has produced in the English colonies such deplorable effects that it was necessary to renounce it prematurely."[30] By the early 1840s many French abolitionists had become so antipathetical to the British apprentice system that they totally dismissed it as not applicable to France's colonies. As mentioned earlier, the secretary of the French abolition society, Isambert, was cheered at the 1840 convention in London when he declared categorically that there would be no apprenticeship in his nation's slave liberation process.[31]

Isambert's assurances to the contrary, not all French emancipationists were against every aspect of the apprenticeship alternative. Apparently, certain moderate French antislavery advocates, agreeing to some extent with French colonists and the government that slaves were far from being adequately prepared for immediate liberty, judged an intermediate regime of some kind as essential. Thus, in the Chamber of Deputies in 1838, Lamartine, while claiming to be a partisan of immediate abolition, called in

27. *Le Courrier français,* May 3, November 2, 1841.
28. Charles Joseph Dussillon, *Considérations sur l'esclavage aux Antilles françaises et son abolition graduelle, suivies d'un aperçu analytique et critique du système d'apprentissage et de ses résultats dans les colonies anglaises* (Paris, [1843]), 76–78.
29. Victor Schoelcher, *Des colonies françaises. Abolition immédiate de l'esclavage* (Paris, 1842), 344, 346.
30. *Le Siècle,* April 14, 1843.
31. *BFAS Reporter,* July 1, 1840; *Le Courrier français,* June 20, 1840; *Le Siècle,* June 30, 1840.

effect for a British-type system with ten years' preparation for slaves; in other words, he was advocating a longer transition period than the one implemented by Britain.[32] As noted, Lamartine continued to favor this approach at least as late as 1840, much to the dismay of British abolitionists listening to his address at the February 10 banquet in Paris.[33] Moreover, Lamartine was not the only French opponent of slavery to perceive positive facets in the apprenticeship plan. The Rémusat Report of 1838 found that neither the British black, planter, nor government had been satisfied with the experience; it conceded, though, that apprenticeship had maintained order and production.[34] The Tocqueville Report of 1839, while calling for simultaneous and universal abolition, suggested, too, that it be followed by a preparatory stage superior to the British model. Tocqueville emphasized that his commission disapproved of several particulars in the British system but believed in the need for a transitory situation to ready slaves for freedom. English apprenticeship, Tocqueville explained, should have concentrated more on educating and moralizing the slave than on just guaranteeing work; and to assure a more effective operation of the project, the British should have avoided giving masters their indemnities before the experience had been concluded. In short, his consultative body recommended for France an apprentice approach in which the state would purchase slaves and act as their tutors.[35] Understandably, both the more radical French emancipationists and their British allies found this proposal to be far too similar to the apprentice program implemented by Britain and therefore to be unacceptable. Still, some abolitionists in the late 1830s had shown an obvious proclivity to accept an amended form of apprenticeship.

The controversy over this system continued within the confines of the Broglie Commission during the early 1840s. Indeed, an examination of the reception that apprenticeship received before this body sheds considerable light on the way in which it was perceived in France at the time. Interestingly enough, what began as a three-sided debate among proslavery elements, radical abolitionists, and moderate abolitionists ended up by taking a novel turn. It became

32. *Le Moniteur universel*, February 16, 1838.
33. Société française pour l'abolition de l'esclavage, *No. 16*, pp. 7–15; *Le Siècle*, February 12, 1840.
34. Rémusat Commission, *Rapport*, 44–45.
35. Tocqueville Commission, *Rapport*, 47–52.

apparent from the commission's discussions that by the 1840s some French humanitarians had become so opposed to apprenticeship that they could consider a continuation of slavery as preferable to it.

Just as colonial representatives had made anti-apprenticeship presentations to the Broglie Commission, those commission members favorable to the colonial cause carried on a concerted attack against the intermediate approach. Mackau launched the campaign by arguing that apprenticeship would not work in France's dependencies because French slaves were not as well prepared for emancipation as England's had been at a comparable stage; consequently, this procedure would result in disturbances and production losses if applied to the French Caribbean. He stressed that apprenticeship would prove "dangerous and impolitic" for France's holdings: "the application of the English model would therefore be a veritable calamity for our colonies." What Mackau appeared to find especially "disappointing with apprenticeship" was its early termination and its use as a means of compensating planters for only half the indemnity owed them.[36] Referring also to the decrease in staple products that had accompanied it, Mackau concluded that apprenticeship was an entirely negative program that, "in a word, satisfied no one." Mackau, like the plantocracy whose position he defended, totally rejected "any emancipation system which would have the British approach for its basis."[37]

Some of the abolitionists on the commission joined in wholeheartedly condemning British apprenticeship. The peer Count Pellegrino Rossi asserted that it had proved contradictory in giving blacks the impression that they were simultaneously free and slave.[38] According to Passy, English apprenticeship had been "the object of almost general disapprobation," as everyone agreed that it had failed in satisfying either the blacks or the whites. Moreover, he held, it had destroyed the rapport between slaves and their owners, had prolonged corporal punishment, and had constituted a disguised form of slavery.[39] It remained, however, for Sade to press

36. Broglie Commission, Minutes, January 3, 1842.
37. *Ibid.*, February 10, March 14, 1842.
38. *Ibid.*, January 31, 1842.
39. *Ibid.*, March 7, 1842.

French emancipationist hatred of apprenticeship to its extreme. Sade charged that the British system had completely failed to make blacks ready for freedom and was tantamount to "the prolongation of slavery." He had become convinced that all members of the commission were aware of "the inconveniences and poor success of the apprentice regime," which had "entirely missed the mark" and which would have the same results in France's colonies. Consequently, Sade proposed that his country adopt a program of eventual complete emancipation similar to England's but with continued slavery substituted for apprenticeship until slaves were able to cope with a state of liberty. He claimed to dislike the idea of prolonging servitude but pointed out that its extension could serve to reduce the amount of compensation eventually due planters by permitting them to exploit their slaves for a longer period in exchange for a lesser indemnity.[40] French abolitionists had learned their lesson all too well from their British mentors. Sade had come to abhor apprenticeship so much that he preferred continued slavery to it.

Although he was a moderate emancipationist who saw some good points in apprenticeship, the president of the Broglie Commission was prepared to defend it only to a certain extent. Besides, Broglie, too, was ready to postpone freeing the slaves. As a result, he rallied to Sade's position after giving apprenticeship what he believed to be its due. Broglie contended that the intermediate regime had "been criticized in an exaggerated fashion"; after all, it had preserved order and production. One reason why it was treated so harshly, he suggested, was because no system is perfect, and this one did have its fault. Another factor behind its negative image, he surmised, was that both English abolitionists and colonists had clamored against it, the former as an infringement on liberty, the latter as a deletion from authority. He added, however, that if France were to adopt the apprenticeship principle, its inconveniences, as exposed by the British case, could be avoided. Although his gradualist approach had brought him this far in justifying apprenticeship, Broglie ended by purporting that the extension of slavery would have the convenience of not confusing blacks about their real situation; and, as Sade had suggested, it could also pro-

40. *Ibid.*, January 31, February 28, May 23, 1842.

vide a means for lowering the indemnity eventually paid to masters. Therefore, he threw his support behind the Sade proposal.[41] Another French abolitionist opposed to immediate slave liberation had shown his preference for the protraction of slavery rather than the adoption of apprenticeship.

The influential Alexis de Tocqueville did speak up in the commission in favor of a transitional period, albeit different from the British one. In effect, he put forth the same sort of alternative that his commission had suggested in 1839. He agreed with Broglie that English apprenticeship "has generally been judged with far too much severity" and that its problems could be avoided in a French version. Furthermore, he admitted, the state of slavery was not conducive to preparing blacks for liberty. Accordingly, Tocqueville proposed that French apprentices be placed under the temporary aegis of the government and paid a salary. This, too, he held, could serve as a device to reduce the amount of compensation to be paid estate owners, for some of the salary could be kept by the government and applied toward the indemnity. Another emancipationist on the commission, Tracy, rallied to Tocqueville's position.[42] Other commission members, though, refused to sanction a project for government ownership of slaves, which they judged too complicated. In the end Tocqueville and Tracy committed themselves to the Sade-Broglie proposition.

In a session in late May, 1842, Broglie summed up the position of the pro-emancipation commission members. He argued that their proposal was "the English system, minus the defects which have compromised its execution." One of the most significant defects of the total British experience, he contended, "has been apprenticeship, that bastard regime, which as a result has rendered more keen the reciprocal irritation between planters and blacks, and which has produced no good, either as a means of preparation [for freedom], or as a prolongation of forced work. . . . This defect the commission has eliminated in admitting that slavery will be continued under its real form, for the time that is recognized necessary to equate apprenticeship, that is, to replace half of the indemnity." The commission, Broglie explained, was advocating the continuation of slavery for ten years, to be followed by five years of what he

41. *Ibid.*, February 28, 1842.
42. *Ibid.*, March 7, 1842.

called *engagement*, during which salaries would be set and former slaves would be constrained to work for a master, though not necessarily their former owner.[43]

As Broglie pointed out in his final report, the majority on the commission recommended ten years of additional servitude, because French slaves were much less ready for freedom than England's had been. Consequently, "French apprenticeship" had to be longer than "English apprenticeship." In reality, instead of proposing a British system pure and simple, the Broglie Report advocated an elongated period of slavery to be followed by a scheme resembling apprenticeship. Obviously, for Broglie and other moderate French emancipationists it was not the concept of apprenticeship as such that was objectionable but the fact that it had not lasted long enough or proved sufficiently effective in controlling the black population. Such a position clearly amounted to a convergence of views between French abolitionists and the opponents of slave liberation. Even this proposal by the majority of the commission, however, did not satisfy those members of the group, headed by Mackau, favorable to the colonies. Instead, they put forth a minority motion calling for emancipation to be delayed for twenty years and effected through progressive and partial rather than rapid and simultaneous procedures.[44]

There is little doubt, then, that by the early 1840s British abolitionist strategies had backfired. By exhorting their French brethren to repudiate apprenticeship, the British had not persuaded them to espouse immediatism. On the contrary, all French emancipationists had come to repudiate the British model, and the moderate faction of the French movement had even opted for a prolongation of slavery. Once again the British example had been taken in the negative rather than positive sense on the other side of the Channel. Moreover, the apprenticeship issue had the effect of exacerbating the divisions within the never very cohesive French antislavery movement between its radical and moderate elements. The radicals might spurn apprenticeship, but most of them favored more rapid freeing of the slaves, not the extension of bondage. Furthermore, by rejecting a British intermediate regime, French abolitionists had reduced the number of options available to them in their

43. *Ibid.*, May 25, 1842.
44. Broglie Commission, *Rapport*, 202, 334–44.

quest for emancipation of some kind. Perhaps the British approach had its deficiencies, but it might have been easier to convince the French public to adopt slave liberation following apprenticeship than to accept complete, immediate emancipation; and, despite its disadvantages, even the British preparatory system should have been preferable from an abolitionist point of view to a considerable extension of slavery. Unfortunately, the objectives of many French emancipationists had come to coincide with those of the plantocrats, whose aim had always been to discredit British apprenticeship and eliminate it as a possible alternative to slavery. In this sense, the French debate over British apprenticeship had resulted in an indubitable setback for abolitionism and another victory for proslavery forces within France and its colonies. The position of French abolitionists on this issue also played into the hands of their government, which was not anxious to adopt a definite emancipation project of any kind.

During the mid-1830s and the early 1840s the French government, too, was closely following the evolution of the apprenticeship problem and its application in Britain's dependencies. It appears that French navy and colonial department officials were dubious about this aspect of the British process even before it went into effect. In a "Note for the Director" of the colonies, a French functionary expressed the opinion in 1833 that apprenticeship based on the British model could not be applied satisfactorily to France's possessions. The adoption of such an approach, he predicted, would destroy the moral authority of masters over slaves, cause insubordination of the latter, and "inevitably lead to disorders." Moreover, he feared that blacks were unlikely to work under apprenticeship.[45] These first French bureaucratic reflections, written with evident concern for colonial interests, seem to have set the stage for later French government evaluations of apprenticeship, to have become institutionalized in the French administrative mind. In a memo on emancipation written in 1835, Director of the Colonies Saint Hilaire reported that British apprenticeship was too severe on blacks. Besides, he suggested, the results of the British system so far, based on information already received from the Caribbean, "are far from rendering desirable its applica-

45. Note for the director, December 27, 1833, in Gén. 206 (1513), ANSOM.

tion in our colonies."[46] This same wariness became evident in the course of a conversation between Isambert of the French abolition society and Saint Hilaire in 1836. In the interview, Saint Hilaire asserted that his ministry was "sincerely abolitionist" but was under pressure from the colonial party—unlike the government in Britain, where pressure came primarily from emancipationists—and unable to pay the indemnity that would be required. He also declared that he was "not a partisan of the English system," adding: "Apprenticeship is worthless. At the end of the experience it will be necessary to have rigorous regulations to assure the continuation of work. This will be a sort of servitude almost as vigorous as the former one."[47] Already in the mid-1830s the French government's impressions of British apprenticeship were decidedly negative.

This attitude on the part of French officials was undoubtedly reinforced by reports emanating from the French observers sent to the British colonies. The French official who made the most favorable statements on apprenticeship was Bernard, who pointed out that it was a useful transitional device. Still, even he remarked that the system was disliked by all parties concerned—the planters, abolitionists, and apprentices.[48] As mentioned earlier, one of the first French evaluators of the British situation, Pardeilhan, had reported on what he saw to be the numerous faults of British apprenticeship, especially its failure to inculcate the work ethic in blacks.[49] Another early account, that of Alphonse Barrot, the French consul in Colombia who was visiting Jamaica, affirmed that the system was detested by English proprietors, who believed that they would be forced to continue to care for their former slaves while the latter would be free to work much less than under slavery; moreover, he predicted, under apprenticeship, "the slave will not advance one step toward civilization."[50] In his assessments on Mauritius, d'Arvoy was equally critical of an institution that he

46. Saint Hilaire, note on slave emancipation prepared for the duc de Broglie and apparently forwarded to Guizot, October 1, 1835, in Guizot Papers, 42AP40, Archives Nationales.
47. Société française pour l'abolition de l'esclavage, *4ᵉ publication,* 52. This conversation was reported by Isambert in the Société's session of June 6, 1836.
48. Report to Minister, April 10, 1836, in Gén. 178 (1418), ANSOM.
49. Report on Demerara, March 1, 1837, in Gén. 165 (1336), ANSOM.
50. Barrot to Minister of Foreign Affairs, June 28, 1834, in Gén. 178 (1418), ANSOM.

viewed as causing blacks to be insubordinate and disinclined to work.[51] The fact that apprenticeship was displaying apparent shortcomings in the spheres of continued labor and productivity must have been of particular interest to a government preoccupied with these questions.

Official French attention to the British situation heightened when it became apparent that the length of apprenticeship would be reduced. An internal navy and colonial ministry note from the summer of 1838 indicated that it was necessary to be especially observant of British colonial developments, for apprenticeship would be over as of August 1, and "by the end of 1838 we will already be in a position to know the results of this great measure, and its first effects on our colonies."[52] In late August the minister sent his governors a request for all possible information on the new situation facing England's territories at the end of the intermediate phase. It was, he attested, necessary to study closely "the new era into which the colonial possessions of England have now entered."[53] Such a policy, of course, was in line with the French government's previously stated objective of observing British actions concerning abolition while making no immediate moves in that direction. Even the procolonial press was willing to suggest in mid-1838 that France was still pursuing its policy of temporizing in the face of the termination of British apprenticeship while doing little to advance slave liberation in French holdings.[54] In reality, though, a combination of circumstances at this time was making the French government seriously reconsider its course of action.

In the late 1830s other factors besides the ending of British apprenticeship emerged to focus the administration's attention on the emancipation problem. In February, 1838, Passy, then vice-president of the Société française pour l'abolition de l'esclavage, formally presented in the Chamber of Deputies a motion intended to lead to the freeing of French slaves. His project, envisaging a process of gradual manumission through the liberation of slave children at birth and the institution of the right for adults to purchase their freedom (rachat), was heatedly debated in the lower

51. Report, September 14, 1837, in Gén. 164 (1332), ANSOM.
52. Draft of July 23, 1838, in Gén. 161 (1322), ANSOM.
53. Minister to Governors, August 28, 1838, in Gén. 144 (1225) and Corr. Gén. 190, ANSOM.
54. Le Bulletin colonial, August 13, 1838.

house, with the government and colonial lobby opposing it. Still, despite the resistance of the administration, the deputies voted to take the Passy proposal into consideration, appointing a commission presided over by Guizot to examine it.[55] The report of this body, made by Rémusat on June 12, 1838, also favored gradual emancipation, citing—as mentioned—the positive aspects of the British system as a whole, including apprenticeship.[56] As a result of these events, the French government, in spite of its own predilections, was obliged to consider, though not necessarily act on, the Passy proposition as approved in the Rémusat Report. In the process it was compelled to reexamine the abolition question and its policy toward it.

The French government's stance on the issue was clarified in a series of notes drawn up in the summer and autumn of 1838. In a dispatch Minister Rosamel sent his governors in August, he referred to the end of apprenticeship as an "event which is as important as it is unforeseen, and whose results will be known by the beginning of the [French legislative] session in 1839," when the Rémusat Report was to be examined again. He observed, too, that "it is a new reason for the government to want to remain free to trace itself the paths it would be best for France to follow." Rosamel then postulated that "it is possible that the questions raised by the Rémusat Report will become magnified by 1839 as a result of what is happening in the English colonies, and that the government could be constrained by the force of things to become immediately preoccupied, no longer with preparatory measures for emancipation, but with the application of this great measure to our possessions." He assured the governors that if the latter were the case his administration would not institute a system of special magistrates as the English had and that freedom for slaves would be accompanied by "indemnity and security" for the masters. As the minister explained, it was necessary to prevent the substitution of "parliamentary initiative for that of the executive power," something that would "interfere with the liberty of action which the latter needs to preserve in a matter of such gravity." Accordingly, the government was preparing proposals for the moralization of

55. *Le Moniteur universel*, February 16, 1838.
56. Rémusat Commission, *Rapport*, 44–45, 47–48, 67–69.

French slaves and the improvement of their situation.[57] Spurred on by developments on the French and English scenes, the government was finally planning to give substance to its promises of ameliorating substantially the state of French slaves. It was also acting to retain its authority and initiative on the slavery question by doing everything possible to deflect the recommendations made by the Chamber of Deputies commissions and avert a crescendo of legislative interventions such as those that had helped persuade the London government to introduce abolition.

A crossed-off passage of a draft version of the dispatch cited in the preceding paragraph clearly shows the connection between England's decision to terminate apprenticeship and the new initiative that officials in Paris were preparing to take. After mentioning that England's move might compel France to consider outright emancipation rather than just ameliorative measures, the minister asked to be informed immediately of any influence England's granting of full liberties might have on the "spirit of the slave population" of France's colonies.[58] Obviously, the French government feared that the abridgment of British apprenticeship might occasion major unrest, or even revolt, in France's possessions, which in turn could oblige the government to act quickly to liberate the slaves. It is noteworthy that the French administration's original anxiety that British actions would cause uprisings in French establishments had not entirely dissipated. An avowal of this kind also suggests that a slave revolt might have been one of the few things that could have persuaded the July Monarchy to move toward at least relatively rapid emancipation.

The cancellation of British apprenticeship did not occasion any noticeable disorders in French territories, even though no strengthening of French colonial garrisons appears to have occurred at this time. As a result, the French government was able to continue pursuing its policy of cautious gradualism in emancipation matters. The minister of the navy and colonies, Rosamel, reassured the *colons* about his government's stance in a "very confidential" letter to Dupin, president of the Council of Delegates. He reiterated his belief that the Rémusat Report would be debated during the next

57. Minister to Governors, August 21, 1838, in Corr. Gén. 1838, ANSOM.
58. Draft of August 21, 1838, dispatch, in Gén. 174 (1389), ANSOM.

legislative session, the discussion being complicated by "a very grave fact": the termination of British apprenticeship and the definitive disappearance of British slavery. He added, however, that to retain control over the matter his ministry was proposing a policy of preparing French slaves for liberation.[59] Evidently, Rosamel believed that this was the best means of circumventing any abolitionist proposal for more immediate freedom for French slaves.

In his reply to Rosamel, Dupin strove to reassure the minister and counter any hasty action on his part. Dupin noted that the minister's decision to prepare French slaves for liberation had been precipitated by the sudden conclusion of apprenticeship in England's holdings; therefore, he suggested, it would be best to await the results of the English experiment before proceeding any further.[60] In fact, the government needed little encouragement to continue on its cautious track. A note Saint Hilaire prepared for presentation to the Council of Ministers at the end of 1838 elaborated on the government's intentions. After citing material sent by Moges that indicated the extent to which work had diminished following emancipation in British dependencies, the director of the colonies assured the Cabinet that, when the Rémusat proposal was discussed after the opening of the new legislative session, the navy and colonial department would be ready to counter with its own proposition: funds would be allocated for religious and elementary education in the colonies, and ordonnances would be drawn up for the implementation of a slave census and for the regulation of voluntary manumissions.[61] Improvements in the plight of French slaves, although still minor in nature, were about to be set in motion by a combination of circumstances in France and the United Kingdom.

In the end, the Rémusat proposal never had the chance to force an alteration in French colonial policy. In early 1839, the Chamber of Deputies was dissolved, and the report, like all other pending parliamentary business, became a dead letter. The abolitionists, though, revived the issue once again. On June 7, 1839, Tracy reintroduced the Passy plan in the lower house, and this time Toc-

59. Minister to Dupin, October 5, 1838, in Gén. 161 (1323), ANSOM.

60. Dupin to Minister, October 10, 1838, in Gén. 161 (1323), ANSOM.

61. Director of Colonies, report to Council of Ministers, December, 1838, in Gén. 161 (1322), ANSOM.

queville prepared the report for the new commission examining the question. Tocqueville's report, as explained above, supported the idea of a more direct approach to emancipation, advocating that the government purchase the slaves, pay half of their value immediately to their owners, and let the slaves work for the masters for an additional ten years to repay the remainder of the compensation due. However, the legislative session recessed before the Tocqueville Report could be discussed by the Chamber of Deputies. Once again the navy and colonial minister was free to revert to his former position and inform his colleagues in the Cabinet that French policy was "to study our neighbors and not imitate them."[62] That the navy and colonial ministry was still somewhat flexible on the entire matter, however, is shown by a note it presented to the Council of Ministers in late 1839. This memo indicated that if the deputies were to accept the conclusions of the Tocqueville Report, the navy and colonial department was ready to enter "spontaneously into the paths . . . which must lead to the great social transformation that England has just achieved in her colonies." The government would move rapidly to prepare the slaves and then introduce in the session of 1841—as the Tocqueville Commission had suggested—a law that would end slavery and provide for an indemnity and the preservation of colonial labor.[63] Perhaps rumors of this memo's existence even led some abolitionist circles to believe that in one of its last meetings in 1839 the Council of Ministers had voted to accept the proposals of the Tocqueville Commission and present an emancipation bill along these lines.[64] Although such a vote seems never to have taken place, apparently the French government in the late 1830s was resigned to moving more quickly toward emancipation if obliged to do so by a slave uprising or concerted abolitionist pressure of the kind that Frenchmen of the time believed had forced the British government to act.

In reality, however, the eventuality that the French government envisaged as a possibility never came to pass. Instead of introduc-

62. Navy and Colonial Minister to Foreign Minister, September 16, 1839, in Corr. Gén. 192, ANSOM.

63. Note for Council of Ministers, November 5, 1939, in Gén. 171 (1376), ANSOM.

64. Reported in *L'Espérance*, January 4, 1840.

ing an emancipation law, it continued its ameliorative program. It issued an ordonnance on January 5, 1840, naming new magistrates to oversee the treatment of slaves; and the Chambers, viewing education and religion as the keys to slave advancement, voted a credit of 650,000 francs in the budgets of 1840 and 1841 to fund these new posts, increase the number of clergy, and build chapels and schools in the colonies. Then, in February, 1840, the ministry fell over the Egyptian Crisis with Britain. The new Cabinet, headed by Thiers, handled the slavery question by forming on March 26, 1840, a royal commission, presided over by Broglie, to examine it. Preoccupied with the Eastern Crisis, the government was clearly marking time on the slavery issue. In this sense, the diplomatic confrontation with Britain was halting progress in the emancipation sphere. Finally, while the Broglie Commission was still holding its meetings, the right-of-search dispute broke out between Paris and London in early 1842. The difficulties over Egypt had revived Anglophobia in France. The right-of-search imbroglio now tended to focus this anti-British sentiment on the colonial and slavery questions. Great Britain's advocacy of emancipation, when associated in French minds with the search problem, would effect a further setback for the French abolitionist cause in the 1840s.

SIX

EFFECT OF THE RIGHT-OF-SEARCH CONTROVERSY

The right-of-search dispute arose from a disagreement over procedures to repress the slave trade, but it had a major effect on French antislavery policy. In fact, this dispute between France and Great Britain had a negative impact on both French perceptions of British emancipation and the development of the French abolitionist movement. The crisis erupted on the French scene in late 1841 and early 1842, though its antecedents can be traced back to the 1830s. Following the establishment of the July Monarchy, the French government had agreed to British entreaties and signed bilateral conventions in 1831 and 1833 to proscribe the transatlantic slave trade by permitting the mutual right to intercept and search merchant vessels on the high seas. This process, part of the rapprochement that had occurred between Britain and France following the July Revolution, operated rather smoothly for a decade and was not of real interest to the French public during the 1830s. The French press, for example, paid little attention to the questions of slavery and the slave trade immediately after the Revolution of 1830 and made sparse editorial comment on the conclusion of the 1831 and 1833 agreements. Furthermore, throughout the 1830s the same press made few references to Britain's campaign against the slave trade, though as a whole it tended to react favorably whenever it did mention it.[1] In view of the response of the

1. For a discussion of the French press's reaction to slave trade repression, see Jennings, "The French Press and Great Britain's Campaign Against the Slave Trade."

press, the Chambers, and pamphlet literature, it is clear that in the 1830s Frenchmen were generally not interested in the Anglo-French campaign against the slave trade. Only after 1840 would the conjuncture of several events set off the right-of-search controversy, bring the French public to question the motivation behind British anti–slave trade efforts, and in so doing tarnish British pro-emancipation policies in French eyes.

The so-called Egyptian Crisis was crucial in the course of Anglo-French relations after 1840. The French government under Thiers backed Mohammed Ali of Egypt in his attempts to retain dominance over Syria until a British-inspired coalition obliged France to abandon its ally and forced Egypt to surrender Syria. The result was a war scare in 1840 on both sides of the Channel that shattered the entente cordiale, which had inspired cooperation between Britain and France since 1830.[2] Worse still, from the point of view of Anglo-French antislavery activities, was the fact that the latent Anglophobia stirred up by this confrontation soured French opinion toward Britain and prepared the terrain for the right-of-search controversy. Nevertheless, there is no evidence suggesting that the Egyptian Crisis as such was a direct cause of, rather than a factor indirectly contributing to, the search dispute.

In fact, this disagreement evolved directly out of a combination of developments concerning repression of the slave trade.[3] By 1840 the British had reinforced their efforts against slave traffic by strengthening cruiser contingents on the African coast and resorting to the use of a tight inshore blockade in an attempt to prevent slavers from landing or taking to sea.[4] Accordingly, an increased number of French merchantmen were intercepted and searched by British naval vessels under the provisions of the 1831 and 1833

2. For these diplomatic developments, see M. S. Anderson, *The Eastern Question, 1774–1923* (London, 1966).

3. The mechanics of joint naval search action are examined by Christopher Lloyd, *The Navy and the Slave Trade: The Suppression of the African Slave Trade in the Nineteenth Century* (1949; rpr. London, 1968); Serge Daget, "British Repression of the Illegal French Slave Trade: Some Considerations," in Henry A. Gemery and Jan S. Hogendorn (eds.), *The Uncommon Market: Essays in the Economic History of the Atlantic Slave Trade* (New York, 1979), 419–42; and Serge Daget, "France, Suppression of the Illegal Trade, and England, 1817–1850," in Eltis and Walvin (eds.), *The Abolition of the Atlantic Slave Trade*, 193–215.

4. These mutations in British cruiser strategy are analyzed by Lloyd, *The Navy and the Slave Trade*, and J. Gallagher, "Fowell Buxton and the New African Policy, 1838–1842," *Cambridge Historical Journal*, X (1950), 36–58.

conventions. Furthermore, the identification of possible slavers was complicated by the fact that at this time more merchantmen were carrying on legitimate trade with the west coast of Africa, with some British and French ships even furnishing African slave stations with European goods later to be exchanged for slaves—an entirely legal procedure at the time.[5] With more vessels plying the African coast, and with increasing difficulties in determining legitimate from illegal commerce or goods, the entire right-of-search system was becoming subject to a certain amount of arbitrariness and thus to charges by merchant ships of unwarranted arrest, harassment, or mistreatment.

By 1840 a growing number of complaints from French merchant captains about being unnecessarily searched began filtering into the French navy and colonial ministry and eventually into the pages of the French press.[6] The problem of British interference with French ships received added publicity in February, 1840, when the British seized as a slaver the *Sénégambie*, a vessel chartered by the French government to recruit *engagés* in Senegal.[7] *Le Bulletin colonial*, for instance, exploded with indignation at the arrest of this ship, a "most arbitrary" action by "the least philanthropic, most spoliatory nation in the world."[8] Occurrences of

5. See Lawrence C. Jennings, "French Policy Toward Trading with African and Brazilian Slave Merchants, 1840–1853," *Journal of African History*, XVII (1976), 515–28.

6. According to documents in the ANSOM, twenty French merchant vessels were visited by British cruisers between 1837 and 1843, sometimes in a manner considered highhanded or insulting by the French (list dated March 3, 1844, in Gén. 146 [1230]).

7. *Engagés* were a limited number of indentured laborers or soldiers who contracted to serve for a set number of years in the colonies. At times French ships even transported to their dependencies "liberated Africans," bought from slavers on the African coast, enfranchised, and then set off as *engagés*; but this policy, too, remained quite limited. By the 1840s Great Britain was adopting a similar policy and transporting to the West Indies freed Africans seized from slavers and landed at Sierra Leone or other coastal points in an attempt to provide adequate labor in the postemancipation sugar colonies. For more detail on these French and British African emigration policies, see Claude Faure, "La garnison européenne du Sénégal et le recrutement des premiers troupes noires, 1779–1858," *Revue d'histoire des colonies françaises*, VIII (1920), 5–108; François Zuccarelli, "Le régime des engagés à temps au Sénégal, 1817–1848," *Cahiers d'études africaines*, II (1962), 420–61; Johnson U. J. Asiegbu, *Slavery and the Politics of Liberation, 1787–1861: A Study of Liberated African Emigration and British Anti-Slavery Policy* (London, 1969); François Renault, *Libération d'esclaves et nouvelle servitude: Les rachats de captifs africains pour le compte des colonies françaises après l'abolition de l'esclavage* (Abidjan and Dakar, 1976).

8. *Le Bulletin colonial*, March 20, 1840.

this kind made the French increasingly aware of the disadvantages of the mutual search agreements and of the apparent heavy-handedness of the British.

In late 1841 a similar incident provided further tinder for the impending conflagration. At this time reports began to reach France about the seizure by the British of the freighter *Le Marabout* of Nantes because she was judged to be carrying an excessive number of planks—one of the numerous criteria that, under the agreement of 1833, constituted grounds for suspicion of slave trading.[9] News of *Le Marabout*'s capture, which spread throughout the French press near the end of December, was accompanied by indications that her crew had been mistreated by the arresting cruiser. French journals, their interest quickened by the *Sénégambie* case, were now provided with evidence tending to demonstrate that the British had arbitrarily employed the right of search on a bona fide French merchantman in an effort to disrupt France's legitimate maritime commerce. Such a conclusion seemed all the more plausible because France was no longer openly engaged in the slave trade—though one might wish to qualify France's providing slave goods or recruiting *engagés* as indirect involvement in this traffic—and none of the French merchantmen seized under the provisions of the 1831 and 1833 conventions had ever been convicted as a slaver. All of the elements required to fuel a crisis between Britain and France over the right of search were falling into place.

The spark that was needed to set off an explosion of French opinion against Anglo-French cooperation in repressing the slave trade was provided when the French learned that a new treaty extending the search powers of British cruisers had been signed in London on December 20, 1841. Unfortunately for the Guizot government, it had acceded to a reinforced search agreement with the British just when the French public had reason to repudiate this procedure. The result was a storm of protest in France, first against the 1841 treaty and then against the right-of-search conventions of 1831 and 1833, a protest that went beyond party lines and included the entire French political spectrum. None of the press—with the exception of Guizot's *Le Journal des débats*, which itself wavered

9. For a factual account of the *Marabout* incident see the old but still useful work by Jean de Maupassant, *Le droit de visite sous Louis-Philippe: L'affaire du "Marabout"* (Bordeaux, 1913).

on the issue—and only a handful of Cabinet members or abolitionists supported Guizot on the right of search by the spring of 1842.
Although this outpouring of public indignation was at its height in
early 1842, it did not abate entirely until the mid-1840s. As a
consequence, the Guizot government was obliged to refuse to
ratify the treaty of 1841, which it had already signed, and to negoti-
ate with Britain the de facto termination of joint search in 1845.[10]
At the same time, these developments led to profound questioning
within France of Britain's philanthropy in attacking both the slave
trade and slavery. Coincidentally, this tendency by the French to
incriminate Britain coincided with similar charges by Spain that
Britain was trying to instigate slave revolts in Cuba and with
claims by the United States that Britain was employing antislavery
tactics to gain domination over Texas, thus marking a growing
international skepticism in the 1840s about British motivation in
slavery-related issues.

French questioning of British intentions was exemplified by
statements in newspapers of the French port cities, particularly
Bordeaux. *L'Indicateur* affirmed that "under the pretext of freeing
blacks," England had attempted to assume "the sovereignty of the
seas." *Le Courrier de la Gironde*, too, bluntly proclaimed that
mutual search was a "pretext" for England to obtain "the domination of the seas." In another instance the daily expressed its conviction that Great Britain, "the least philanthropic nation in the
world," was committing "veritable acts of piracy" to "annihilate
our commerce with Africa."[11] The legitimist *La Guienne* was
equally persuaded that England was exploiting the right of search
in an attempt to monopolize colonial production, adding that
"philanthropy was the best means England could find to harm our
navigation and annihilate our commercial relations with nations
beyond the seas." In similar fashion *Le Mémorial bordelais*
charged that the English dissimulated their "odious Machia-
velianism" and "insatiable ambition under the . . . cloak of fraud-
ulent philanthropy." The newspaper contended that in France

10. For a discussion of the right-of-search controversy during the early 1840s, see
Lawrence C. Jennings, "France, Great Britain, and the Repression of the Slave
Trade, 1841–1845," *French Historical Studies*, X (1977), 101–25.
11. *L'Indicateur*, June 26, 1842; *Le Courrier de la Gironde*, October 5, January 4,
27, 1842.

"everyone is perfectly informed" about "these grand negrophilic sentiments which England affects"; thus, "the philanthropy which [the British] government feigns can no longer fool anyone." Britain's actions had led *Le Mémorial* to believe that "there is something as sacred for France as the liberty of her blacks, her own liberty, the liberty of the seas."[12] The newspaper's indictment of British motives had led it to assimilate the slave trade with slavery and to suggest that the preservation of French national interests from British encroachment justified the maintenance of both.

Other port city organs joined the Bordeaux press in attacking British philanthropists along these same lines. A republican-oriented opponent of servitude, *Le Journal de Rouen*, indignantly exclaimed that the right of search was "nothing but philanthropic juggling to mask the ambitious designs of the nation which covets the absolute domination of the seas." *Le Sémaphore de Marseille*, representing France's second port for West Indian trade after Le Havre and her leading center for African trade, developed in detail the charge that "under the false cloak of . . . humanity" England hoped to "usurp the exclusive monopoly of the commerce of Guinea."[13] *L'Armoricain* of Brest was also convinced that Great Britain, "a nation basely envious of our prosperity," was employing repression of the slave trade as a "pretext" to "interfere with our commerce and suppress it in the future." Many port city journals appeared to be in agreement with the contention of *La Charente-Inférieure* (La Rochelle) that England, "that essentially mercantile nation," was using "this holy philanthropy" as a "mask" to cover its interference with French commercial relations, as a "humanitarian pretext to ruin her rivals."[14] In the process these publications were tarnishing both Britain's image and the abolitionist cause for which the nation stood.

As a result of the search affair, Parisian dailies, like *La Presse*, were as prepared as their provincial counterparts to maintain that

12. *La Guienne*, March 16, May 12, 1842; *Le Mémorial bordelais*, April 15, November 30, December 18, 1842, February 20, 1844.

13. *Le Journal de Rouen*, September 20, 1842; *Le Sémaphore de Marseille*, September 9, January 4, 13, 1842. For comparative tables on the shipping of the major French port cities with the slave colonies, see Jennings, "La presse havraise et l'esclavage," 68–71.

14. *L'Armoricain*, April 19, January 15, 1842; *La Charente-Inférieure*, June 8, 1845.

Britain was less devoted to altruistic aims than to that "maritime predominance toward which she works unceasingly." The events of 1841 and 1842 led *Le Commerce* to exclaim: "No, England is not motivated by love for negroes, whom she mocks and exploits. . . . It is a commercial monopoly that she is dissimulating under this philanthropic formula."[15] Such declarations might be expected from procolonial organs, but other liberal or republican journals of the capital, usual advocates of the antislavery cause, made similar utterances. *Le Charivari* proclaimed that "philanthropy [was] an arm" for Albion to use against competitors; and *La Patrie* maintained that "under the false front of philanthropy" England treated her commercial competitors "more harshly than the slavers [treat] their victims." *Le Courrier français*, a staunch proponent of joint search a decade earlier, now expressed serious doubts about England's selflessness, concluding, like *Le Mémorial bordelais*, that "the liberty of the seas is as important as the liberty of blacks."[16] Caught up in the furor of the times, even pro-abolitionist spokesmen were prepared to castigate Britain's intentions to the point of disassociating themselves from the British-inspired anti–slave trade and antislavery causes. The search affair had the important effect of giving even French liberal and republican elements second thoughts about British disinterestedness in slavery-related issues.

French disillusionment with Britain at this time manifested itself in other matters touching on British humanitarianism. That is, the negative atmosphere permeating from the mutual search problem led Frenchmen to suggest that Britain's philanthropic aura was also belied by her less-than-humane treatment of other peoples—Irish, Indians, Chinese, liberated Africans—and the working class within Britain itself. Such arguments were not entirely new in France. Already in the mid-1830s, for example, at a time when it was still favorable to emancipation, *L'Indicateur* of Bordeaux had questioned British altruism in light of England's treatment of the Irish.[17] Such charges became much more prevalent, though, when the right-of-search controversy brought more Frenchmen to suspect the purity of British motives.

15. *La Presse*, February 18, 1842; *Le Commerce*, May 2, 1842.
16. *Le Charivari*, October 28–29, 1842; *La Patrie*, May 6, 1842; *Le Courrier français*, January 31, April 12, 1842.
17. *L'Indicateur*, October 11, 1835.

Following the outbreak of the mutual search dispute, *Le Mémorial bordelais* wondered how England could be so philanthropic concerning the abolition of slavery when she maintained white slaves in India—Britain did not officially terminate slavery there until 1843—and treated both the Irish and its own poor worse than slaves.[18] At the end of 1842 the same journal asked why "the false philanthropy of England . . . could not show a little less pity for the plight of slaves and busy itself a little more with [English] proletarians whom it allowed to die of hunger, and the Irish whom it kept in the most frightful misery." In reality, the paper affirmed, "no one is duped" by the false interest that "Albion" showed for "the children of Guinea"; what England actually desired was "to destroy the sugar cane culture" of the West Indies and make "the entire world tributary to her possessions in India."[19] Other Bordeaux dailies adopted a similar line. *Le Courrier de la Gironde* remarked that the real test for British "philanthropy" was whether it always pressed for slave liberation, even when this infringed on Britain's own interests. The newspaper could not believe the latter to be true, for England still tolerated slavery in India. Thus, there were "other things than philanthropy in the abolitionist zeal" of England. *La Guienne* expressed similar sentiments in different terms when it paraphrased a statement from one of Jollivet's booklets and suggested that "the English abolitionist society would do well to preoccupy itself a little less with the abolition of slavery in French colonies, and a little more with the abolition of slavery in India."[20]

The French press outside Bordeaux also expanded on these themes. The Catholic *L'Univers* (Paris), a self-proclaimed proponent of slave liberation, queried whether England "is not compromising her efforts to persuade other peoples to concur in the aboli-

18. *Le Mémorial bordelais*, March 8, 1842. The argument that white workers experienced a lower standard of living than black slaves was an old one in proslavery circles. See David Brion Davis, *The Problem of Slavery in Western Culture* (Ithaca, 1966), 202, 335–36; and Davis, *The Problem of Slavery in the Age of Revolution*, 275. A considerable amount of comparative work has been done recently on aspects of British and American wage and chattel labor. See, for example, Marcus Cunliffe, *Chattel and Wage Slavery: The Anglo-American Context* (Athens, Ga., 1979), and Betty Fladeland, *Abolitionists and Working Class Problems in the Age of Industrialization* (Baton Rouge, 1984).

19. *Le Mémorial bordelais*, December 1, 1842.

20. *Le Courrier de la Gironde*, February 20, 1842; *La Guienne*, March 17, 1842; Jollivet, *De la philanthropie anglaise*, 48.

tion of slavery, when one sees her retaining in India four million unfortunate slaves." *La Patrie* proclaimed that England's policies in India, China (where the British were fighting the Opium War), and Ireland proved that "England practiced humaneness only for her own profit." In fact, England's altruistic pose was intended "to annihilate the few resources which remain for our slave colonies." *Le Charivari* concurred that England's abolition of the slave trade and slavery were not selfless acts, for she still had forty million red slaves in India (there was little consensus among French organs on these figures) and millions of white slaves in her own factories. Accordingly, British philanthropy was a mere ploy to interfere with other nations' commerce.[21]

Another factor rendering Frenchmen dubious about the authenticity of British humanitarianism was the manner in which French perceptions of Britain's African emigration policy were altered in conjunction with the right-of-search crisis.[22] As previously demonstrated, an integral part of the process leading to French disenchantment with joint search procedures had been the British capture of a French vessel the *Sénégambie* engaged in France's engagé program. As a result, the French were highly indignant when disclosures were made during the right-of-search debate about British ships also transporting "liberated Africans" to the British Caribbean. A French colonial defender and former delegate of Guiana, Favard, saw no difference between the actions of the *Sénégambie* and those sanctioned by the British African emigration plan.[23] *Le Commerce*, for its part, ironically employed the heading "English philanthropy" for articles in which it denounced Britain's "disguised slave trade" of African workers.[24] French emancipationists also reacted negatively to this British procedure which they realized was having adverse effects on both the British and French antislavery cause. A French correspondent for the BFASS—probably Isambert—implored his British confederates to press for the

21. *L'Univers*, February 25, 1842; *La Patrie*, December 25, 1841; *Le Charivari*, March 28–29, 1842.
22. For a discussion of French views on this problem, see Lawrence C. Jennings, "French Reaction to the 'Disguised British Slave Trade': France and British African Emigration Projects, 1840–1864," *Cahiers d'études africaines*, XVIII (1978), 201–13.
23. Favard, *Examen des résultats*, 40–41.
24. *Le Commerce*, August 29, September 6, 1842.

termination of Indian slavery and of African emigration. Such alterations in English policy, he hoped, would "take from our adversaries a subject of recrimination, which they are continually stirring up to mislead and irritate public opinion."[25] A French abolitionist was wisely attempting to convince his British coworkers to call for the revocation of procedures that were alienating Frenchmen from British humanitarianism.

On other occasions French abolitionists were more harsh or forthright in their criticism of British measures. In one of the articles that he published anonymously in *Le Siècle*, Tocqueville accused the British of establishing a new sort of slave trade by importing both African and Indian laborers to their dependencies.[26] The French abolitionist society's official publication doubted England's right to seize the *Sénégambie*, pointed out that British vessels were engaged in similar dubious recruitments, and added that England's actions, "far from serving the cause of abolition in France," were "doing enormous harm to it by exciting a just susceptibility." It then admonished the English: "Above all, it is necessary to respect the honor of nations."[27] The noted abolitionist Victor Schoelcher was equally brusque in his judgment. In a letter to *Le Siècle* he denounced the London government for obliging African workers to leave Sierra Leone, the British African depot for blacks seized from slavers. "The Cabinet of Saint James," he asserted, "under the influence of egotistical preoccupations, is abandoning the cause of black men." Such a development, he indicated, was most unfortunate, for "England is thereby sacrificing all moral force to achieve the destruction of slavery, which she had energetically begun."[28] In light of the right-of-search imbroglio, Britain's actions toward other peoples and her African emigration policy had caused even French abolitionists to doubt British motives and cast aspersions on the sincerity of British philanthropy. Well-established ties were being strained between British and French aboli-

---

25. Anonymous letter published in the *BFAS Reporter*, June 1, 1842.

26. *Le Siècle*, November 22, 1843. Besides transporting African emigrants, the British—and the French, to a much more limited extent—were recruiting free Indian workers for their sugar establishments. For this, see especially Hugh Tinker, *A New System of Slavery: The Export of Indian Labour Oversea, 1830–1920* (London, 1974).

27. Société française pour l'abolition de l'esclavage, *No. 19*, p. 53.

28. *Le Siècle*, October 18, 1842.

tionists; their moral union was weakening. French proponents of abolition themselves were prepared to admit that these developments augured ill for the French emancipationist movement. This was especially true because many Frenchmen tended to assimilate the slave trade to slavery in the early 1840s.

In examining French newspapers, pamphlets, and legislative debates in the early 1840s, following the outbreak of the right-of-search conflict, one is struck by the number of occasions on which the terms *slavery* and *slave trade* are confused, used synonymously, or interconnected by both proslavery and antislavery factions. It was, of course, in the interest of colonial spokesmen to confound these two closely related structures when denouncing Britain's motives. Their willingness to do so is demonstrated in many of their utterances. In a booklet whose aim was to denigrate the British example, Favard insisted that the right of search, like the Egyptian Crisis of 1840, had awakened his fellow countrymen's "sentiment of nationality." In the light of England's machinations concerning mutual search, he continued, the entire British record of abolishing colonial slavery should be reexamined, and Frenchmen should no longer follow blindly in England's footsteps.[29] A similar brochure by Edmond de Kellermann, duc de Valmy, claimed that the right-of-search problem had confirmed French suspicions that the English had not acted disinterestedly in abolishing either the slave trade or slavery.[30] In the Chamber of Deputies a representative from Bordeaux, Jean Etienne Ducos, joined fellow deputies Valmy and Adolphe Augustin Marie Billault in questioning Britain's motives in general.[31] The legitimist *La Quotidienne* charged that England wished to ruin France's colonies, either by employing search procedures or by pressing for the rapid abolition of slavery. While writing on the mutual search issue another legitimist organ, *La Gazette de France* (Paris) also insisted that England "wishes that we emancipate our slaves before the appropriate time at the risk of ruining our colonies."[32] In an article on both the right of search and slavery *Le Commerce* stressed what

29. Favard, *Examen des résultats*, 5–6, 45–46.
30. Edmond de Kellermann, duc de Valmy, *Note sur le droit de visite* (Paris, [1842]), 8–9.
31. *Le Moniteur universel*, January 31, February 1, 2, 1843.
32. *La Quotidienne*, February 1, 1845; *La Gazette de France*, February 27, 1842.

it called "the secret motives of British philanthropy," which, under "the entirely generous facade of suppressing slavery," hoped to "destroy work" in France's possessions. *Le Courrier de la Gironde* revealed identical convictions in emphasizing that Britain's long-range aim was to "destroy the colonies of the West." This Bordeaux newspaper was persuaded that England's pursuit of the right of search and of "the forced abolition of slavery lead directly to this objective."[33] French colonial advocates were obviously exploiting the right-of-search crisis to besmirch the universal British campaign against slavery. Undoubtedly their efforts were assisted by the growing diplomatic tension dividing France from Great Britain by the mid-1840s. Franco-British efforts to revive the entente of the 1830s after the Eastern Crisis of 1840 had been strained by the right-of-search affair, shaken by the dispute over Tahiti in 1844, and destroyed by the Spanish Marriages question in 1846.[34] The British and their philanthropy had become tainted in French eyes, much to the glee of French apostles of slavery.

Simultaneously, French proslavery forces employed the tactic of discrediting French emancipationists by portraying them as either naïve followers or willing dupes of the British. During the height of the mutual search controversy the French abolitionist plan to invite an English delegation to a major public assembly in Paris enabled *Le Courrier de la Gironde* to call the Société françaisé pour l'abolition de l'esclavage "a club of Anglo-French negrophiles." According to the newspaper, the Société was unpatriotic and "acting only under foreign influence."[35] Other journals leveled comparable indictments of French philanthropists. *La Presse*, alleging that more foreigners than Frenchmen had attended the meeting in Paris, feigned amazement that a group with a non-French majority could sit in the antechambers of the National Assembly—where many of the Société's sessions were held—and "raise questions menacing the existence of our colonies." *La Gazette de France* suggested that, in light of England's actions, French abolitionists

33. *Le Commerce*, December 10, 1842; *Le Courrier de la Gironde*, March 10, 1842.
34. For background on these incidents, see J. R. Baldwin, "England and the French Seizure of the Society Islands," *Journal of Modern History*, X (1938), 212–31; and Roger Bullen, *Palmerston, Guizot and the Collapse of the Entente Cordiale* (London, 1974).
35. *Le Courrier de la Gironde*, February 25, March 16, May 14, 1842.

either were well intentioned but uninformed or were inspired by Anglomania.[36] *Le Mémorial bordelais* was less tactful in publishing a note from Martinique which purported that the British and their allies, the French emancipationists, were encouraging blacks to cut whites' throats by calling for an end to slavery. The legitimist *La France* (Paris), for its part, insinuated that the newly founded republican daily *La Réforme* (Paris), a staunch adversary of servitude, was in the pay of British abolitionists.[37] In one of his pamphlets Dupin made the same accusation of abolitionists in general. He asked how any Frenchmen who had a sense of patriotism could "consent to being the collaborators of England, the clients of her pretensions, the advocates of her errors, the imitative promoters of even her aborted experiences."[38] French colons were as prepared as Dupin to exaggerate British influence on French emancipationists. A committee of the Colonial Council of Guadeloupe affirmed that "slave emancipation in the western colonies is an English idea" and that a "host of the same missionaries" had crossed "the Channel to make propaganda for abolition." The result had been the formation of "the Anglo-French society for the abolition of slavery," whose very existence constituted "a great scandal."[39] It remained for *La Quotidienne*, when discussing the right of search as a English device to ruin France's dependencies, to unleash one of the most ignoble attacks on French emancipationists. It proclaimed that it would "not cease to denounce . . . the party of scroungers and tremblers" in France "who deliver the interests and the honor of the fatherland to the foreigner."[40] At a time when they were most vulnerable because of their relationship with their British associates, French abolitionists were being portrayed by their enemies as lackeys of the British and traitors to their nation.

It is noteworthy that in the midst of the fray caused by the mutual search dispute some French emancipationists did indeed come to the defense of Great Britain. In the 1842 debate on the issue in the Chamber of Deputies, Isambert supported Guizot

36. *La Presse,* January 20, 1843; *La Gazette de France,* January 1, 1843.
37. *Le Mémorial bordelais,* October 26, 1844; *La France,* November 1, 1843.
38. Dupin, *Seconde Mémoire,* 15–16.
39. Colonial Council of Guadeloupe, reports dated 1844, in Gen. 171 (1379), ANSOM.
40. *La Quotidienne,* February 1, 1845.

when the French foreign minister vouched for Britain's disinterestedness in eradicating the slave trade. In front of the same
body a year later Agénor de Gasparin also insisted that it was "not
serious" to see an English plot behind suppression of slavery and
the slave trade. The English abolitionist movement, he assured his
listeners, was led by "good" and "generous men."[41] During the
Paris abolitionist meeting attended by British representatives on
March 9, 1842, Passy replied to British affirmations of altruism by
totally misrepresenting the facts and declaring "that no one in
France, except perhaps some men lacking enlightenment, put in
doubt the sincerity and generosity of the motives which direct the
English abolitionist societies and their delegates." Odilon Barrot,
too, testified that most British emancipationists were not proponents of the right of search, that their aim was to terminate the
slave trade by eliminating slavery. Speaking for the French host
organization, Barrot declaimed: "we pay homage to the purity and
fervor of your convictions," knowing full well that "no ulterior
motives direct you."[42] Ironically, as Barrot's remarks suggest, at
the very time—the 1840s—when many British abolitionists had
become disenchanted with their government's espousal of search
tactics as an effective and humane means of repressing the slave
trade, French emancipationists felt compelled to defend their British colleagues over this issue.

Some French newspapers also vouched for British humanitarianism. Guizot's organ, Le Journal des débats, declared that in
terminating bondage "England had only selfless views," that never
had a nation accomplished "as prodigious a sacrifice" as spending
the equivalent of 500 million francs to abolish slavery. Two years
later the daily repeated the theme that "in history" Great Britain
would "have the glory" of having been "the first" country to
achieve the abolition of black slavery.[43] In a similar vein the official
publication of the French abolitionist society averred that the British achievement was "one of the most honorable works of the
century."[44] In his submissions to Le Siècle Tocqueville defended
the disinterestedness of British actions and affirmed that it would

---

41. *Le Moniteur universel*, January 23, 1842, July 29, 1843.
42. Société française pour l'abolition de l'esclavage, *No. 19*, pp. 5, 16.
43. *Le Journal des débats*, April 12, 1842, October 3, 1844.
44. *L'Abolitioniste français*, January–February, 1845.

be foolhardy to believe England had destroyed her own prospering territories and paid out a huge indemnity just to undermine the tropical staple production of other states. Finally, the radical *Réforme* published an article by Schoelcher, who, despite his displeasure over Britain's African emigration policy, declared English slave liberation to be "a generous measure which will provide the renown of their country in the nineteenth century."[45] Notwithstanding the right-of-search crisis, then, some French promoters of emancipation were as willing as in the 1830s to praise and defend Britain's motives in abolishing slavery.

It is significant, however, that many French emancipationists showed less enthusiasm for their British co-workers and their accomplishment following the outbreak of the right-of-search episode. Although some humanitarians, such as Gasparin, defended British intentions during the debate over the question, even they tended to vouch for the altruism of the English abolitionists rather than that of the British government. A liberal newspaper, *La Patrie*, followed this same line of reasoning when it declared that English emancipationists had been inspired by "a surge of religious charity" but that the London government had capitalized on the situation in order to pursue its own less laudable objectives.[46] Other French antislavery proponents strove to dissociate themselves from the British in a variety of ways. The Catholic *Univers* suggested that the French abolitionist cause could best be served by a withdrawal of English influence from it, for "this question has nothing to gain in France from an invasion of English Protestant philanthropy."[47] *L'Abolitioniste français* itself attempted at times to keep its distance from British emancipationists and assert the independence of the French organization. According to this organ, while "the enemies of emancipation would like it to be believed that French abolitionists are in the train of the English," this was not true; France had abolished servitude in the fourteenth century and had taken the lead in destroying slavery during the French Revolution. *La Réforme* repeated these assertions, that "slave emancipation is a revolutionary idea and not an English one."[48] In

45. *Le Siècle*, November 9, 1843; *La Réforme*, March 21, 1844.
46. *La Patrie*, October 4, 1842.
47. *L'Univers*, March 3, 1842.
48. *L'Abolitioniste français*, March–April, 1844; *La Réforme*, January 2, 1845.

the Chamber of Deputies in 1845 both Tocqueville and Isambert reiterated the stand that the freeing of slaves was a French concept, dating back to the eighteenth century; Tocqueville went so far as to suggest that the British initiative was the "product of a French idea."[49] As the mutual search crisis endured, erstwhile defenders of Britain's altruism felt obliged to strike a defensive pose and assert their independence from British influence. When Dupin remarked in the Chamber of Peers that patriotism would cause Frenchmen to reject abolitionism because of its foreign inspiration, *L'Abolitioniste* countered that "this [British] influence is felt less than ever in France."[50] That the French abolition society itself was prepared at times to renounce its British antecedents is clear from the motion it debated during its session of February 5, 1845. On this occasion it discussed whether to submit a petition to the Chamber of Deputies to "protest that abolition is a French idea, which the irritating debates that have supervened since 1841 as a result of the right of search are extraneous and cannot but prejudice."[51] As a result of the search controversy French emancipationists had become burdened with and embarrassed by the British example they had invoked in positive terms so often in the past. By the 1840s it was becoming apparent that in France, as in the United States, British efforts to encourage and assist the abolitionist movement were backfiring to some extent.[52]

Not only was the right-of-search conflict causing many French humanitarians to assert their independence from Great Britain. By churning up French nationalistic sentiment, it was also alienating Frenchmen from the British emancipation model. As a result, even staunch supporters of slave liberation in France were having second thoughts about the wisdom of rapid, immediate antislavery measures as advocated by the British. This can be seen quite clearly in the transformation that occurred in the attitudes of three

49. *Le Moniteur universel*, May 31, June 1, 1845.
50. *L'Abolitioniste français*, January–February, 1845.
51. *Ibid.*
52. For a discussion of the process whereby British assistance to American abolitionists eventually caused a backlash in the United States in the 1830s and 1840s and thus proved detrimental in some ways to the American emancipationist cause, see the works by Temperley, *British Antislavery*; Rice, *The Scots Abolitionists*; Christine Bolt, *The Anti-Slavery Movement and Reconstruction: A Study in Anglo-American Co-Operation, 1833–1877* (London, 1969); and Betty Fladeland, *Men and Brothers: Anglo-American Anti-Slavery Co-Operation* (Urbana, Ill., 1972).

pro-abolitionist organs, *Le Constitutionnel, Le National,* and *Le Siècle,* toward British emancipation specifically and slave liberation in general during the period 1841 through 1845.

Le Constitutionnel had rendered fervent praise to the British precedent in the 1830s; and in the mid-1840s the daily was still defending the production record of Britain's colonies. As late as February, 1841, the newspaper wrote that England had given France "a great example" that "it is necessary to follow, and the sooner the better." Nevertheless, the right-of-search episode resulted in a noticeable wavering in the journal's attitude toward the British achievement. When the crisis broke out *Le Constitutionnel* announced that "philanthropy is only a pretext" for England's actions. It added shortly thereafter that no one in France wanted the slave trade, and few desired the retention of slavery, but neither did anyone wish to see their eradication "paid for with the sacrifice of our interests and honor." It was well known that England did nothing contrary to her interests; consequently, France should be careful to "abolish slavery, but not diminish the power of our country."[53] Some three months later *Le Constitutionnel* had become convinced that it was illusory to view British pressure for emancipation as simply a humanitarian impulse. The paper proclaimed that French emancipationism was disinterested, for France had no "vast continent of India" to supply her with colonial products. "But what France intends to do for the rehabilitation of blacks, she must not accomplish at the expense of her own dignity. If we place questions of humaneness very highly, we place questions pertaining to our country even higher"; and France's honor had been tarnished by England's mutual search tactics. Speaking in terms reminiscent of the colonialist press, the daily now claimed that England had "a different cause to defend than that of the Negroes, her own cause," that of "her possessions in India."[54]

By the autumn of 1842 *Le Constitutionnel* was asserting that France had no ulterior motives in abolishing slavery and the slave trade but that the right-of-search controversy had raised up "public indignation" and shown Frenchmen that England was maneuvering only to further her own aims. Noting that the right-of-search conflict had caused a division in the debate on French emancipa-

53. *Le Constitutionnel,* February 25, 1841, January 6, 23, 1842.
54. *Ibid.,* May 5, 26, 1842.

tion, it now proclaimed its adherence to the government's objective of taking the necessary time to prepare slaves for liberty.[55] In 1844 the journal not only repeated this stance, but acquiesced in charges made by the Bordeaux press that the English had encouraged French abolitionists to send incendiary writings to the French West Indies; *Le Constitutionnel* agreed that for years the British had worked for the demise of France's colonial establishment for the benefit of India.[56] By 1845 the paper was insisting that Britain's advocacy of universal abolition was a "philanthropy which is at the same time a political system." *Le Constitutionnel* had come to assume that "France will postpone and adjourn all her generous projects if emancipation is spoken of not as a spontaneous, free act, but as satisfaction given to a foreign people."[57] This evaluation reflected the alteration that the right-of-search controversy had forged in the newspaper's mentality concerning emancipation and also, undoubtedly, in the minds of many Frenchmen in the 1840s.

Although the moderate republican *Le National* always maintained a love-hate relationship with Britain—applauding its liberalism but castigating its aristocracy—it, too, effusively praised British slave liberation in the 1830s and as late as 1841. After the outbreak of the right-of-search conflict, however, the daily's attitude also underwent an abrupt change. *Le National* now proclaimed that England cared little for the rights of humanity, that it had long meditated a plan "to sterilize the Americas for the profit of [India]." Simultaneously, this organ denounced rumors—which proved false—that the July Monarchy might abolish slavery as a concession to England, exclaiming that to do so would sully French honor. Instead, France must eliminate bondage on her own, for to "accomplish" this "under English injunction would be to stigmatize it forever" in French eyes.[58] By the mid-1840s the newspaper's perception of British intentions had darkened further. *Le National* now envisaged British antislavery as "a philanthropic mask" used by England to monopolize tropical commerce. Although the daily insisted that it was still favorable to emancipations it referred disparagingly to "the societies of agitators estab-

55. *Ibid.*, October 19, 29, 1842.
56. *Ibid.*, June 5, October 29, 1844.
57. *Ibid.*, February 6, March 29, 1845.
58. *Le National*, February 28, March 28, April 19, 1842.

lished in London with the avowed intention of stirring up the black race everywhere."[59] On another occasion the journal was kinder to British abolitionists, portraying them as mere dupes of the "peddlers of London" who exploited this "holy cause" for their own profit. As a whole, though, *Le National* had apparently become convinced that in abolishing slavery England simply wanted to provoke "a civil war in all the colonies" where slavery persisted.[60] From being an advocate of British philanthropy and slave liberation in general, this paper had evolved to a point at which deep suspicion of Britain's actions made its own commitment to abolition waver.

A similar evolution occurred in the attitude of *Le Siècle*. Such a development is highly significant, for this daily was a steadfast abolitionist organ, one of the first French newspapers to advocate immediatism rather than gradualism, a journal that opened its columns to such emancipationists as Tocqueville and Schoelcher. As soon as the right-of-search controversy broke out *Le Siècle* stressed its disdain for slavery and the slave trade but asserted that it had equal "aversion" for a nation that, "under the mask of humaneness," encroached on the rights of others. The newspaper subscribed fully to the theme that, while British abolitionists were well intentioned, the British government envisaged the repression of the slave trade as a means to maintain maritime and commercial hegemony, enabling it to develop its holdings in India. A few months later the daily reemphasized its conviction that the eradication of slavery and the slave trade was "a religious and moral act" for the English people, though the London government had its own objectives: to eliminate sugar and cotton production in the Americas and restrict freedom on the seas.[61] Concurrently, while continuing to underscore its own opposition to slavery, it indicated that "England, who has emancipated her slaves with ostentation, possesses white slaves in India about whom she does not speak." By the autumn of 1842 the newspaper was prepared to insist, on behalf of slave-owning nations, "that the right to emancipate [slaves] or retain them in servitude is one of internal sovereignty with which foreign countries cannot meddle."[62]

59. *Ibid.*, February 3, April 5, 1845.
60. *Ibid.*, August 22, 1844, February 21, 1845.
61. *Le Siècle*, January 4, February 7, May 10, 1842.
62. *Ibid.*, March 6, September 25, 1842.

Having recoiled from what it pictured as overbearing British proselytism, *Le Siècle* took pains to define its position on British antislavery. The organ explained that the London government had acquiesced to slave liberation when it could "no longer resist this religious and philanthropic movement which agitated England" but had then hastened "to exploit it for the advantage of its maritime supremacy." Motivated by a spirit of self-righteousness, the English cried out whenever anyone criticized mutual search procedures: "You do not want the abolition of the slave trade, you do not want the emancipation of blacks!" To this the daily replied on the part of Frenchmen: "We have been dupes of this phraseology for too long. We wish the freeing of the Negroes and the suppression of the slave trade with the most complete sincerity, but we wish to attain this goal without infringing upon the liberty of commerce and the independence of flags."[63] While retaining its abolitionism, already in 1842 *Le Siècle* was breaking with what it perceived as British policy on this issue.

The following year *Le Siècle* ran a series of anonymous articles by Tocqueville that were favorable overall to the British experience, showing that the paper, though open to divergent opinions, remained committed in principle to emancipationism. Still, the journal returned to its indictment of Britain's intentions in a major article printed in 1845, when the right-of-search debate again reached a crescendo in France. Elaborating on its earlier themes, it asserted that the English nation might honestly say it was acting selflessly concerning slavery and the slave trade but that the British government "would lie" in making such a claim. The London Cabinet had "merely a mediocre concern for the liberty of blacks" and a real interest only in its supremacy on the world scene. The newspaper now propounded that "veritable philanthropy has never played more than a secondary role in the determinations of England."[64] In another instance it referred to the "hypocrisy" of the British administration, which "covered its own ambition under the great principles of justice and humanity." *Le Siècle* also reasserted its position that the question of slave liberation was a French internal one to be decided only by the French Chambers.[65]

63. *Ibid.,* October 3, 1842.
64. *Ibid.,* March 22, July 17, 1845.
65. *Ibid.,* November 17, 1844, April 5, 1845.

The pro-abolitionist daily had become so jaundiced toward Britain that, on hearing rumors that Britain coveted Cuba, it expressed its preference for continued Spanish control of the island, even though it admitted that British occupation would have led to the destruction of Cuban slavery. The newspaper rationalized its stance by the specious argument that slavery in Cuba was "a fact" rather than "a principle" and that it would soon be abolished there anyway.[66] Le Siècle, undoubtedly like many Frenchmen, had become so alienated from Britain as a result of the right-of-search affair that it was prepared to see the universal antislavery movement receive a temporary reversal rather than accede to a move that might profit the British government.

This does not mean, of course, that Le Siècle, Le National, Le Constitutionnel, and other papers of pro-abolitionist tendencies abandoned the emancipation cause outright following the right-of-search episode or that all of the French press turned away from the British example. Indeed, certain adamant antislavery advocates, such as L'Abolitioniste français, the radical Réforme, and the marginal, Protestant Semeur, remained basically favorable to the British model even in the late 1840s.[67] Still, their devotion could not compensate in terms of opinion building for the wavering or desertion of such mass-circulation dailies as Le Constitutionnel and Le Siècle.[68] The crisis certainly tended to make many organs of public opinion wary of British philanthropy and, thus, cautious in their approach to the slavery question as a whole. In fact, the reaction against the right of search broke the increasing abolitionist momentum in France, which could have led the French movement more rapidly toward immediate emancipation. Without a doubt, by the mid-1840s the British example of slave liberation was being negated in most French eyes, even those of most abolitionists. These developments also dealt a severe blow to a French emancipa-

---

66. Ibid., February 20, 1845.

67. For Le Semeur, see Drescher, "Two Variants of Anti-Slavery," in Bolt and Drescher (eds.), Anti-Slavery, Religion and Reform, 53.

68. In 1846 Le Siècle published a daily average of 32,885 copies and Le Constitutionnel, 24,771, with Le National and La Réforme printing only 4,280 and 1,860 issues, respectively. For 1846 publication statistics on French newspapers, see Jean-Pierre Aguet, "Le tirage des quotidiens de Paris sous la Monarchie de Juillet," Revue suisse d'histoire, X (1960), 216–86. For an indication of how circulation had evolved by 1848, see Lawrence C. Jennings, "The Parisian Press and French Foreign Affairs in 1848," Canadian Journal of History, VII (1972), 119–47.

tionist organization whose historic ties to Great Britain were too close to deny or renounce, even if all French emancipationists had been willing to do so.

French humanitarian spokesmen were quite aware of the setback that the circumstances surrounding the right-of-search problem had inflicted on French antislavery efforts. Shortly after the outbreak of the crisis, Odilon Barrot made a prophetic statement in a speech delivered during the abolitionist meeting of March 9, 1842, attended by the British delegation. Although he defended British altruism, Barrot exclaimed at one point: "Let us take care not to confuse public sympathies for slave emancipation with the no less respectable susceptibilities of national honor. Our cause will gain nothing from such a conflict." He continued by warning his listeners that "to place sentiments of humanity in competition with national pride, to constitute a conflict between two noble passions, would not create a force favorable to the abolition of slavery, but raise up a great danger to it." Similarly, in the summer of 1842 Isambert informed Scoble, secretary of the BFASS from early 1842 to 1852, that "the vulgar confound" the slavery and slave trade questions, that "public opinion is everywhere in such a state that we dare not speak of the abolition of slavery."[69] Already at the beginning of the mutual search imbroglio French emancipationists were pointing out the interconnection between the slave trade repression and slave liberation questions, and predicting how the former would affect the latter.

By 1843 other abolitionists were confirming the realization of the process foreseen by Barrot and Isambert. In a booklet favorable to emancipation—albeit of the gradual variety—Dussillon still advocated following the British example but noted that the "tyrannical vexations" of England in connection with the right-of-search affair had turned public opinion in France against Great Britain. According to Dussillon, "the discussion of the right of search" had "profoundly irritated" French sentiment and augmented the "indifference" toward emancipation "which is unfortunately only too apparent" in France.[70] The following year Bissette, one of the few

69. Barrot's speech was reported in both *Le Siècle*, March 12, 1842, and Société française pour l'abolition de l'esclavage, *No. 19*, pp. 48–49; Isambert to Scoble, August 1, 1842, G103, Rhodes House Anti-Slavery Papers.
70. Dussillon, *Considérations sur l'esclavage*, 12–13, 104.

French proponents of immediatism in the early 1840s, corroborated Dussillon's observation that anti-British feeling had had a negative effect on French abolitionism. In a letter written to his British friend Scoble, he asserted that French statesmen "see everywhere [and] always the influence of England, and this absurd idea paralyzes the efforts" of French antislavery forces. Moreover, he observed, the French Cabinet, little inclined toward freeing slaves in the first place, took advantage of this situation to prolong servitude under the pretext of yielding to the pressure of justly indignant public opinion.[71]

In 1845 another emancipationist repeated these same contentions. Speaking in the Chamber of Peers, Count Auguste Arthur Beugnot insisted that "France no longer has the same dispositions concerning the liberation of slaves" as before. "Previously she quivered at the mention of emancipation, when one spoke of breaking the chains of slaves: today she only views this question with indifference, with disdain. To the contrary she is preoccupied with different thoughts. The right of search, opposition to the designs of England, that is what absorbs her entirely. In a sense the emancipation of slaves is placed on the *ad referendum* protocol, thrown back to another time."[72] As late as the spring of 1847 Bissette's new antislavery journal attributed the failure of French emancipation to the fact that defenders of slavery "deftly exploited the storm" caused by the right-of-search conflict to discredit the abolitionists, to mislead the public, and to deflect attention from the slavery issue.[73] Quite simply, the mutual search conflict was permitting French authorities to table the emancipation question.

Perhaps the most detailed analysis of the interworking of the problems of slavery and the repression of slave trade was made by the abolitionist Tracy when acting as a member of the Broglie Commission on slavery. While discussing the possibility of indemnifying slave owners, Tracy pointed out that compensation of this kind depended on the willingness of the French legislative bodies. He noted, however, that "one should not dissimulate the fact that the repugnance of the Chambers to launch into a costly system of

71. Bissette to Scoble, April 19, 1844, C13/117, Rhodes House Anti-Slavery Papers.
72. *Le Moniteur universel*, April 5. 1845.
73. *La Revue abolitioniste*, 53–54.

emancipation" would be "complicated henceforth by a political obstacle which appears, for some time now, to have taken on a serious character." He was referring to

> the actual state of feelings in the heart of the Chambers, concerning the questions of the slave trade and the emancipation of slaves, which find themselves connected with English policy. A visible reaction is manifesting itself against this policy, and, from a sort of infatuation with England, opinion seems to have passed to a repulsion which appears to be attached especially to everything which could resemble a consequence of the influence of England in [French] maritime and colonial issues. Ideas which seem called upon to prevail for a long time about what is referred to as British Machiavellianism perhaps are preparing veritable difficulties for the solution of the problem of slavery, and especially for the adoption of large and decisive measures.

Tracy believed that the opposition of the Guizot government to the voting of compensatory funds could eventually change, but "what will not be modified so easily, one must fear, is the estrangement of the public powers from every measure which could seem to be inspired by the example of England."[74] As Tracy astutely observed, the right-of-search conflict had caused such mass revulsion to British antislavery and anti–slave trade policies that Frenchmen could no longer envisage British slave liberation as a model worthy of imitation by France. Instead, French alienation from British abolitionism would strengthen the French government's resolve to approach the slavery problem slowly, cautiously, and gradually, to seek a French rather than English solution to the emancipation question.

74. Broglie Commission, Minutes, February 14, 1842.

SEVEN

REJECTION AND WANING OF
THE BRITISH EXAMPLE

In the early 1840s a variety of circumstances predisposed the French government to exploit for its own purposes the setback that the right-of-search controversy had dealt the abolitionists. In some ways the Soult-Guizot Cabinet followed in the footsteps of the Thiers ministry that preceded it in matters concerning slavery. Preoccupied with the Egyptian Crisis of 1840, the Thiers administration not only postponed the emancipation question by the appointment of the Broglie Commission to examine slavery, but also began to fortify Paris out of fear that war with a coalition led by the British could result in another invasion of France. Already in the 1830s navy and colonial ministry officials had believed that French budget deficits would make it impossible to compensate colonists and free the slaves. Now, the enormous expenditures associated with fortification building, combined with subsequent heavy government investment in railway construction, greatly indebted the French treasury and limited the possibility that the Thiers or Guizot Cabinets would augment this debt by funding the lesser priority of emancipation. Abolitionists themselves were keenly aware that "our financial situation imposes circumspection" on the authorities, that the Chambers were unlikely "to saddle themselves with a new tax to hasten" emancipation "while all their resources are engaged ten years in advance by the immense works which the fortification of Paris and the railroads necessitate."[1] These financial constraints, along with the firm

1. See statements by Paul de Gasparin in the Chambers (*Le Moniteur universel*, April 25, 1847) and Dussillon in his booklet (*Considérations sur l'esclavage*, 104–105).

commitment of the French navy and colonial ministry to gradualism, appear to have been long-term factors influencing French
slavery policy in the 1840s. Nevertheless, the mutual search problem also had undeniably important consequences on government
policy. Indeed, shortly before the outbreak of the dispute over this
issue, the Guizot administration—probably in an attempt to retain the initiative and head off further abolitionist demands—
seemed prepared to consider implementing slave liberation.

Evidence suggests that in 1841 the French government was still
entertaining the idea put forth by the navy and colonial department in 1839 of introducing an emancipation bill before the end of
the 1841 legislative session. In March, 1841, Guizot informed the
aged Clarkson that it was his Cabinet's "intention . . . to present
the outline of a law before the end of the present session which will
lay the foundation for this great measure," the abolition of slavery.[2]
In June of the same year Isambert expressed his conviction that the
navy and colonial minister, Duperré, was preparing an emancipation law.[3] The session ended on June 25, 1841, without such legislation having been introduced, perhaps because the Chambers had
been preoccupied during their last weeks with financial measures
to alleviate the huge deficits caused by military and defense spending. Emancipationist disappointment was so great that by the end
of 1841 both French and British antislavery circles had come to
suspect that the Guizot administration was actually encouraging
Broglie to buy time by prolonging his commission's deliberations.[4]
Undoubtedly because of what French abolitionists perceived as
procrastination by the government, in early 1842 the Société française pour l'abolition de l'esclavage made a decision that portended
renewed emancipationist pressure for freeing the slaves. Given the
government's apparent willingness during the period from 1839 to
the spring of 1841 to act on the slave liberation issue if obliged to do
so, it seems likely that the Guizot administration would have been
prepared to yield to persistent and concerted abolitionist demands
in 1842 if the mutual search crisis had not intervened.

In its session of January 5, 1842, the French abolition society
adopted a motion proposed by Odilon Barrot that French eman-

2. BFASS Minute Books, March 25, 1841.
3. Letter of Isambert to Tredgold, dated June 22, in *BFAS Reporter*, June 30, 1841.
4. *Le Constitutionnel*, December 19, 1841; *BFAS Reporter*, December 29, 1841.

cipationists deviate from their tradition of holding small closed-door meetings and organize instead a public antislavery assembly in Paris on March 7. At the same time the Société decided to invite foreign delegations to attend, just as the BFASS had done in its great London convention of June, 1840.[5] The French were obviously borrowing a page from their British brethren. When Isambert informed the BFASS of the Société's intentions and formally invited its attendance, British abolitionists "rejoiced at the decision to hold a [public] meeting in Paris," a procedure that had had such "good effects" in England. The BFASS was certain that this "must give a powerful impulse to the cause of [French] emancipation."[6] On both sides of the Channel it seemed clear that the French antislavery society had decided to alter its tactics and adopt the British approach of stirring up public sentiment through mass meetings.

In defending their actions later on, French abolitionists claimed that their invitation to the British had been made before they became aware of the Guizot government's agreement to the treaty of December 20, 1841, extending the right of search.[7] This assertion is belied by a letter from Isambert to Tredgold, who had preceded Scoble as secretary of the BFASS. The letter, dated January 6, 1842, and read in the BFASS meeting of January 11, made a precise reference to the search crisis. In fact, Isambert's missive suggested that British attendance might have a salutary effect, convincing French public opinion that England's "great work of emancipation . . . is not the result of the calculations of a government for the purposes of prejudicing the colonies of other nations, but simply a work of civilization and humanity." The Société deemed the moment especially propitious for a mass meeting because such a meeting might sway French voters in the summer elections to press for the eradication of slavery.[8] Perhaps French abolitionists had calculated that their British cohorts could actually help defuse the crisis in France by reassuring Frenchmen that they were not directly implicated in the search question—that, indeed, most

5. Société française pour l'abolition de l'esclavage, *No. 19*, p. 66.
6. *BFAS Reporter*, January 12, February 23, 1842; BFASS Minute Books, January 11, 1842.
7. Société française pour l'abolition de l'esclavage, *No. 19*, p. 66.
8. BFASS Minute Books, January 11, 1842.

British emancipationists now advocated the universal abolition of slavery as the only effective means of terminating the slave trade.[9] At the least, the French abolition society had not taken the search dispute seriously enough to believe it necessary to discourage British attendance at the March assembly, even after the controversy had reached its height in France. Although it might have been natural for French abolitionists to desire British assistance at an event that marked their espousal of British antislavery tactics, they had totally misjudged the effect the right-of-search incident, compounded by the presence of English emancipationists in Paris, would have on French attitudes toward slave liberation.

In late February, 1842, after a month and a half of uproar in France over the search affair, the Guizot Cabinet dashed abolitionist illusions about the holding of a mass meeting. It informed the Société that some "150 to 200 troublemakers" intended to disrupt the assembly by shouting "down with the English" and that it would be best not to hold a public gathering. The Société's executives, knowing perfectly well how the government operated, interpreted this as an outright ban on their meeting and canceled it. As the French emancipationists bitterly remarked, if the government had been prepared to tolerate the assembly it could have offered to provide the necessary security for it rather than encouraging its nullification.[10] Believing that the right-of-search conflict had dissolved any support the abolitionists might have had, the French administration evidently believed it could act with impunity in rebuffing the Société's initiatives. In effect, it had taken advantage of the right-of-search affair to quash an abolitionist maneuver that would have had the dual disadvantages of setting a precedent for French internal politics—in which public meetings were restricted—and presaging the formation of a mass-oriented, British-style French abolition society.

As British representatives were already in Paris to attend the assembly, they were invited instead to a private banquet on March 9 offered in their honor by their French hosts. One British emancipationist, Sturge, refused to participate in such a compromise and returned home in a huff.[11] As a whole, though, the British

9. Société française pour l'abolition de l'esclavage, *No. 19*, p. 67.
10. *Ibid.*, 67–69.
11. Temperley, *British Antislavery*, 186.

delegation was given a cordial reception by the French group; and, as already explained, the two abolitionist organizations exchanged pledges of support and admiration at their joint function. Still, the French abolition society now reverted to its former role as a small, quasi-parliamentary, largely elitist body that had little influence on the public. French emancipationists had not only been taught a lesson by their government but had also lost their best chance to transform themselves into an effective mass organization. In this sense, the right-of-search episode had enabled the government to deliver a blow to the antislavery movement that broke its initiative and set its development back several years.

French abolitionist spokesmen were well aware of the significance of their government's move and its impact on their association. *Le Siècle* exclaimed that the authorities had dropped their "mask of humanity" in banishing the assembly. An anonymous letter in the early June issue of the *BFAS Reporter* from a correspondent in Paris—in fact, Isambert—complained that the proscription of the public meeting had blocked massive conversions to the French antislavery cause. It continued by charging that the administration had obviously hoped to prevent the Société from going beyond the press in propagandizing its principles. Thus, the informant surmised, by his actions Guizot had "succeeded" in postponing the presentation of a draft law on emancipation for several legislative sessions. Two weeks later the British journal published another letter from its Paris contributor which pointed out that the French legislative session of 1842 had closed "in full re-action against emancipation," something which indicated "that [the French] government only desires to gain time, in order to disembarrass itself of the question."[12] In other words, the outbreak of the mutual search affair in late 1841 and early 1842 had provided an opportunity for the Guizot Cabinet to curtail the activity of the French abolition society and adjourn the emancipation question.

Other evidence besides the evaluations of abolitionists indicates that after the outbreak of the search crisis the French government began to consider rejecting entirely the rapid emancipation option advocated by the British. To begin with, in 1842 and 1843 the most important officials of the Ministry of the Navy and Colonies in

12. *Le Siècle*, March 3, 1842; *BFAS Reporter*, June 1, 15, 1842.

charge of matters related to slavery were replaced by procolonial advocates. Director of the Colonies Saint Hilaire, a conservative on the issue during most of the previous decade, had become more amenable to the idea of slave liberation by the late 1830s. In 1842, however, he retired; and a deputy from the Gironde and former *négociant* in Bordeaux, Joseph Henri Galos, was appointed to his office. A French correspondent of the British abolitionists, again probably Isambert, claimed that Saint Hilaire had become "favorable to emancipation" but had been "obliged to resign, in consequence of the dislike shown towards him, and of the impotency to which he was reduced, the [French] colonial offices being filled with men who are avowed adversaries of emancipation."[13] If this was the case, Galos was better suited than Saint Hilaire to function in the surroundings. Then, in 1843, the moderate Duperré was removed as minister, replaced temporarily by Admiral Roussin, and then replaced permanently by Admiral Mackau. The latter, the staunchest defender of slavery on the Broglie Commission, would control the navy and colonial portfolio from 1843 to the spring of 1847. As mentioned, Jubelin, another noted proponent of the colonial ideal, was also promoted—in 1844—to the high echelons of the bureaucracy, where he would serve as assistant to Mackau as undersecretary of state for the navy and colonial department. With this sort of entourage holding power in the navy and colonial ministry, it was apparent that a British approach to slave liberation had little chance of being considered seriously in France for some time.

This tendency away from rapid emancipation was confirmed by other developments in 1843 and 1844. The Broglie Commission finally issued its report in 1843, presenting the government with plans for both gradual and immediate abolition, though even the project for immediate emancipation called for a ten-year delay, to be followed by a five-year apprenticeship. The Guizot Cabinet, however, acted on neither of these proposals, for the Broglie Commission's report, like those of the Rémusat and Tocqueville Commissions preceding it, was merely a consultative study, which did not bind the administration. An utterance by Mackau in the Chamber of Deputies in 1844 indicates that the French government's inactivity on the slavery question in the early 1840s had

13. *BFAS Reporter*, April 20, 1842.

been directly encouraged by the search controversy. When Agénor de Gasparin questioned the minister as to why no moves had been taken toward slave liberation despite the appearance of the Broglie document, Mackau blurted out that, with the right of search still being debated, he was unprepared to discuss the emancipation problem because he "in no way expected" that "the question of the abolition of slavery" would be brought before the legislative tribune.[14] Bissette's organ went so far as to suggest that the government and the plantocrats had been in collusion in using the right-of-search controversy to concentrate attention on the slave trade issue to the detriment of the slavery issue.[15] What is certain is that the continuation of the mutual search dispute had precluded any immediate government action on emancipation.

The persistence of the abolitionists, who once again raised the question in the Chambers in May, 1844, afforded Guizot the opportunity to spurn once more the British precedent and laud the gradualist approach. Guizot declared that the English experience "leaves much to be desired," that France would proceed toward abolition by avoiding British "errors" and by achieving slave liberation with "better conditions" than those imposed by England. In other words, he claimed that France would improve on the British accomplishment. At the same time, he stressed the impossibility of seriously considering immediate emancipation.[16] Commenting on the French foreign minister's pronouncements, the pro-Guizot *Journal des débats* explained that France was working toward the freeing of slaves without committing the "errors" that had marked the record of "a rival nation." Even the abolitionist-oriented *Constitutionnel* now adopted this line. According to this newspaper, the English "had faced problems and disappointments which it is necessary to avoid; we should profit from their experience to act differently and better than they did."[17] Formerly fervent abolitionist spokesmen were now quite prepared to accept the institutionalization of the gradualist process.

In the session in which Guizot rejected the British example, his colleague Mackau supported him by tabling the Broglie Commis-

14. *Le Moniteur universel*, January 24, 1844.
15. *La Revue abolitioniste*, 54.
16. *Le Moniteur universel*, May 5, 1844.
17. *Le Journal des débats*, May 5, 1844; *Le Constitutionnel*, May 5, 1844.

sion proposals and announcing that he would present to the Chambers an amelioration plan to follow up and expand on the legislation passed in 1840. Although such a move implicitly acknowledged that this legislation had proved ineffective, Mackau introduced a draft bill on May 14, 1844, that called for measures guaranteeing the better treatment of slaves, providing for improved religious and primary education for blacks, and offering slaves the possibility to purchase their freedom. Not only would France not consider the sort of program passed by Britain in 1833, but the policy outlined by Mackau in the mid-1840s amounted to little more than the ameliorative plan the British colonial secretary, Lord Henry Bathurst, had—with little success—encouraged the British colonies to implement in 1823. According to the radical abolitionist Félice, the French project was not even as advanced as the British proposal of 1823, which had produced nothing of substance and no real improvement for British slaves.[18]

When the debate on the Mackau bill opened during the spring, 1845, legislative session, a diplomatic incident permitted French apostles of slavery to contend that even this gradualist approach had been inspired by Britain and was therefore unacceptable. In early 1845 a two-man Anglo-French commission had been appointed—with the abolitionists Stephen Lushington and Broglie representing their respective nations—to end the right-of-search impasse by finding an alternative means of repressing the slave trade. Their meetings in London eventually culminated in the bilateral treaty of May 29, 1845, by which mutual search procedures were replaced by an agreement calling for each country to police its own merchantmen off the slave coasts. In the midst of the negotiations, however, the British emancipationists, hoping to strike a blow against slavery throughout the world, issued a well-intentioned statement calling on their government to seize the opportunity to press for the freeing of the slaves in French possessions as a part of any settlement.[19] When Lushington did broach this matter in the course of the discussions, Broglie rapidly deflected the move by insisting that "the greatest harm of the right of search, in my opinion, was that as long as it continued, the words

18. Félice, *Emancipation immédiate et complète des esclaves*, 43–44.
19. BFASS Minute Books, February 7, 21, May 2, 1845.

abolition of slavery could no longer be pronounced" in France. He added that the best way to render emancipation "impossible" in his country was to make it in any way dependent on the right-of-search issue.[20] Once again a French official was bearing witness to the close negative relationship between mutual search and slave liberation in France.

French procolonial advocates, though, were unaware of their government's outright rejection of the London abolitionists' initiative; and when rumors about their overture began to spread in France, the colonial lobby seized upon it to menace Mackau's ameliorative proposals. General Cubières, who confessed in the Chamber of Peers on April 4 to be sympathetic to antiabolitionism—and who later was found guilty of corruption—suggested that the Paris government had been encouraged by the government in London to propose the Mackau bill. Another determined colonial advocate, the prince de Moskowa, intervened in support of Cubières by insisting that Mackau's legislation had originated as a concession to Britain. When the measure was discussed in the Chamber of Deputies a month and a half later, Jollivet also characterized the draft law as an allowance "made to appease the English government."[21] Mackau himself interjected to deny these charges by emphasizing that they were untrue, that his motions were tied to earlier deliberations in the Chambers, and that they were the culmination of a policy followed for years by the navy and colonial department. Nevertheless, four days later another procolonial orator, Berryer, again insinuated in the lower house that the proposal was of English inspiration, adding the timeworn accusation that Britain wished to ruin France's West Indian dependencies for the benefit of India.[22] The plantocratic attack on the Mackau bill was so great that even French abolitionists felt obliged to vote for it to save the legislation and at least bring about short-term improvements in the plight of colonial slaves.

The deliberations on the Mackau bill of 1845 afforded two French emancipationists another opportunity to invoke and defend the British achievement. Ledru-Rollin appealed to his fellow

20. Broglie to Guizot, March 19, 1845, in Guizot Papers, 42AP214, Archives Nationales.
21. *Le Moniteur universel,* April 5, May 30, 1845.
22. *Ibid.,* May 30, June 3, 1845.

deputies to "be just" and admit that English philanthropy had not been prompted by "a narrow and mean sentiment of rivalry." Montalembert also assured his countrymen that England was acting out of "the love of humanity."[23] Other abolitionists, however, made comments that, while appealing for slave liberation, implicitly acknowledged the anti-British accusations of the colonial party. Count Joseph Marie Portalis rose in the Chamber of Peers on April 8 to ask whether, even if England had been inspired by a combination of humanitarian and egotistical intentions in abolishing slavery, this would be reason for France to betray its noble mission of liberty and refuse to free its slaves for "irritating considerations of national rivalry." In late May, Agénor de Gasparin observed that, "when England achieves a just and good act, even if for selfish reasons, France should not renounce it."[24] Contentions of these kinds, while intended to assure passage of the Mackau law, show to what extent French abolitionists were on the defensive and alienated from the British position. Furthermore, they indicate that after the right-of-search controversy many emancipationists were prepared to rally to the government's gradualist approach.

The law of 1845 was passed by both Chambers and became the basis for French slavery policy for the remainder of the July Monarchy. British abolitionists correctly assessed the moderate nature of this legislation and the reversal it inflicted on the slave liberation cause in France. The *BFAS Reporter* congratulated Gasparin for the manner in which he "did justice to the results of the English abolition act" but bemoaned the fact that he had adhered to, and even supported, emancipation through "self-redemption," or the right of slaves to purchase their freedom. Indeed, the British abolitionist organ was highly critical of the entire Mackau law, a "measure of amelioration" rather than a "measure of emancipation," a "painful and miserable disappointment" that was totally "useless." It also expressed its "regret that the abolitionists of France can do nothing more effectual for the advancement of the great interests which are at stake."[25] French emancipationist support for the Mackau law, and the entire right-of-search episode, had

23. *Ibid.*, June 3, 1845; Montalembert's speech was reported in *La Réforme*, April 8, 1845.
24. *Le Moniteur universel*, April 9, May 31, 1845.
25. *BFAS Reporter*, April 16, June 25, 1845.

caused British and French antislavery forces to question and doubt each other.

Although British abolitionists despaired at times and issued occasional remarks that unwittingly must have further alienated their cross-Channel colleagues, during the 1840s the BFASS continued its somewhat sporadic efforts to inspire and assist the French movement. Despite the setback dealt the latter by the banning of its March, 1842, public assembly, British emancipationists also retained their basically optimistic attitude toward the situation in France. Perhaps encouraged by Isambert's letter of January 6, 1842, the British delegation to Paris profited from its attendance at the March 9 banquet by assuring Frenchmen of its disinterestedness. Thus, Forster proclaimed that "the principles of the English and Foreign [Anti-Slavery] Society are of a purely moral, pacific and religious nature; they have nothing to do with the right of search, which is an international governmental question." Members of the deputation also delivered an address, dated February 28, from the London society which guaranteed their hosts that "the abolitionists of Great Britain are animated neither by commercial considerations, nor by a desire of national aggrandizement."[26] Concurrently, the British used the occasion to spur on their cohorts toward immediatism. Addresses presented at the Paris gathering from the abolition societies of Southampton and Newcastle on Tyne invited Frenchmen to "reject an intermediary state" or gradualism and to move rapidly toward their goal, while the abolition society of Leeds called on French emancipationists to appeal to public opinion.[27] Even when the delegation returned to Britain its members attempted to dissimulate their dissatisfaction with the cancellation of the public assembly. The Reverend John Hinton reported that he and his fellow representatives had been cordially received by their French co-workers and that "notwithstanding their disappointment in regard to the public meeting, much good will be likely to result in forwarding the cause of universal emancipation."[28] Here, of course, Hinton was mistaken. The presence of British abolitionists in Paris during the midst of the search contro-

26. Société française pour l'abolition de l'esclavage, No. 19, pp. 5, 22.
27. Ibid., 27–29.
28. BFASS Minute Books, March 18, 1842.

versy had certainly been counterproductive and harmful to the French antislavery movement.

In fact, both British and French emancipationists apparently came to realize that it would be best during the height of the crisis to loosen their mutual ties. An examination of the BFASS Minute Books, along with comparable French documentation, indicates that abolitionists on both sides of the Channel seemed to become preoccupied with their own problems and less active in Anglo-French cooperative moves during the period from early 1842 through early 1844, a tendency that can only be attributed to the atmosphere created by the right-of-search conflict. To be sure, intercourse between the two groups did not cease. During the BFASS meetings of June 24 and July 8, 1842, the British organization stressed the need for strengthening abolitionism in France by "gaining access to the French periodical press"; on August 26, 1842, Scoble announced that he had received a private letter from Isambert; on March 31, 1843, a message was drafted for Clarkson to send to the Société; on August 4, 1843, Alexander spoke of perhaps visiting France as part of a continental tour; and on December 29, 1843, Forster read dispatches he had received from Isambert and "Odillon [sic] Barrot."[29] The entries concerning France in the BFASS Minute Books, though, are few in number and sparse in detail compared with those prior to March, 1842, and after the first months of 1845, when the British reacted to the introduction of the Mackau bill. In the late spring of 1842 the *BFAS Reporter* avowed its frustration with the July Monarchy's "course of re-action in relation to slavery," though in 1843 it recouped its spirits temporarily when it expressed its belief that the issuing of the Broglie Report might revive abolitionist initiative in France.[30]

During this same period many Frenchmen, as mentioned above, tended to feel that their best course lay in deemphasizing their British connections. It is noteworthy that only one delegate of the French abolition society, an uninfluential one, Amedée Thayer, arrived (and he was late) to attend the General Anti-Slavery Conference of 1843 in London, a meeting billed as a sequence to the

29. *Ibid.*, June 24, July 8, August 26, 1842, March 31, August 4, December 29, 1843.

30. *BFAS Reporter,* June 15, 1842, April 19, 1843.

World Anti-Slavery Convention of 1840. Thayer did not play an active role in the assembly, but a nondelegate, Léon Faucher, the liberal editor of *Le Courrier français*, who participated on a personal basis, spoke up—with Browning acting as interpreter—to express regret at the "alienation" between France and Britain and vouch for the sincerity of British intentions.[31] The French did not interrupt their contacts with their British associates at this time, for, as secretary of the Société, Isambert wrote regularly to his counterparts in the BFASS between 1839 and 1846, but the tenor of his messages altered noticeably. After the outbreak of the right-of-search dispute, his letters displayed a feeling of resignation and dejection about conditions in France, less interest in the situation in Britain and its colonies, and a tendency to blame Tory parliamentarians for supporting the Guizot Cabinet and thus encouraging "the anti-liberal system that weighs on us." In 1845, also, the frequency of Isambert's communications with London declined somewhat. When Scoble spoke with the French abolitionist in Paris in October, 1845, Isambert asked him to assure his British colleagues "that the best feelings existed on the part of himself and his friends toward their fellow labourers [the British], and that his silence had arisen from purely prudential motives."[32] Isambert's "prudential motives" were not specified in the BFASS minutes, but it seems most likely that they were related to the mutual search controversy and the French abolitionists' desire at this time to give the French public no excuse to identify them further with the British.

In 1844, however, British emancipationists once again saw signs of hope developing in France. Despite its discouragement about the tenor of the debates within the Broglie Commission, the *BFAS Reporter* remarked early in 1844 that news from France "is more cheering than any which has hitherto come into our possession." One cause for the journal's ebullience was the petition campaign "for entire and immediate abolition" launched by Parisian workers

31. *Ibid.*, June 14, 28, 1843; *Proceedings of the General Anti-Slavery Convention, Called by the Committee of the British and Foreign Anti-Slavery Society and Held in London, from Tuesday, June 13th, to Tuesday, June 20th, 1843* (1843; rpr. Miami, 1969), 195–96, 348.
32. Isambert to Scoble, July 29, 1844, G103, Rhodes House Anti-Slavery Papers; BFASS Minute Books, October, 1845 (according to Temperley [*British Antislavery,* 187–88], the exact date of this entry is October 17).

in 1844 through their journal *L'Union*. The *Reporter* estimated that such petitions would attract "not less than 10,000 names," a development "of special interest because it is a popular movement, and brings into action that very element which we have long deemed most useful, and wanting, to the advancement of the cause of abolition in France." Another point that pleased the *Reporter* was the appearance for the first time under the July Monarchy of a significant and regularly published emancipationist periodical, *L'Abolitioniste français*.[33] Indeed, the British were not foreign to the appearance of this publication, the official organ of the Société française pour l'abolition de l'esclavage. On June 13, 1845, the secretary of the BFASS, Scoble, informed his French equivalent, Isambert, that the British society would renew its subscription—indicating that a similar arrangement was already in effect—for 110 copies of "*L'Abolitioniste française* [sic]," 100 copies for distribution in France and 10 copies for forwarding to England, with Isambert being authorized to draw on the treasury of the British organization for the corresponding sum.[34] The aid that the British society furnished *L'Abolitioniste* had undoubtedly been critical for the founding of the journal, for when Scoble spoke to Isambert in France in the autumn of 1845 the latter "observed that [*L'Abolitioniste*] could now stand alone with the assistance afforded by the Society's subscription." Furthermore, in 1844 the BFASS paid the Paris publishers Firmin Didot £584.45 for the publication of 2,000 copies of the French version of a pamphlet by Alexander and Scoble, *Liberté immédiate et absolue ou esclavage. Observations sur le rapport de M. le duc de Broglie . . . adressées à tous les Français*.[35] The British had become actively involved in assisting French abolitionism by subsidizing its publications.

Increased British abolitionist involvement with France also manifested itself in other ways. For one thing, British emancipationists redoubled their missions to France. For another, the British, increasingly disappointed with the accomplishments of the Société française pour l'abolition de l'esclavage, began to seek con-

---

33. *BFAS Reporter*, February 7, May 29, 1844. The *Reporter*'s optimism was misplaced, for the petitions of 1844 drew less than 10,000 signatures and were isolated occurrences that were not followed up in any significant way until 1846–47.

34. BFASS Minute Books, June 13, 1845.

35. *Ibid.*, October 4, [17], 1845.

nections with and offer encouragement to other antislavery elements in France more favorable to immediatism. Both of these processes emerged in 1844 and 1845.

In March, 1844, the secretary and the treasurer of the BFASS, Scoble and Alexander, visited France, arranged for the publication of their booklet, and made numerous contacts, especially with lawyers, Catholic clergymen, and men of letters who might be prepared to issue treatises advocating immediate emancipation.[36] On March 29 the two executives of the BFASS joined with Forster and Joseph Gurney in organizing a meeting with more than fifty leading French abolitionists at the *hôtel* Bedford on the rue Saint-Honoré in Paris. Here Gurney harangued the group for over an hour about the need for complete and immediate slave liberation based on the principle that slavery was contrary to the fundamental precepts of Christianity.[37] Also in 1844 Gurney, using as intermediaries the Toulousan Protestant banker brothers F. L. and A. Courtois, approached Guillaume de Félice of the Protestant faculty of Montauban in southern France. Gurney suggested that Félice become the British society's "agent for the abolition of slavery in France." Although Félice did commit himself to producing antislavery pamphlets on a part-time basis, he was compelled to decline Gurney's proposition because of his heavy teaching schedule.[38] Evidently, the BFASS was attempting to establish close ties with French emancipationists of the Protestant faith who were disenchanted with gradualism and who might bring to the French cause the same fiery conviction that had marked British Evangelicalism.[39]

The expansion of the BFASS's overture to French abolitionists was underlined again in December, 1844, when the British organi-

36. *BFAS Reporter,* May 29, 1844.
37. Reported in *Le Lien* (Paris), April 6, 1844.
38. Félice to F. L. and A. Courtois, C157/66, Rhodes House Anti-Slavery Papers. The best discussions available so far on the participation of Protestants in the French abolitionist movement are those by Tudesq, *Les grands notables,* and Drescher, "Two Variants of Anti-Slavery," in Bolt and Drescher (eds.), *Anti-Slavery, Religion and Reform,* 43–63.
39. Most recent analyses of the British abolitionist movement stress the role played by religion. See in particular, however, besides the study by Drescher, "Two Variants of Anti-Slavery," two articles by Roger Anstey: "Religion and British Slave Emancipation," in Eltis and Walvin (eds.), *The Abolition of the Atlantic Slave Trade,* 37–61; and "Parliamentary Reform, Methodism and Anti-Slavery Politics," *Slavery and Abolition,* II (1981), 209–26.

zation decided to send its yearly letter encouraging universal emancipation, not only to the Société française pour l'abolition de l'esclavage, but to important individuals, such as Gasparin and Ledru-Rollin. Then, during a London meeting on June 6, 1845, after the right-of-search problem had been resolved, a French abolitionist, Caillet, lectured the BFASS about the state of the antislavery cause in France, "the necessity of employing the press to advance it," and the particular need for British philanthropists to visit his country.[40] The termination of the mutual search controversy, along with the institutionalization of gradualism in France through the Mackau law of 1845, had obviously convinced British and some French abolitionists that the time had come for a new emancipationist offensive. When the BFASS issued its annual message of encouragement to Frenchmen on February 6, 1846, to coincide with the opening of the French legislative session, it referred to the law of 1845 as "thoroughly objectionable in principle" and declared that now that the search dispute had ended, "the general question of abolition can be discussed with calm, and at the same time with all the seriousness that its great importance requires."[41] British emancipationists were again acknowledging the pernicious effect the crisis had had upon French abolitionism and at the same time were hoping for a renewal of French antislavery initiative now that the issue had been settled.

In the meantime, in July, 1845, a leading British abolitionist, Forster, had again visited France, this time with his wife. Upon his return, he reported with apparent disappointment to the BFASS that "it appeared that [French] Anti-Slavery operations are mostly confined to Paris and that great ignorance exists in the provinces relating to the question." Forster was underscoring the ineffectiveness of the French emancipationists' efforts and their total lack of a provincial organizational network on the British model. He added, however, that there were "encouraging circumstances which led him to conclude that Anti-Slavery exertions in the provinces would be well repaid," for he expected the General Council of the Meurthe et Moselle department to take up the question at its next meeting. Apparently the British were unaware

40. BFASS Minute Books, December 20, 1844, June 6, 1845.
41. *L'Abolitioniste français*, 2ᵉ livraison, 1846; *BFAS Reporter*, April 1, 1846.

that several French departments, though not Meurthe et Moselle, had called for emancipation in their annual statement of "wishes" [*voeux*] to the administration in Paris from 1836 on, without these moves' having had any discernible effect on French government policy. Once again, then, and despite their numerous contacts, the British were demonstrating that they were still quite ignorant of happenings in France concerning slavery. Nevertheless, at the end of the same session of the BFASS, the secretary of the organization mentioned the possibility of journeying to Montauban; and he was encouraged to do so by the society.[42] A month later, when elaborating further on his plans, Scoble announced that he definitely would visit southern France, seeking an interview with Isambert along the way.[43] The British were vigorously pursuing their policy of traveling to the Continent to make contacts with their French counterparts.

During the October, 1845, meeting of the BFASS Scoble reported in detail on his trip to France. He had spent three days in Paris collecting information on the Mackau law and two days at Isambert's country residence, where the latter explained to him the reasons for French emancipationist support for passage of the 1845 legislation. He then went for nine days to the Protestant stronghold of Montauban, spending most of his time with "M. de Félice, Professor of Moral Philosophy," the emerging abolitionist contacted the previous year by Gurney. While in Montauban, Scoble discussed emancipationism with Félice, "setting the ground upon which it shall henceforth be based by himself and his friends, viz., that slavery is a crime before God and ought therefore to be abolished." Scoble recounted: "On this subject [Félice] will prepare a pamphlet forthwith. After which an attempt will be made to organize Committees on that principle." Following his visit to Montauban, Scoble stayed four days in Toulouse "and was promised the hearty co-operation of the Courtois frères," owners of the most important bank in that city—and still one of the leading Toulousan banking institutions today—"who rejoice that the question will now be placed on the right ground." Next Scoble spent one day in Saverdun, near Toulouse, carrying on discussions

42. BFASS Minute Books, July 4, August 1, 1845. For earlier statements by French general councils, see Gén. 156 (1301), ANSOM.
43. BFASS Minute Books, September 5, 1845.

with certain pastors, but especially with M. Laurens, "an influential member of the *Consil général* of Lot and Garonne [department], who will also lend his best assistance to the cause." Scoble related that he ended his trip to France with short excursions to Bordeaux and Nantes, being "promised the aid of Pastor Laharpe" at the former city and meeting with other pastors in the latter.[44] After having encouraged Frenchmen to adopt the British tactics of public meetings, petitioning, and pamphlet writing in an attempt to mobilize French opinion, the British were now advising their co-workers to stress the religious message that had proved so successful in Great Britain.

In recounting the details of his French trip, Scoble insisted that "at the several places" at which he had sojourned he had had the opportunity

> of meeting at private soirées many influential persons . . . all of which will co-operate on the ground of immediate and entire emancipation. The plan proposed is first to issue M. de Félice's pamphlet, then to organize, and afterward, to move the Protestant Consistorie [*sic*] and the *conseils-généraux* throughout France to petition the Chambers, and then by a succession of well-written and judicious pamphlets to awaken every portion of society to take an interest in the question, to accomplish which the friends of the Anti-Slavery cause in France will require the cordial sympathy and generous support of the Abolitionists in Great Britain.[45]

In his report Scoble gave the impression that he had almost single-handedly managed to establish a parallel abolitionist organization in France that would work toward the British principle of immediate slave liberation without indemnity. The British had not yet realized that without an efficient indigenous religious or organizational network in France to support such a hastily imposed structure it could not possibly succeed.

During the next two years the BFASS continued to assist individual French emancipationists inclined toward immediatism. When the British society heard in the spring of 1846 that the booklet Scoble had solicited from Félice, *Emancipation immédiate et complète des esclaves. Appel aux abolitionists* [*sic*], had been finished and was being published, it proposed to pay Félice's ex-

44. *Ibid.*, October [17], 1845.
45. *Ibid.*

penses for drawing up an address "to the electoral bodies of France" in favor of abolition. A year and a half later Forster personally offered to defray the costs of a new edition of Félice's pamphlet aimed at a wider audience.[46] Then, in December, 1846, the London group noted that Bissette was circulating petitions for "immediate and entire abolition" in Paris but that he "was straitened for want of funds in procuring signatures in the country districts." Accordingly, it proceeded "to vote him the sum of ten pounds to be applied to that purpose." A month later Bissette acknowledged receipt of the ten pounds and "strongly recommended . . . the support of a new periodical" he was founding, "the *Revue abolitioniste* to be devoted to the cause of immediate emancipation to which Professor de Félice and others had promised their assistance." Consequently, Forster proposed, and the committee adopted, a motion that three hundred pounds be devoted to that monthly for the next three months.[47] Little did Forster and his colleagues realize that Bissette's new *Revue* would publish only the three issues directly subsidized by the British before folding, a clear indication that the French immediatist cause still had scant popular support in France in the spring of 1847.

Obviously pleased with the founding of another French emancipationist journal, the BFASS also made a new overture to the Société française pour l'abolition de l'esclavage, "urging upon them the importance of moving upon the principle of immediate and entire abolition." Following these same lines, Forster visited Paris and encouraged "Paul de Gasparin—brother of Agénor—and Gustave de Beaumont . . . to prepare a pamphlet containing the substance" of the latest debates in the French Chambers on emancipation for distribution to the General Councils of the departments. This was viewed as a means to appeal for the support of these bodies when they next assembled, in October. At the same time, Forster met with Dutrône and Lutheroth, the former an official of the French abolition society, the latter a long-standing member. While reporting to London the heartening news that Dutrône "spoke approvingly of" Bissette—giving the impression that cooperation was possible between the Société and the imme-

46. *Ibid.*, April 24, 1846; Félice to Scoble, December 8, 1847, C157/70, Rhodes House Anti-Slavery Papers.
47. BFASS Minute Books, December 18, 1846, January 22, 1847.

diatists—Forster also displayed evident dismay "that the French Committee [the Société] met but rarely."[48] By late 1847 Bissette had "drawn upon" the BFASS for twelve pounds to defray "expenses" incurred in issuing four other petitions and had been granted an additional thirty pounds to enable him to travel to the provinces.[49] Indeed, it appears that by 1847 the BFASS had forged closer ties with the Bissette-Félice faction of French emancipationists than with the Société française pour l'abolition de l'esclavage.

An examination of the letters that both Félice and Bissette sent to the BFASS indicates that as time went on the ties the two men established with the London society tended increasingly to become those of financial dependency. After having willingly accepted British subsidies in the mid-1840s, in 1846 Félice advocated a concerted effort by the British society to seek out French abolitionists and financially assist the publication and distribution of their works. Not only did the British organization not follow up on this, but Félice's suggestion appears to have soured his relationship with London; by 1847 Félice was complaining about having had no word from his British benefactors "for a long time."[50] Similarly, from 1840 to 1847 Bissette constantly pestered the BFASS to defray his travel or publication costs, either in the form of outright grants or through the sale of subscriptions. Already in 1840 and 1841 Bissette's urgent pleas for widespread aid from the British abolitionists for the publication of his *Revue des colonies*—which ultimately ceased appearing in 1842, apparently for lack of funds—elicited only a disappointing 50-franc subscription each from Sturge and Alexander. As the decade progressed, the British continued to accord Bissette some of the financial assistance he solicited, but at times they granted it grudgingly; and by 1847 Bissette too was bemoaning the fact that the British were no longer corresponding with him as regularly as previously.[51] Evidently the BFASS, while generous in supporting the French emancipationists, had limits to its liberality and had hoped that its French counter-

48. *Ibid.*, January 22, June 26, 1847.
49. *Ibid.*, August 27, December 10, 1847.
50. Félice to [Scoble], July 21, 1846, May 8, 1847, C157/68, 69, Rhodes House Anti-Slavery Papers.
51. See the entire series of exchanges between Bissette and Scoble spanning the period 1840–47 in C13/110-27 and C5/44-49, *ibid.*

parts would show more initiative in developing their own sources of funding. The repeated requests for financial assistance by Félice and Bissette demonstrated, not only their financial dependence upon the British, but the extent to which the immediatist French abolitionists lacked a basis for support within their own country.

Forster's negative assessment of the French abolitionist society, along with the financial difficulties of the Bissette-Félice faction, must have shaken somewhat the general optimism of British emancipationists about their ability to advance the antislavery ideal within France. There were other reasons, too, for the BFASS to feel dejected about the course of developments in France between 1845 and 1847. The *BFAS Reporter* displayed increased disillusionment as it came to realize that the French government was acting with extreme slowness even in implementing the ameliorations provided for by the Mackau law. As explained, already in June, 1845, the British journal had denounced the Mackau bill as useless. When the first ordonnances implementing some of the measures outlined by the legislation were published in early November, 1845, "after four month's delay," the *Reporter* exclaimed that "we do not hesitate to say that a more contemptible juggle was never played off upon a people or upon a legislature, even by the most eminent professors of the art of thimble-rig." The abolitionist organ explained that the ordonnances covered only part of the legislation, and this "in a manner miserably mean and unsatisfactory. The tendency of the ordinances is rather to obstruct the redemption of slaves than to promote it, rather to consolidate the system of slavery than to break it up. They might have been drawn up by M. Jollivet himself," for they "indicate the prevalence in the Cabinet of the very spirit by which he is animated." The *Reporter* charged that Mackau had completely forgotten his promises and that his actions were "nothing short of a deliberate insult to the French Chambers and the French nation." The newspaper was so infuriated that it totally lost its composure with the outburst that Mackau "is not an honest man, but a man of trick and trickery," whose words were "a studied effort to deceive." Besides, it added, "the whole French government" was "implicated in his hypocrisy and deceitfulness." In the journal's opinion, "it is now too plain that the 'rulers' of France do not mean to abolish colonial slavery." It hoped, though, that French emancipationists would call Mackau "to a rigorous account."[52] In the late summer of 1847 the *Reporter* was more persuaded than ever that the "schemes of amelioration" adopted by the July Monarchy "amount almost to nothing."[53] Although despairing about the situation, the BFASS obviously hoped that French abolitionists would challenge their government and force it to alter its ways.

Active British support for the antislavery movement in France during the years 1844 through 1847 had had some undeniably positive results. British financial aid had certainly assisted the French abolitionist publications *L'Abolitioniste français* and *La Revue abolitioniste* during the difficult early stage of their development, though the initial steps in their foundation had been taken by Frenchmen. British intervention also had evidently encouraged Félice's actions and facilitated Bissette's participation in the petition campaign, albeit both men had already been active emancipationists before Scoble's visit and had not been converted to the cause by British endeavors. That the British strategy of petitioning had inspired French abolitionists in their own somewhat limited petition campaigns is certain. In referring to the petitions, *L'Abolitioniste français* acknowledged this in asserting that in France, "as in England, it will be necessary for the government to act, when here, as in England, the voice of the people will have proclaimed its all powerful will." On another occasion, too, the periodical invoked the British precedent, pointing out that the English had obtained slave liberation through petitions and that the French could do the same.[54] Still, it should be noted that it was primarily disenchantment with the Mackau law, rather than proddings from the British, that inspired Frenchmen to undertake the petition campaigns of 1846 and 1847. In fact, the French had already petitioned against slavery on a much more limited basis in the 1830s and 1840s, with little consequence. The British, then, had been helpful in encouraging French abolitionists behind the scenes. Obviously, Britain's public image had been so tarnished in France by the right-of-search affair that any substantial amount of open, well-publicized intervention by the British would have proved counterproductive in the 1840s.

52. *BFAS Reporter*, November 12, 1845.
53. *Ibid.*, September 1, 1847.
54. *L'Abolitioniste français*, 6e livraison, 1846, 6e livraison, 1847.

In some ways, though, British exhortations to the French had come to naught. Scoble's hopes for forming other committees throughout the provinces on the principle of immediatism were never realized. The Société française pour l'abolition de l'esclavage remained the only significant abolitionist organization in France until the end of the July Monarchy, despite the emergence of an embryonic daughter society in Lyon by 1847 and the existence of the loosely connected Félice-Bissette coalition and a small circle around Schoelcher. British hopes to stimulate the formation of a Protestant antislavery network never materialized in France because of the small number of Protestants. Without a Protestant infrastructure on the British model to organize opinion and press for immediatism, British exhortations to stress the unholy nature of slavery also fell short in France. Furthermore, there is no evidence indicating that British efforts to persuade French departmental councils to call for an end to slavery had any measurable effect on either these bodies or the Paris government. Even the petition campaigns on which the British placed so much hope did not result in petitions numerically important enough to sway the authorities. As a recent study has shown, in England one adult in five signed petitions for emancipation, while in France not one in a thousand did so in 1847.[55] The British might have flattered themselves about stimulating and assisting abolitionism in France, but the French movements never received nearly as much support as their British counterparts. In spite of British efforts, an effective abolitionist mobilization never occurred in France, and therefore emancipationism had little success in influencing French slavery policy profoundly prior to 1848.

British disappointment with the course of developments in France during the period 1845 through 1847 was certainly compounded by what the BFASS perceived as the shortcomings of the Société française pour l'abolition de l'esclavage. In the spring of 1846 the British organization sent an address to the French society prodding it again to opt for immediatism. In reply, the Paris group simply stated that "we are perfectly well aware of the inefficiency of the legislative enactments passed in the Sessions of 1845" and of "the means that are adopted to elude them." The Société added

55. Drescher, "Public Opinion and the Destruction of British Slavery," in Walvin (ed.), *Slavery and British Society*, 26–29.

that it was collecting facts "to prove to the legislature" that the situation facing slaves was worsening rather than improving. It pledged to continue "our task until the final triumph of the holy cause we have embraced with you," though it warned that "we have to contend against great obstacles."[56] As late as 1846 the Paris group was still bound to its policy of acting through the press and legislature to persuade the government to alter its course on the slavery question. Moreover, despite Dutrône's kind words to Scoble concerning Bissette, the black emancipationist complained to Scoble in January, 1847, about the uncooperative attitude of the French abolition society, a body that he said had afforded him no "assistance," "encouragement," or even "moral support" in his efforts to circulate immediatist petitions.[57] Racial or class bias also seems to have broadened the chasm between Bissette and the Société, for Gustave de Beaumont explained to a British antislavery advocate in 1844 that Bissette was not a member of the abolition society because "he is a colored man!" According to Félice, the Société had even made "negative reports" to the BFASS about Bissette, something that might have contributed to the estrangement between the London organization and the free man of color by the late 1840s.[58] The continuing disunity between French abolitionists was also fostered by the exclusive, legalistic approach of the Société and its preference for operating through its established channels.

All of this must have intensified British exasperation with the French abolition society, influencing the *BFAS Reporter* to issue a rather curt evaluation of the French organization in the late summer of 1847. Describing the Paris association as being formed by the "most eminent statesmen and philanthropists," the *Reporter* outlined the history of the Société and remarked: "They did not, however, organize on the principle of immediate and entire abolition—in fact they had no plan, at least they never presented one to the Chambers—but they provoked frequent discussions there, and were instrumental in circulating a large amount of information on the subject of slavery, and of exhorting from the Government and

56. *L'Abolitioniste français*, 2e livraison 1846; *BFAS Reporter*, April 1, 1846.
57. Bissette to Scoble, January 19, 1847, C13/119, Rhodes House Anti-Slavery Papers.
58. Quoted in Drescher, *Dilemmas of Democracy*, 163; Félice to [Scoble], December 8, 1847, C157/70, Rhodes House Anti-Slavery Papers.

the Chambers a decision that slavery ought and must be abolished."[59] The *Reporter* had accurately defined the Société as an elitist group acting through parliament and the printed page, with at best a nebulous policy of its own. Less than a year before the Revolution of 1848 overthrew the July Monarchy and brought an abrupt end to slavery, the French abolition society had not reached the organizational or theoretical stage its British counterpart had attained in 1831.

Some signs of change were noticeable, however, within the Société française pour l'abolition de l'esclavage during the last year of Louis Philippe's reign. The organization rallied to and supported the petition campaign of early 1847, which had been animated by Bissette; and by the end of the year, it had drafted its own petition for circulation.[60] An indication of the factors influencing French abolitionists to reconsider their position was given when Paul de Gasparin, a member of the Société, presented a petition in the Chamber of Deputies in the spring of 1847 advocating immediate emancipation. Gasparin proclaimed his agreement with the petitioners: preparatory measures had proved unsuccessful in England's colonies; the laws of 1845 demonstrated that amelioration was not working in France's establishments; and now the French government should move rapidly toward slave liberation.[61] In the meantime, in January, 1847, the BFASS had sent its usual address to the Paris organization to encourage it to adopt immediatism. It is noteworthy that this time the French body did not reply forthwith, an indication that it was either too preoccupied, too disorganized, or too undecided to do so. When in September it finally made its response—shortly after the *BFAS Reporter* had printed its critical history of the Société—the BFASS had reason to rejoice. The letter to London from Dutrône, now secretary, and Passy, first vice-president, not only denounced the inefficiency of the "measures . . . adopted by the French Chamber and Government to ameliorate the condition of the slaves" but announced that after long hesitation the Société had adopted immediate and complete emancipation as its goal. Apparently it was their disappointment

---

59. *BFAS Reporter*, September 1, 1847.
60. Félice to [Scoble], December 8, 1847, C157/70, Rhodes House Anti-Slavery Papers.
61. *Le Moniteur universel*, April 25, 1847.

with the 1845 legislation and the support it still received that determined most French abolitionists to espouse immediatism, not the exhortations from their British cohorts to do so. Nevertheless, the BFASS was finally able to express its "great satisfaction," its "great pleasure" concerning French developments.[62]

In fact, though, the apparent victory of the British approach amidst French abolitionists was a shallow one. Opposition to emancipationism in France and especially to immediate abolitionism on the British model was still very evident. That the stronghold of this opposition was now within the Chamber of Peers became clear in March, 1847, when this body refused to consider petitions for simultaneous slave liberation. Although Montalembert defended immediatism during the debate in the upper house, Beugnot, the moderate abolitionist reporter on the petitions, reminded his audience that their nation had rejected England's procedure of setting a date for emancipation and providing for an indemnity; instead, France was firmly committed to the policy of improving the position of slaves and preparing them for freedom. While the Chamber of Peers supported the Mackau law, the Chamber of Deputies adopted a different, though somewhat ambiguous, stand on the matter when it discussed the petitions and abolitionism later in the spring. The deputies adopted a resolution proposed by the reporter of their commission on the petitions, Paul de Gasparin, which suggested that the government go beyond the 1845 legislation and fix a time and conditions for emancipation.[63] Such a resolution delivered an oblique criticism of current government policy, but even the abolitionists did not consider this a triumph.[64] For its part, the Guizot ministry, unmoved by the Chamber of Deputies' resolution, proclaimed its intention to abide by the Mackau legislation and give it more time to produce favorable effects.[65] By the autumn of 1847 the majority of French abolitionists might have opted for the essentials of the British system, but they still did not have the popular support that could have enabled them to impose rapid slave liberation on the authorities.

62. BFASS Minute Books, October 1, 1847; L'Abolitioniste français, 5ᵉ livraison, 1847; BFAS Reporter, December 1, 1847.
63. Le Moniteur universel, March 31, April 25, 27, 1847.
64. L'Abolitioniste français, 2–4ᵉ livraison, 1847.
65. Le Moniteur universel, March 31, April 25, 27, 1847.

In sum, they had been singularly unsuccessful in winning over the French government to their point of view. In contrast, a significant proportion of the colonial lobby saw eye to eye with the administration on matters relating to emancipation.

Although they had opposed the Mackau law when it was being discussed by the Chambers, following its adoption many colonial spokesmen rallied behind it, fully realizing that it posed no imminent menace to slavery. Thus, the colonial council of Martinique wrote to the king in early 1848 to repeat the much-used argument that the English solution had been a disaster even with greater preparation for slaves than that now prevailing in France's holdings. Dupin also reminded the navy and colonial minister that the Broglie Commission had stressed the difference between the French and British situations and that French dependencies were not nearly as well prepared for freeing the slaves as the English ones had been.[66] Although it is difficult to sound the French government's reaction to these colonial entreaties, it seems that they merely reinforced the navy and colonial department's stance on slavery. Despite the fact that Mackau was replaced as minister by Napoléon Lannes, duc de Montebello in 1847, the Ministry of the Navy and Colonies was evidently as wary as ever of emancipation in the British style.

In this respect, a colonial newspaper, L'Avenir de Pointe-à-Pitre, reported that at a dinner with some colons in the autumn of 1847, Galos, director of the colonies since 1842, remarked that England's "great error" had been to abolish slavery without sufficient preparation for her slaves.[67] This testimony, added to the general tenor of government policy, indicates that Montebello and his subordinates were still firmly committed to Mackau's gradualist program. In fact, the Guizot ministry's attitude toward slave liberation would not change measurably until the Revolution of 1848 overthrew the July Monarchy in late February and established the Second Republic.

The February Revolution brought to power as members of the Provisional Government such abolitionists as François Arago (navy and colonial minister), Lamartine (foreign minister), Ledru-

66. Colonial Council of Martinique to King Louis Philippe, January 8, 1848, in Gén. 173 (1388), Dupin to Minister, May 4, 1846, in Gén. 192 (1499), ANSOM.
67. November 3, 1847, in Gén. 170 (1375), ANSOM.

Rollin, Crémieux, and Etienne Joseph Louis Garnier-Pagès. They almost immediately followed Schoelcher's advice—Schoelcher himself had been appointed undersecretary of state in the navy and colonial ministry and placed in charge of the colonies—and announced the formation on March 4 of a commission "to prepare in the shortest possible delay . . . immediate emancipation in all the colonies of the Republic."[68] This commission, presided over and completely dominated by Schoelcher in person, worked with determination and zeal to eradicate slavery completely from the French colonies. A thorough perusal of the minutes of this body's meetings demonstrates that Schoelcher and his associates based their decision to liberate the slaves on their own republican principles and their recognition of the failure of the July Monarchy's policies rather than on the British precedent. The commission did cite problems with British apprenticeship when rejecting outright this option; and when colonial spokesmen testified before it, the debate was resumed over the extent to which British abolition had interfered with production. Sturge and Alexander also appeared before the commission on March 13 to encourage it to proclaim emancipation as soon as possible. In reality, though, the commission made scant reference to the British example.[69] Brief mention of Britain can be found on only 18 of the 302 printed pages of its minutes; in the commission's attached 8-page report, no mention whatsoever of Britain is made. At this time of revolutionary innovation and republican idealism the British antislavery example seemed distant indeed. In this sense, the decision to eradicate slavery in 1848 was more analogous to the French move of 1794 than to the British act of 1833.

Schoelcher's commission labored less than two months before presenting the government with a decree, promulgated on April

---

68. *Le Moniteur universel*, March 5, 1848. For analyses of French slave liberation in 1848, see Gaston Martin, *L'abolition de l'esclavage, 27 avril 1848* (Paris, 1948); Emile Tersen, "La commission d'abolition de l'esclavage, 4 mars–21 juillet 1848," *Actes du congrès historique du centenaire de la Révolution de 1848* (Paris, 1948), 295–301; Jacques Adélaïde-Merlande, "La commission d'abolition de l'esclavage," *Bulletin de la Société d'histoire de la Guadeloupe*, nos. 53–54 (1982), 3–34; Léo Elisabeth, *L'abolition de l'esclavage à la Martinique* (Fort-de-France, 1983); and M. A. Fisher-Blanchet, "Les travaux de la commission d'indemnité coloniale en 1848," *Espaces caraïbes*, I (1983), 37–56.

69. *Procès-verbaux, rapports et projets de décrets de la commission instituée pour préparer l'acte d'abolition immédiate de l'esclavage* (Paris, 1848), 5, 18, 24, 27, 49.

27, that called for the complete and immediate abolition of slavery. Accordingly, servitude ceased in all of the French colonies before the end of 1848. The indemnity for slave owners, however, was not announced by the government until the spring of 1849. It proved to be much less generous than the British one, granting 126 million francs for the 248,560 French colonial slaves—including a few thousand in Senegal—or an average of approximately 507 francs per slave, even though the commission had calculated that the real value of a slave in 1848 was 1,085 francs.[70]

Already in the spring of 1848 French republicans were pointing with pride to their accomplishment of immediate slave liberation. Lamartine was finally able to tell Sturge and Alexander, when he met with them in Paris in March, that "we congratulate ourselves on being . . . in harmony with the noble sentiments of England, which a long time ago freed the black race in her colonies." That the British were highly pleased with the French achievement is evident. The *BFAS Reporter* exclaimed early in April that it was "delighted" with the "marvelous events" in France.[71] On receiving a copy of the French emancipation decree the BFASS sent an address to the minister of the navy and colonies, Arago, expressing "the gratification of the [British antislavery] Committee at this noble act of national justice and humanity."[72] The Revolution of 1848 had finally enabled the French to improve on the British model and free the slaves without the intermediate stage of apprenticeship.

Although British emancipationists received the ultimate satisfaction of seeing their French counterparts adopt immediatism in 1847 and then abolish slavery in 1848 as officials of the new republican regime, the fact remains that it had been a totally extraneous event, a revolution, that made French slave liberation possible. French abolitionism under the July Monarchy had failed, despite—or perhaps because of—British support. Indeed, it is apparent that by the late 1840s the British emancipation example was

70. Martin, *Histoire de l'esclavage dans les colonies françaises*, 295–96; Cochin, *L'abolition de l'esclavage*, 128–34.
71. *BFAS Reporter*, April 1, 1848. For discussion of Lamartine's role in the new republican government, see Lawrence C. Jennings, *France and Europe in 1848: A Study of French Foreign Affairs in Time of Crisis* (Oxford, 1973), and William Fortescue, *Alphonse de Lamartine: A Political Biography* (New York, 1983).
72. BFASS Minute Books, April 28, 1848.

definitely waning in France. Following the end of the right-of-search crisis, and with the adoption of the Mackau law of 1845, Frenchmen of both abolitionist and procolonial persuasion tended to refer much less often than before to the British experience, a tendency that continued, as already explained, into 1848.

A detailed examination of the French press, abolitionist writings, and documents in the navy and colonial archives shows a noted decline in references to Great Britain in the period 1845 through 1848. At this time the French press heatedly debated the Mackau law and its application but rarely mentioned Britain in connection with these questions. Such a stance was perhaps to be expected from the colonial press, which could no longer exploit the search dispute and which was basically pleased that a non-British—and nonimmediatist—solution had been adopted for France's dependencies. However, this same decline of interest in Britain was apparent in abolitionist publications. By the late 1840s *La Réforme*, an advocate of immediatism, had become the French daily most preoccupied with the French slavery problem. It published numerous articles on this issue from 1845 on, but very few of them made any reference to the British model. Similarly, *L'Abolitioniste français*, which in 1844 had printed many entries drawn from the British experience, seldom alluded to the British precedent in 1847. By this time *L'Abolitioniste* was dwelling almost exclusively on the situation in France's own colonies. The same was true of other antislavery writings. Victor Schoelcher, for example, published a long two-volume assessment of the French slavery and emancipation problems in 1847, consisting partially of excerpts from newspaper articles he had written in the previous two years. Among the 1,015 pages of text, only 48 mentioned the British system in any way, and 7 of these were of a negative connotation, denouncing English colonial immigration schemes.[73] Even Bissette, despite his close ties with British abolitionism, rarely referred to the British approach in *La Revue abolitioniste*, the periodical that he put out—with financial assistance from London— in early 1847. Once France had adopted what everyone perceived as a long-term, non-British solution for her colonies, the British precedent became distant and hardly relevant even to French antislav-

73. Schoelcher, *Histoire de l'esclavage*, II, 409–16.

ery advocates. The promulgation of the Mackau law, following the right-of-search controversy, had given Frenchmen a new frame of reference for emancipation to replace the British one.

Documents in the navy and colonial archives also largely ignore British developments in the late 1840s, while covering in detail the diverse ramifications of Mackau's 1845 legislation. This is true both of position papers and correspondence to and from the colonies. In the case of the annual statements of wishes of the departmental General Councils, a noticeable regression in the number of references to British emancipation had also occurred by the late 1840s. Since the mid-1830s some of these bodies, obviously inspired by abolitionists, had repeated in almost mechanical fashion their desire for slave liberation in their annual statements. From 1836 to 1842, for example, the departments of the Nord, the Allier, and the Loiret had regularly made brief allusions to the British emancipation process. By the late 1840s, though, while these and other French departments continued to call for an end to servitude, their invocation of British actions had practically ceased. In 1847, twenty-four department councils appealed for the freeing of the slaves, but only one, the Gers—perhaps because of British emancipationist visits to the southwest—mentioned Great Britain. Quite indicatively, the Nord, the Allier, and the Loiret all ceased citing Britain between 1840 and 1844, the time of the right-of-search dispute.[74]

This same tendency to de-emphasize French abolitionist connections with Britain was evident in petitions submitted to the government in 1847 in favor of immediate slave liberation, even though the petitioning approach rested on a British precedent. These appeals did not stress Britain's example, though they did indicate that additional ameliorative measures had not helped British slaves. More significantly, however, one reference to England in the petitions suggested that the retention of French colonial slaves was not prudent because in case of war the English could intervene to raise up French slaves against their masters.[75] By the late 1840s not only were Frenchmen turning away from the British achievement, but when they did mention it they often did

74. Gén. 156 (1301), ANSOM.
75. Gén. 197 (1489), ANSOM.

so in a sense that portrayed Britain as a menace rather than a model.

This tendency to view British antislavery policies in what could be construed as negative rather than positive terms had become quite common by the latter part of the July Monarchy. Indeed, the concept that holding slaves could endanger France's colonial possessions in case of war with Britain is traceable back to the Revolutionary and Napoleonic epochs. It was apparently revived in the mid-1830s, when French emancipationists were attempting to impress on their government the need to move toward slave liberation. As part of a petition to the Chamber of Peers in 1835 the abolitionists de Valcourt, Jules Delaborde, and Lutheroth pointed out the "danger" that the British example posed for French colonies still retaining slaves. Two months later Isambert reiterated this theme in the Chamber of Deputies.[76] Perhaps through Isambert's influence, as of 1836 some of the statements of wishes sent in annually to Paris by the departmental General Councils repeated the notion that abolition was necessary for the security of French *colons* now that England had freed her slaves. Tracy reinforced the argument during debates in the Chamber of Deputies when he insisted that the existence of freedom just a few kilometers away from France's possessions placed the latter in a possibly "violent situation."[77]

Passy refined the theme that England's actions posed a danger to the internal stability of France's Caribbean establishment when he suggested during discussions in the lower house in 1835 that once apprenticeship ended and British blacks were entirely free nothing could prevent some of them from landing on Martinique from Dominica or Saint Lucia "to preach insurrection, and if need be, bring arms . . . war and revolt." Three months later he again insisted in the same body that in case of a maritime war with Britain a "few hundred blacks" from the British West Indies could "raise up" France's slave population, resulting in "a flow of tears and blood" in France's holdings.[78] The idea of a British menace to France's dependencies in time of war was driven home again to

76. *Le Moniteur universel,* February 25, April 23, 1835.
77. Gén. 156 (1301), ANSOM; *Le Moniteur universel,* May 26, 1836.
78. *Le Moniteur universel,* April 23, February 16, 1835.

Frenchmen at the height of the Eastern Crisis of 1840 when London newspapers suggested that their government could instigate slave revolts in the French Caribbean if France and Britain were to go to war.[79] At a time of reemerging Anglophobia in France, Britain was being pictured as posing a physical threat to French possessions if they persisted in permitting slavery.

When the outbreak of the right-of-search controversy heightened anti-British sentiment in France, it would have been wise for French abolitionists to desist from portraying Great Britain as an impending danger to France's slave colonies. Instead, French emancipationists not only continued but emphasized this contention, apparently hoping that the tension surrounding the right-of-search conflict might frighten Frenchmen into abandoning slavery. Thus the Broglie Commission's report suggested that in case of war France would lose her territories, which constituted important commercial and military stations, because of their retention of slavery.[80] Le Siècle also insisted that conflict with England could stir up the Negroes in France's possessions, causing bloodshed and disaster therein. In the articles that he wrote for Le Siècle Tocqueville repeated the theme that France's colonies would be menaced by an external threat if slaves were not freed.[81] Obviously, French emancipationists had not come to realize that in light of the mutual search dispute references such as these to Britain were counterproductive for the French antislavery cause.

Arguments of this kind were used even more frequently by French abolitionists during the debates on the petition campaign and the Mackau law in 1844 and 1845. In discussions in the Chamber of Deputies Ledru-Rollin supported Agénor de Gasparin's claim that in case of hostilities Great Britain would bring liberty to France's slaves. Similar assertions were made by the Parisian press. La Réforme stressed that England could cause slave revolts in France's territories in time of war, while Le National dramatically declared that war would render French slave liberation "terrible and bloody," for England would "launch armies of blacks" on

79. A statement to this effect was made by Ledru-Rollin in the course of a discussion on slavery in the Chamber of Deputies on May 4, 1844 (Le Moniteur universel, May 5, 1844).

80. Broglie Commission, Rapport, 49–50.

81. Le Siècle, April 3, October 23, 1843.

neighboring French holdings to bring "liberty . . . in the midst of massacres."[82] Then, during the Chamber of Peers' discussion on slavery in early April, 1845, Duke François Gabriel d'Harcourt spoke of how vulnerable France's slave establishments would be during a Franco-British confrontation; Montalembert, too, predicted that once hostilities broke out, England could give the signal for a French slave uprising; and Passy seconded the latter's contention. The report on the Mackau law by Jules de Lasteyrie in the lower house in May, 1845, also underscored the theme that in wartime there would be "no security" in France's possessions, because slaves could be encouraged to revolt by the British.[83] Quite predictably, colonial spokesmen were quick to seize upon such arguments and exploit them as evidence that Britain had not freed her slaves for humanitarian reasons but in order to menace French colonial stability in times of international tension.[84] It appears that French abolitionists, unable to sway their opponents with positive references to Britain's philanthropic achievement, were often tempted to employ the notion of a British threat in a desperate effort to advance their cause.

Interestingly, Tocqueville, who had himself conjured up the English specter in his articles in Le Siècle in 1843, had altered his tactics by 1845. In May of that year, while speaking in the Chamber of Deputies, he denied that France would lose her colonies to England if hostilities were to occur while servitude still existed; instead, in an evident effort to de-emphasize fear of Britain, he now contended that conflict with Britain would force French colons to free their slaves precipitously. Thus, it would be wiser to act before such an eventuality and liberate French slaves under conditions more favorable to the colonies.[85] Perhaps the perspicacious Tocqueville had seen the disadvantage of invoking an open British menace to France's possessions at a time when Frenchmen still associated Britain with rapid emancipation. In retrospect, it seems that the majority of French abolitionist spokesmen had made a

82. Le Moniteur universel, May 5, 1844; La Réforme, May 4, 1844; Le National, May 5, 1844.
83. Le Moniteur universel, April 5, 8, 1845; Jules de Lasteyrie, report of May 22, 1845, in Gén. 143 (1214), ANSOM.
84. Martinique Colonial Council, session of July 17, 1847, in Corr. Gén., Martinique 121, ANSOM.
85. Le Moniteur universel, May 31, 1845.

major strategic error in reinforcing the negative, threatening aspect of Britain's policy when the right-of-search controversy had already impressed this image on the French mentality. The persistent use of this argument concerning Britain's antislavery campaign shows the extent to which even French emancipationists, who logically should have been defending the British example, shared the reservations concerning British motives that had come to mark the French mind.

It is noteworthy, too, that French abolitionists appeared somewhat reluctant to employ the argument that honor obliged France to imitate or improve on Britain's humanitarian record by rapidly liberating French slaves. As the duc d'Harcourt asked in the Chamber of Peers, why was not France's feeling of rivalry with England expressed by its trying to "outdo" Britain in the emancipation question?[86] That the British abolitionists themselves had hoped that France would attempt to rival Britain in slave liberation matters is shown by a statement to this effect made by Daniel O'Connell during the 1840 abolitionist convention in London.[87] This method of approaching the slavery problem might, one could expect, have had good results in a country where sentiments toward Britain were often mingled with chauvinism, pride, and competitiveness. Such a strategy might have had a definite appeal to Frenchmen of varying persuasions concerning abolitionism. For instance, *L'Indicateur*, a proslavery daily by the 1840s, was prepared at one point to accept the thesis that France, which had always "marched at the head of progress in Europe," should not permit itself to be "out-distanced" by England in implementing emancipation.[88] If such an approach could gain adherence from elements in Bordeaux, it should have had a definite tactical appeal to French antislavery advocates.

Throughout the July Monarchy some French abolitionists did indeed incite their fellow countrymen to react with a sentiment of national honor to the slavery issue. As early as 1835 the *Journal de Rouen* suggested that it was unworthy of France to fall behind any nation in philanthropic matters, while *Le Courrier français* queried whether "France could remain behind England" on aboli-

---

86. *Ibid.*, April 5, 1845.
87. Quoted by *Le Courrier français*, June 28, 1840.
88. *L'Indicateur*, April 11, 1845.

tionism, France having always taken the lead in liberty.[89] In his booklet Montrol also insisted that "France cannot lag behind any civilization."[90] At the same time Tracy suggested in the Chamber of Deputies that if his nation must rival England, it should do so in the antislavery sphere. A year later Lamartine declared to the same body that "a people like us should be indignant to await the example of England" in proclaiming "human liberty."[91] When the French abolition society appealed to the General Councils of the departments in 1836 and 1837 to openly espouse emancipation, it also emphasized that this was a "question of national honor and justice."[92]

Sentiments of this kind persisted into the 1840s. In a letter that Isambert sent to Tredgold in 1841 he maintained that "the honour of France can no longer suffer [slavery's] continuance."[93] Speaking before the Chamber of Deputies in 1844, Ledru-Rollin exclaimed dramatically that France could not be satisfied with vague assurances about eventual emancipation when England had already led the way in this domain: "We cannot, in the name of humanity, in the name of French honor and dignity, we cannot." Montalembert, when addressing the Chamber of Peers a year later, was as poignant in his evocation of French integrity, remarking that "I am humiliated and chagrined to think that the great revolution [slave liberation] has taken place under a different banner than that of France." Isambert uttered similar sentiments in the lower house in 1846 when he admitted his humiliation over France's having fallen so far behind England on the slavery issue.[94] *L'Abolitioniste français*, too, referred on several occasions during the first years of its publication to the theme of French honor. Finally, Schoelcher ended the first volume of his *Histoire de l'esclavage pendant les deux dernières années* by stressing the shame that France incurred by lagging behind other European powers in the emancipation process.[95] Other scattered references to this theme could also be

89. *Le Journal de Rouen*, April 25, 1835; *Le Courrier français*, February 4, 7, 1835.
90. Montrol, *Des colonies anglaises*, 1.
91. *Le Moniteur universel*, April 24, 1835, May 26, 1836.
92. Société française pour l'abolition de l'esclavage, *4ᵉ publication*, vii; No. 5, p. 3.
93. Isambert to Tredgold, letter dated May 18, *BFAS Reporter*, June 2, 1841.
94. *Le Moniteur universel*, May 5, 1844, April 8, 1845, May 16, 1846.
95. Schoelcher, *Histoire de l'esclavage*, I, 547.

found. Still, it is amazing that it was not employed more often or more systematically. Rarely was it elaborated on to any extent or used as a central element in the attack on French slavery.

Perhaps French abolitionists employed this argument sparingly because they did not wish either to antagonize their allies or to exacerbate the strain between Paris and London. It is noteworthy that the French antislavery activists Félice and Bissette, who were dependent on their ties to the BFASS, did not touch on this topic in their works, published in 1846 and 1847, respectively, apparently out of deference to Great Britain. Most French emancipationists, however, were apparently reluctant to stress this approach because to do so amounted to admitting French insufficiencies or backwardness in relationship to Britain, an avowal that even they were reluctant to make. Nationalistic sensitivity of this kind would also help to explain the repeated, and largely groundless, assurances given by French abolitionists to their British colleagues and benefactors that French emancipationism was making marked progress. Furthermore, it might elucidate the tendency of French antislavery spokesmen, such as Lamartine, Tocqueville, Isambert, and *L'Abolitioniste français*, to hedge over French shortcomings by alleging that their country had been the first to abolish slavery—during the French Revolution—or that emancipation had originally been a French idea. Especially after the right-of-search controversy, French abolitionists were hesitant to admit either that France had fallen behind Britain or that national honor required France to imitate the British.

Clearly, the rivalry that marked Franco-British relations in the 1840s had had detrimental effects on the French antislavery movement. Even French emancipationists had come to harbor too many suspicions of British motives to employ the example of British slave liberation in the most positive manner possible. By the last years of the July Monarchy the British abolitionist experience had become tarnished in French eyes or discounted as no longer relevant. British emancipationists had been overly optimistic in the 1830s when they proclaimed that the British precedent of freeing colonial slaves would inevitably bring France to follow Britain's lead. In fact, the overall effect of the British example on France proved to be more negative than positive.

CONCLUSION

In some ways British slave liberation had a profound effect on the growth of abolitionism in France. The British example proved that slavery could be ended in a peaceful and effective manner, thus enabling French humanitarians to broach the question of eliminating servitude in France's colonies. French emancipationists were inspired by the British precedent to found the French abolitionist society, to take the issue before the legislature, and to propagate their ideals through the written word. British philanthropists not only assisted their French cohorts by furnishing them with publications and data on the positive aspects of the British experience, but communicated directly with them, sent representatives to counsel them, and provided funds for some of their undertakings. There is little doubt that the French antislavery movement would have encountered severe theoretical and logistical difficulties without the encouragement and support it received from the British. Indeed, if the French had not benefited from the inspiration and succor provided by the British, French emancipationism would undoubtedly have taken many more years to coalesce into a meaningful, operational organization.

In other ways, though, British efforts to aid the French abolitionists proved disappointing. British emancipationists were unable to influence their French colleagues to construct a popular rather than elitist structure. The French were either unable or unwilling to launch a successful petition or public meeting campaign. As a result, they were never able to mobilize opinion, as the British had, to press for the destruction of slavery. Even the gradual trend toward immediatism that emerged in abolitionist circles after 1840 can be attributed much less to British exhortations than to the apparent shortcomings of the French government's extremely gradualistic approach. In fact, British intervention in favor of immediatism probably contributed to the division within the French movement, which tended to weaken it considerably in the 1840s. It appears, too, that the most noteworthy negative aspect of British slave liberation, decreased productivity, induced some moderate French abolitionists to opt for gradualism. The British example of granting an indemnity and establishing apprenticeship also seems to have persuaded a faction of the French movement that the freeing of slaves could not or should not be achieved in the British fashion. Finally, the French reaction against Britain as a result of the right-of-search crisis was a major element influencing a number of French emancipationists to embrace the gradualistic approach, to turn away from the model advocated by the British. In sum, the British precedent had not proved totally convincing or appealing even to French abolitionists.

Although British efforts had both positive and negative effects on French antislavery advocates, they tended, ironically, to fortify rather than weaken the proslavery cause in France. The British accomplishment stimulated French defenders of slavery into increased and more effective activities. The plethora of publications and statistics on the British experience provided the French plantocracy with a massive amount of information, which could be employed selectively or even out of context against the principle of emancipation. French proponents of slavery could use the British documentation to demonstrate that the British action had been dangerous, disruptive, impractical, detrimental economically. Applying this experience to the French scene, they could argue that the freeing of French slaves, too, would prove disastrous for production, destructive to the colonies, and overly expensive for mainland France. Indeed, now that historians of the 1980s are stressing the economic setback that slave liberation dealt the British establishments, it is interesting to note that French colonial sympathizers clearly perceived this development in the 1830s and used it to help dissuade the French government from imitating Britain. The French colonial lobby also profited immensely from the anti-British backlash caused by the right-of-search controversy. This body was able to exploit the Anglophobia concomitant with the search dispute to sully British altruism and discredit a French antislavery organization dependent on the British. In a sense, the British achievement did oblige French colonial interests to alter their stance on slavery enough to acknowledge that abolition must be realized some day, but this brought them to adopt the even more defendable position that the freeing of the slaves should be postponed as long as possible. In the long run, despite British hopes to the contrary, the British precedent did not undermine the structure of slavery in France's colonial holdings.

The French government, too, reacted in an extremely cautious manner to the British emancipation record. The British action afforded French officials an excuse to defer slave liberation and at the same time provided them with justification for this decision. This dilatory stance soon became ensconced as policy; and the French government implemented a program of ameliorating the position of French slaves rather than freeing them in the British fashion. Taking note of the negative rather than positive results of the British process, French Cabinets became convinced in the 1830s that they must avoid adopting the ineffective British apprenticeship system and a financially prohibitive indemnity plan. Then, in the 1840s, the Anglophobia aroused by the mutual search controversy enabled the French administration to set aside entirely the British precedent. French officials, like French *colons*, totally rejected the British example and espoused instead a policy of extreme gradualism, which would remain in place for the duration of the July Monarchy.

In retrospect, it is clear that there are several reasons why abolitionism failed in France while succeeding in Great Britain. Unlike their British equivalents, most French emancipationists remained elitist, conservative, and deeply divided to the end. Then, too, the evangelical Protestant elements that had so stimulated the British antislavery cause were too small a minority in France to be meaningful. Moreover, in France the *notable* dominated government, apprehensive about reform of any kind, tended to be obsessed with the plantocratic concerns of maintaining production and protecting colonial rights. Furthermore, the July Monarchy committed funds to railway building and the fortification of Paris rather than to compensating slave owners or restructuring the colonial economy. There is little doubt, however, that one of the foremost factors braking the development of abolitionism in France was the overall negative impression British emancipation made on the French mentality. In Great Britain public pressure had influenced the ruling elite to eradicate slavery, but in France negative perceptions of the British experience tended to withdraw popular support from the French emancipationist movement and emasculate it. Contrary to the expectations of British abolitionists, as a whole the British example impeded rather than advanced the French struggle against slavery.

BIBLIOGRAPHY

PRIMARY SOURCES

Archives

Archives départementales de la Loire-Atlantique, Nantes
  Archives de la Chambre de Commerce de Nantes
Archives des Affaires Etrangères, Paris
  Correspondance politique
  Mémoires et documents
  Personnel dossiers
Archives Nationales, Paris
  Guizot Papers
Archives Nationales, Section Outre-Mer, Aix-en-Provence
  Correspondance Générale
  Généralités
Bodleian Library, Oxford
  Rhodes House Anti-Slavery Papers
Service historique de la Marine, Vincennes
  Personnel dossiers

Newspapers

Bordeaux
  Le Courrier de la Gironde, 1837–48
  La Guienne, 1830–48
  L'Indicateur, 1830–48
  Le Mémorial bordelais, 1830–48
Brest
  L'Armoricain, 1835–36, 1841–45
Le Havre
  Le Courrier du Havre, 1839–40
  Le Journal du Havre, 1830–48

London
  British and Foreign Anti-Slavery Reporter, 1840–48
  Times, 1841–45
Marseille
  Le Sémaphore de Marseille, 1831–45
Nantes
  Le Breton, 1831–45, 1847–48
  Le National de l'Ouest, 1841–45
Paris
  L'Abolitioniste [sic] *français*, 1844–48
  Le Bulletin colonial, 1836–38, 1840
  Le Charivari, 1842–45
  Le Constitutionnel, 1830–48
  Le Courrier français, 1830–43
  L'Espérance, 1839–48
  La France, 1842–43
  La Gazette de France, 1842–45
  Le Globe, 1841–45
  Journal de la Société de la morale chrétienne, 1834
  Le Journal des débats, 1830–48
  Le Journal du commerce, then *Le Commerce*, 1830–45
  Le Lien, 1841–48
  Le Moniteur du commerce, then *La Paix*, 1833–37
  Le Moniteur universel, 1830–48
  Le National, 1830–48
  L'Outre-mer, 1836, 1839–40
  La Patrie, 1841–45
  La Presse, 1836–48
  La Quotidienne, 1831, 1834, 1841–45
  La Réforme, 1843–48
  La Revue abolitioniste [sic], 1847
  La Revue de Paris, 1832
  La Revue des colonies, 1834–35
  La Revue du dix-neuvième siècle, 1836–37
  La Revue mensuelle d'économie politique, 1833–34
  Le Siècle, 1836–48
  Le Temps, 1830–42
  L'Univers, 1841–42

La Rochelle
  La Charente-Inférieure, 1837–39, 1841–45
Rouen
  Le Journal de Rouen, 1830–33, 1835–36, 1842–45
  Le Mémorial de Rouen, 1842–45

Printed Documents

France. Administration des douanes. *Tableau décennal du commerce de la France avec ses colonies et les puissances étrangères, 1837–1846.* Paris, 1848.

France. Ministère de la marine et des colonies. *Abolition de l'esclavage dans les colonies anglaises.* 5 vols. Paris, 1840–43.

——. *Commission instituée, par décision royale du 26 mai 1840, pour l'examen des questions relatives à l'esclavage et à la constitution publique des colonies. Procès-verbaux.* Paris, 1840–42.

——. *Commission instituée par décision royale du 26 mai 1840 . . . Rapport.* Paris, 1843.

——. *Etats de population pour 1834.* Paris, 1836.

——. *Tableau de population, de culture et de navigation. . . .* Paris, 1844, 1851.

Minutes of the Proceedings of the General Anti-Slavery Convention Called by the Committee of the British and Foreign Anti-Slavery Society Held in London on the 12th of June, 1840. London, 1840.

Proceedings of the General Anti-Slavery Convention, Called by the Committee of the British and Foreign Anti-Slavery Society and Held in London, from Tuesday, June 13th, to Tuesday, June 20th, 1843. 1843; rpr. Miami, 1969.

Procès-verbaux, rapports et projets de décrets de la commission institutuée pour préparer l'acte d'abolition immédiate de l'esclavage. Paris, 1848.

Books and Pamphlets

Alexander, George W., and John Scoble. *Liberté immédiate et absolue ou l'esclavage. Observations sur le rapport de M. le duc de Broglie . . . adressées à tous les Français.* Paris, 1844.

Chazelles, le comte de. *Emancipation, transformation. Le sys-*

*tème anglais, le système français. Mémoire adressé à la Cham-
bre des députés à l'occasion du projet de loi concernant la régime des esclaves dans les colonies françaises.* Paris, 1845.

Dupin, Baron Charles. *Second mémoire. Situation comparée des
colonies françaises et des colonies anglaises.* Paris, 1844.

Dussillon, Charles Joseph. *Considérations sur l'esclavage aux
Antilles françaises et son abolition graduelle, suivies d'un aperçu analytique et critique du système d'apprentissage et de ses
résultats dans les colonies anglaises.* Paris, [1843].

Favard, M. *De l'abolition de l'esclavage dans les colonies françaises.* N.p., [1838].

————. *Examen des résultats produits par l'émancipation des
noirs dans les colonies anglaises.* Paris, 1842.

Félice, Guillaume de. *Emancipation immédiate et complète des
esclaves. Appel aux abolitionistes [sic].* Paris, 1846.

Gasparin, Agénor de. *De l'affranchissement des esclaves et de ses
rapports avec la politique actuelle.* Paris, 1839.

Jollivet, Thomas Marie Adolphe. *L'émancipation anglaise jugée
par ses résultats. Analyses des documents officiels imprimés par
l'ordre de M. le Ministre de la marine et des colonies.* Paris,
1842.

————. *Des missions en France de la Société abolitioniste [sic]
anglaise et étrangère.* Paris, 1841.

————. *A MM. les habitànts de la Louisianne [sic].* Paris, 1843.

————. *Parallèle entre les colonies françaises et les colonies anglaises.* Paris, 1842.

————. *De la philanthropie anglaise.* Paris, 1842.

————. *Question des sucres dans la Chambre des communes
d'Angleterre. Du travail libre et du travail forcé, leur influence
sur la production coloniale.* Paris, 1841.

Kellermann, Edmond de, duc de Valmy. *Note sur le droit de visite.*
Paris, [1842].

Lacharière, André de. *De l'affranchissement des esclaves dans les
colonies françaises.* Paris, 1836.

Layrle, Marie Jean François, Capitaine de vaisseau. *Abolition de
l'esclavage dans les colonies anglaises.* Paris, 1842.

Lechevalier, Jules. *Rapport sur les questions coloniales . . . à la
suite d'un voyage fait aux Antilles et aux Guyanes pendant les
années 1838 et 1839.* 2 vols. Paris, 1843–44.

Macaulay, Zachary. *Détails sur l'émancipation des esclaves dans les colonies anglaises, pendant les années 1834 et 1835.* Paris, 1836.

_____. *Faits et renseignements provant les avantages du travail libre sur le travail forcé, et indiquant les moyens les plus propres à hâter l'abolition de l'esclavage dans les colonies européennes.* Paris, 1835.

_____. *Haïti, ou renseignements authentiques sur l'abolition de l'esclavage et de ses résultats, à Saint-Domingue et à la Guadeloupe.* Paris, 1835.

_____. *Suite des détails sur l'émancipation des esclaves dans les colonies anglaises pendant les années 1835 et 1836.* Paris, 1836.

_____. *Tableau de l'esclavage tel qu'il existe dans les colonies françaises.* Paris, 1835.

Milliroux, Félix. *Demerary, transition de l'esclavage à la liberté. Colonies françaises, future abolition.* Paris, 1843.

Montrol, François Mongin de. *Des colonies anglaises depuis l'émancipation des esclaves et de l'influence de cette émancipation sur les colonies françaises.* Second publication of the Société française pour l'abolition de l'esclavage. Paris, 1835.

Schoelcher, Victor. *Colonies étrangères et Haïti. Résultats de l'émancipation anglaise.* 2 vols. Paris, 1842–43.

_____. *Des colonies françaises. Abolition immédiate de l'esclavage.* Paris, 1842.

_____. *Histoire de l'esclavage pendant les deux dernières années.* 2 vols. Paris, 1847.

Société française pour l'abolition de l'esclavage. *No. 1. Prospectus.* Paris, 1835.

_____. *4e publication.* Paris, [1836].

_____. *No. 5. Année 1837.* Paris, 1837.

_____. *No. 8. Année 1838.* Paris, June, 1838.

_____. *No. 9. Rapport fait au nom de la commission chargée de l'examen de la proposition de M. Passy, sur le sort des esclaves dans les colonies françaises.* Paris, 1838.

_____. *No. 11.* Paris, November, 1838.

_____. *No. 12.* Paris, February, 1839.

_____. *No. 13.* Paris, July, 1839.

_____. *No. 14. Rapport fait au nom de la commission chargée d'examiner la proposition de M. de Tracy, relative aux esclaves des colonies, par A. de Tocqueville.* Paris, 1839.

———. *No. 16. Banquet offert à la députation de la Société centrale britannique pour l'abolition universelle de l'esclavage, 10 février 1840.* Paris, March, 1840.

———. *No. 17.* Paris, April, 1840.

———. *No. 19.* Paris, April, 1842.

Sully-Brunet, E. *Considérations sur le système colonial et le plan d'abolition de l'esclavage.* Paris, 1840.

SECONDARY SOURCES

Books

Anderson, M. S. *The Eastern Question, 1774–1928.* London, 1966.

Anstey, Roger. *The Atlantic Slave Trade and British Abolition, 1760–1810.* Atlantic Heights, N.J., 1975.

Asiegbu, Johnson U. J. *Slavery and the Politics of Liberation, 1787–1861: A Study of Liberated African Emigration and British Anti-Slavery Policy.* London, 1969.

Bolt, Christine. *The Anti-Slavery Movement and Reconstruction: A Study in Anglo-American Co-Operation, 1833–1877.* London, 1969.

Bolt, Christine, and Seymour Drescher, eds. *Anti-Slavery, Religion and Reform: Essays in Memory of Roger Anstey.* Folkstone, Kent, 1980.

Braunstein, Dieter. *Französische Kolonialpolitik, 1830–1852: Expansion, Verwaltung, Wirtschaft, Mission.* Wiesbaden, 1983.

Bullen, Roger. *Palmerston, Guizot and the Collapse of the Entente Cordiale.* London, 1974.

Burn, William L. *Emancipation and Apprenticeship in the British West Indies.* London, 1937.

Cochin, Augustin. *L'abolition de l'esclavage.* 1861; rpr. Fort-de-France, 1979.

Cohen, William B. *The French Encounter with Africans: White Response to Blacks, 1530–1880.* Bloomington, Ind., 1980.

Cunliffe, Marcus. *Chattel and Wage Slavery: The Anglo-American Context.* Athens, Ga., 1979.

Davis, David Brion. *The Problem of Slavery in the Age of Revolution, 1770–1823.* Ithaca, 1975.

_____. *The Problem of Slavery in Western Culture*. Ithaca, 1966.

_____. *Slavery and Human Progress*. Oxford, 1984.

Deerr, Noel. *The History of Sugar*. 2 vols. London, 1949–50.

Drescher, Seymour. *Capitalism and Antislavery: British Popular Mobilization in Comparative Perspective*. London, 1986.

_____. *Dilemmas of Democracy: Tocqueville and Modernization*. Pittsburgh, 1968.

_____. *Econocide: British Slavery in the Era of Abolition*. Pittsburgh, 1977.

_____, ed. *Tocqueville and Beaumont on Social Reform*. New York, 1968.

Duchêne, Albert. *La politique coloniale de la France. Le ministère des colonies depuis Richelieu*. Paris, 1928.

Elisabeth, Léo. *L'abolition de l'esclavage à la Martinique*. Fort-de-France, 1983.

Eltis, David. *Economic Growth and the Ending of the Transatlantic Slave Trade*. New York, 1987.

Eltis, David, and James Walvin, eds. *The Abolition of the Atlantic Slave Trade: Origins and Effects in Africa and the Americas*. Madison, Wisc., 1981.

Fladeland, Betty. *Abolitionists and Working Class Problems in the Age of Industrialization*. Baton Rouge, 1984.

_____. *Men and Brothers: Anglo-American Anti-Slavery Co-Operation*. Urbana, Ill., 1972.

Fortescue, William. *Alphonse de Lamartine: A Political Biography*. New York, 1983.

Gisler, Antoine. *L'esclavage aux Antilles françaises (XVIIe–XIXe siècle)*. 1965; rpr. Paris, 1981.

Green, William A. *British Slave Emancipation: The Sugar Colonies and the Great Experiment, 1830–1870*. Oxford, 1976.

Jennings, Lawrence C. *France and Europe in 1848: A Study of French Foreign Affairs in Time of Crisis*. Oxford, 1973.

Klingberg, Frank J. *The Anti-Slavery Movement in England*. 1933; rpr. London, 1964.

Lloyd, Christopher. *The Navy and the Slave Trade: The Suppression of the African Slave Trade in the Nineteenth Century*. 1949; rpr. London, 1968.

Martin, Gaston. *L'abolition de l'esclavage, 27 avril 1848*. Paris, 1948.

———. *Histoire de l'esclavage dans les colonies françaises*. Paris, 1948.

Mathieson, William Law. *British Slave Emancipation, 1838–1849*. 1932; rpr. New York, 1967.

———. *British Slavery and Its Abolition, 1823–1838*. 1926; rpr. New York, 1967.

Maupassant, Jean de. *Le droit de visite sous Louis-Philippe: L'affaire du "Marabout."* Bordeaux, 1913.

Mellor, George R. *British Imperial Trusteeship, 1783–1850*. London, 1951.

Merk, Frederick. *Slavery and the Annexation of Texas*. New York, 1972.

Murray, D. J. *The West Indies and the Development of Colonial Government*. Oxford, 1965.

Renault, François. *Libération d'esclaves et nouvelle servitude: Les rachats de captifs africains pour le compte des colonies françaises après l'abolition de l'esclavage*. Abidjan and Dakar, 1976.

Rice, C. Duncan. *The Scots Abolitionists, 1833–1861*. Baton Rouge, 1981.

Scarano, Francisco A. *Sugar and Slavery in Puerto Rico: The Plantation Economy of Ponce, 1800–1850*. Madison, Wisc. 1984.

Schefer, Christian. *La politique coloniale de la Monarchie de Juillet: L'Algérie et l'évolution de la colonisation française*. Paris, 1928.

Schnakenbourg, Christian. *La crise du système esclavagiste, 1835–1847*. Paris, 1980. Vol. I of *Histoire de l'industrie sucrière en Guadeloupe*.

Stein, Robert Louis. *Léger Félicité Sonthonax: The Lost Sentinel of the Republic*. Cranbury, N.J., 1985.

Temperley, Howard. *British Antislavery, 1830–1870*. Columbia, S.C., 1972.

Tinker, Hugh. *A New System of Slavery: The Export of Indian Labour Overseas, 1830–1920*. London, 1974.

Tudesq, André-Jean. *Les grands notables en France: Etude historique d'une psychologie sociale*. 2 vols. Paris, 1964.

Walvin, James, ed. *Slavery and British Society, 1776–1846*. London, 1982.

Articles, Theses, Dissertations, Papers

Adélaïde-Merlande, Jacques. "La commission d'abolition de l'esclavage." *Bulletin de la Sociéte d'histoire de la Guadeloupe*, nos. 53–54 (1984), 3–34.

Aguet, Jean-Pierre. "Le tirage des quotidiens de Paris sous la Monarchie de Juillet." *Revue suisse d'histoire*, X (1960), 216–86.

Anstey, Roger. "Parliamentary Reform, Methodism and Anti-Slavery Politics." *Slavery and Abolition*, II (1981), 209–26.

Baldwin, J. R. "England and the French Seizure of the Society Islands." *Journal of Modern History*, X (1938), 212–31.

Boesche, Roger. "Tocqueville and *Le Commerce:* A Newspaper Expressing His Unusual Liberalism." *Journal of the History of Ideas*, XLIV (1983), 277–92.

Chatillon, Dr. Marcel. "Les premières années de la suppression de l'esclavage (1834–1840) dans les colonies anglaises, d'après les rapports des enquêteurs royaux français." *Colloque d'histoire antillaise* (Pointe-à-Pitre, 1969), 23–36.

Curtin, Philip D. "The British Sugar Duties and West Indian Prosperity." *Journal of Economic History*, XIV (1954), 157–73.

Daget, Serge. "British Repression of the Illegal French Slave Trade: Some Considerations." In *The Uncommon Market: Essays in the Economic History of the Atlantic Slave Trade*, edited by Henry A. Gemery and Jan S. Hogendorn. New York, 1979.

————. "La France et l'abolition de la traite des Noirs de 1814 à 1831: Introduction à l'étude de la répression de la traite des Noirs au XIXe siècle." Doctorat de 3e cycle, Paris, 1969.

————. "Les mots esclave, nègre, Noir, et les jugements de valeur sur la traite negrière dans la littérature abolitionniste française de 1770 à 1845." *Revue française d'histoire d'outre-mer*, LX (1973), 511–48.

Davis, David Brion. "The Emergence of Immediatism in British and American Anti-Slavery Thought." *Mississippi Valley Historical Review*, XLIX (1962–63), 209–30.

Debbasch, Yvan. "Poésie et traite: L'opinion française sur le commerce négrier au début du XIXe siècle." *Revue française d'histoire d'outre-mer*, XLVIII (1961), 311–52.

Engerman, Stanley L. "Coerced and Free Labor: Property Rights and the Development of the Labor Force." *Annales: économies, sociétes, civilisations,* forthcoming in French translation.

———. "Contract Labor, Sugar, and Technology in the Nineteenth Century." *Journal of Economic History,* XLIII (1983), 635–59.

———. "Economic Aspects of the Adjustment to Emancipation in the United States and the British West Indies." *Journal of Interdisciplinary History,* XIII (1982), 191–220.

———. "Economic Change and Contract Labor in the British Caribbean: The End of Slavery and the Adjustment to Emancipation." *Explorations in Economic History,* XXI (1984), 133–50.

Faure, Claude. "La granison européenne du Sénégal et le recrutement des premiers troupes noirs, 1779–1858." *Revue d'histoire des colonies françaises,* VIII (1920), 5–108.

Fisher-Blanchet, M. A. "Les travaux de la commission d'indemnité coloniale en 1848." *Espace caraïbes,* I (1983), 37–56.

Gallagher, J. "Fowell Buxton and the New African Policy, 1838–1842." *Cambridge Historical Journal,* X (1950), 36–58.

Gobert, David L., and Jerome S. Handler, eds. and trans. "Barbados in the Apprenticeship Period: The Report of a French Colonial Official." *Journal of the Barbados Museum and Historical Society,* XXXVI (1980), 108–28.

———. "Barbados in the Post-Apprenticeship Period: The Observations of a French Naval Officer." *Journal of the Barbados Museum and Historical Society,* XXXV (1978), 243–66, XXVI (1979), 4–15.

Gross, Izhak. "Parliament and the Abolition of Negro Apprenticeship, 1835–1838." *English Historical Review,* XCVI (1981), 560–76.

Hayward, Jack. "From Utopian Socialism, via Abolitionism to the Colonisation of French Guiana: Jules Lechevalier's West Indian Fiasco, 1838–44." Unpublished paper presented to the Colloque International sur la traite des Noirs, Nantes, 1985.

Jennings, Lawrence C. "L'abolition de l'esclavage par la IIe République et ses effets en Louisiane, 1848–1858." *Revue française d'histoire d'outre-mer,* LVI (1969), 375–97.

———. "France, Great Britain and the Repression of the Slave Trade, 1841–1845." *French Historical Studies,* X (1977), 101–25.

———. "French Perceptions of British Slave Emancipation: A

French Observer's Views on the Post-Emancipation British Caribbean." *French Colonial Studies*, III (1979), 72–85.

_____. "French Policy Toward Trading with African and Brazilian Slave Merchants, 1840–1853." *Journal of African History*, XVII (1976), 515–28.

_____. "The French Press and Great Britain's Campaign Against the Slave Trade, 1830–1848." *Revue française d'histoire d'outremer*, LXVII (1980), 5–24.

_____. "French Reaction to the 'Disguised British Slave Trade': France and British African Emigration Projects, 1840–1864." *Cahiers d'études africaines*, XVIII (1978), 201–13.

_____. "French Views on Slavery and Abolitionism in the United States, 1830–1848." *Slavery and Abolition*, IV (1983), 19–40.

_____. "The Parisian Press and French Foreign Affairs in 1848." *Canadian Journal of History*, VII (1972), 119–47.

_____. "La presse havraise et l'esclavage." *Revue historique*, CCLXXII (1984), 45–71.

_____. "Réflexions d'un observateur sur l'émancipation des esclaves britanniques à l'île Maurice." *Revue d'histoire moderne et contemporaine*, XXIX (1982), 462–70.

_____. "Slave Trade Repression and the Abolition of French Slavery." Unpublished paper presented to the Colloque International sur la traite des Noirs, Nantes, 1985.

Kennedy, Melvin Dow. "The Suppression of the African Slave Trade to the French Colonies and Its Aftermath, 1814–1848." Ph.D. dissertation, University of Chicago, 1947.

Kennon, Donald R. " 'An Apple of Discord': The Woman Question at the World's Anti-Slavery Convention of 1840." *Slavery and Abolition*, V (1984), 244–66.

Maynard, Donald. "The World's Anti-Slavery Convention of 1840." *Mississippi Valley Historical Review*, XLVII (1960), 452–79.

Quinney, Valerie. "Decisions on Slavery, the Slave Trade, and Civil Rights for Negroes in the Early French Revolution." *Journal of Negro History*, LV (1970), 117–30.

Resnick, Daniel P. "The Société des amis des noirs and the Abolition of Slavery." *French Historical Studies*, VII (1972), 558–69.

Stein, Robert Louis. "The Revolution of 1789 and the Abolition of Slavery." *Canadian Journal of History*, XVII (1982), 447–67.

Tersen, Emile. "La commission d'abolition de l'esclavage, 4 mars–21 juillet 1848." *Actes du congrès historique du centenaire de la Révolution de 1848*. Paris, 1948.

Tyrrell, Alex. "The 'Moral Radical Party' and the Anglo-Jamaican Campaign for the Abolition of the Negro Apprenticeship System." *English Historical Review*, XCIX (1984), 481–502.

Wilkins, Joe. "Window on Freedom: South Carolina's Response to British West Indian Slave Emancipation, 1833–1834." *South Carolina Historical Magazine*, LXXXV (1984), 135–44.

Zuccarelli, François. "Le régime des engagés à temps au Sénégal, 1817–1848." *Cahiers d'études africaines*, II (1962), 420–61.

Index

DATE DUE